PLATINUM EDITION

3

Series Director: Diane Larsen-Freeman

GRAMMAR DIMENSIONS

FORM, MEANING, and USE

Stephen H. Thewlis

Center for International Programs
Saint Mary's College of California

H·H Heinle & Heinle
Thomson Learning™

Australia • Canada • Denmark • Japan • Mexico • New Zealand
Philippines • Puerto Rico • Singapore • Spain • United Kingdom • United States

Acquisition Editor: Eric Bredenberg
Senior Developmental Editor: Amy Lawler
Production Editor: Michael Burggren
Senior Marketing Manager: Charlotte Sturdy
Manufacturing Coordinator: Mary Beth Hennebury
Composition/Project Management: The PRD Group, Inc.
Text Design: Sue Gerould, Perspectives
Cover Design: Hannus Design Associates
Printer: Quebecor World/Taunton

For permission to use material from this text, contact us:
web   www.thomsonrights.com
fax   1-800-730-2215
phone   1-800-730-2214

Heinle & Heinle Publishers
20 Park Plaza
Boston, MA 02116

UK/EUROPE/MIDDLE EAST:
Thomson Learning
Berkshire House
168-173 High Holborn
London, WC1V 7AA, United Kingdom

ASIA (excluding Japan):
Thomson Learning
60 Albert Street #15-01
Albert Complex
Singapore 189969

AUSTRALIA/NEW ZEALAND:
Nelson/Thomson Learning
102 Dodds Street
South Melbourne
Victoria 3205 Australia

LATIN AMERICA:
Thomson Learning
Seneca, 53
Colonia Polanco
11560 México D.F. México

JAPAN:
Thomson Learning
Palaceside Building, 5F
1-1-1 Hitotsubashi, Chiyoda-ku
Tokyo 100 0003, Japan

CANADA:
Nelson/Thomson Learning
1120 Birchmount Road
Scarborough, Ontario
Canada M1K 5G4

SPAIN:
Thomson Learning
Calle Magallanes, 25
28015-Madrid
Espana

ISBN: 0-8384-0277-1

 This book is printed on acid-free recycled paper.

Printed in the United States of America
3 4 5 6 7 8 9   04 03 02 01

keila
(770) 458-8313

A Special Thanks

The series director, authors, and publisher would like to thank the following individuals who offered many helpful insights and suggestions for change throughout the development of *Grammar Dimensions, Platinum Edition.*

Jane Berger
*Solano Community College,
 California*
Mary Bottega
San Jose State University
Mary Brooks
Eastern Washington University
Christina Broucqsault
*California State Polytechnic
 University*
José Carmona
Hudson Community College
Susan Carnell
*University of Texas at
 Arlington*
Susana Christie
San Diego State University
Diana Christopher
Georgetown University
Gwendolyn Cooper
Rutgers University
Sue Cozzarelli
EF International, San Diego
Catherine Crystal
Laney College, California
Kevin Cross
University of San Francisco
Julie Damron
*Interlink at Valparaiso
 University, Indiana*
Glen Deckert
Eastern Michigan University
Eric Dwyer
*University of Texas at
 Austin*
Ann Eubank
Jefferson Community College
Alice Fine
UCLA Extension
Alicia Going
*The English Language Study
 Center, Oregon*
Molly Gould
University of Delaware
Maren M. Hargis
San Diego Mesa College
Mary Herbert
*University of California, Davis
 Extension*

Jane Hilbert
*ELS Language Center, Florida
 International University*
Eli Hinkel
Xavier University
Kathy Hitchcox
*International English Institute,
 Fresno*
Joyce Hutchings
Georgetown University
Heather Jeddy
*Northern Virginia Community
 College*
Judi Keen
*University of California, Davis,
 and Sacramento City College*
Karli Kelber
*American Language Institute,
 New York University*
Anne Kornfeld
LaGuardia Community College
Kay Longmire
*Interlink at Valparaiso
 University, Indiana*
Robin Longshaw
Rhode Island School of Design
Bernadette McGlynn
*ELS Language Center,
St. Joseph's University*
Billy McGowan
Aspect International, Boston
Margaret Mehran
Queens College
Richard Moore
University of Washington
Karen Moreno
*Teikyo Post University,
 Connecticut*
Gino Muzzetti
*Santa Rosa Junior College,
 California*
Mary Nance-Tager
*LaGuardia Community College,
 City University of New York*
Karen O'Neill
San Jose State University
Mary O'Neal
*Northern Virginia Community
 College*

Nancy Pagliara
*Northern Virginia Community
 College*
Keith Pharis
Southern Illinois University
Amy Parker
*ELS Language Center, San
 Francisco*
Margene Petersen
*ELS Language Center,
 Philadelphia*
Nancy Pfingstag
*University of North Carolina,
 Charlotte*
Sally Prieto
*Grand Rapids Community
 College*
India Plough
Michigan State University
Mostafa Rahbar
*University of Tennessee at
 Knoxville*
Dudley Reynolds
Indiana University
Ann Salzman
*University of Illinois at Urbana-
 Champaign*
Jennifer Schmidt
San Francisco State University
Cynthia Schuemann
Miami-Dade Community College
Jennifer Schultz
*Golden Gate University,
 California*
Mary Beth Selbo
*Wright College, City Colleges of
 Chicago*
Stephen Sheeran
*Bishop's University, Lenoxville,
 Quebec*
Kathy Sherak
San Francisco State University
Keith Smith
*ELS Language Center, San
 Francisco*
Helen Solorzano
Northeastern University

Contents

A Word from Diane Larsen-Freeman, Series Director

Before *Grammar Dimensions* was published, teachers would always ask me, "What is the role of grammar in a communicative approach?" These teachers recognized the importance of teaching grammar, but they associated grammar with form and communication with meaning, and thus could not see how the two easily fit together. *Grammar Dimensions* was created to help teachers and students appreciate the fact that grammar is not just about form. While grammar does indeed involve form, in order to communicate, language users also need to know the meaning of the forms and when to use them appropriately. In fact, it is sometimes not the form, but the *meaning* or *appropriate use* of a grammatical structure that represents the greatest long-term learning challenge for students. For instance, learning when it is appropriate to use the present perfect tense instead of the past tense, or being able to use two-word or phrasal verbs meaningfully, represent formidable challenges for ESL students.

The three dimensions of form, meaning, and use can be depicted in a pie chart with their interrelationship illustrated by the three arrows:

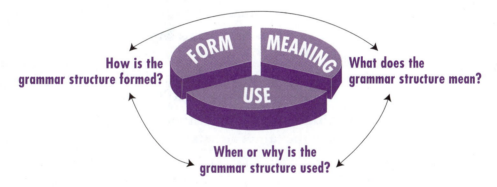

Helping students learn to use grammatical structures accurately, meaningfully, and appropriately is the fundamental goal of *Grammar Dimensions.* It is consistent with the goal of helping students to communicate meaningfully in English, and one that recognizes the undeniable interdependence of grammar and communication.

Enjoy the Platinum Edition!

To learn more about form, meaning, and use, read *The Grammar Book: An ESL/EFL Teacher's Course,* Second Edition, by Marianne Celce-Murcia and Diane Larsen-Freeman, also from Heinle & Heinle. It helps both prospective and practicing teachers of ESL/EFL enhance their understanding of English grammar, expand their skills in linguistic analysis, and develop a pedagogical approach to teaching English grammar that builds on the three dimensions. ISBN: 0-8384-4725-2.

Welcome to Grammar Dimensions, Platinum Edition!

The most comprehensive communicative grammar series available.

Updated and revised, *Grammar Dimensions, Platinum Edition,* makes teaching grammar easy and more effective than ever. Clear grammar explanations, a wealth of exercises, lively communicative activities, technology resources, and fully annotated Teacher's Editions help both beginning and experienced teachers give their students the practice and skills they need to communicate accurately, meaningfully, and appropriately.

Grammar Dimensions, Platinum Edition, is:

Communicative	• Students practice the **form, meaning,** and **use** of each grammar structure.
	• **Improved! A variety of communicative activities** helps students practice grammar and communication in tandem, eliciting self-expression and personalized practice.
	• Students learn to communicate accurately, meaningfully, and appropriately.
Comprehensive	• **Improved!** Grammar is presented in **clear charts.**
	• **A wealth of exercises** helps students practice and master their new language.
	• **The Workbook** provides extra practice and helps students prepare for the TOEFL® Test.
	• **Engaging listening activities** on audiocassette further reinforce the target structure.
	• **New! Enclosed CD-ROM** includes over 500 activities and gives students even more practice in mastering grammar and its use in language. **FREE!**
Clear	• **Improved! Simplified grammar explanations** help both students and teachers easily understand and comprehend each language structure.
	• **Improved! A fresh new design** makes each activity engaging.
	• **New! Communicative activities** ("the Purple Pages") are now labeled with the skill being practiced.
	• **New!** The Teacher's Edition has **page references** for the Student Book and Workbook, minimizing extra preparation time.

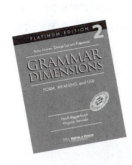

User Friendly for Students	• **Contextualized grammar explanations and examples** help students understand the target language.
	• **New! Goals** at the beginning of each unit focus students' attention on the learning they will do.
	• **Sample phrases and sentences** model the appropriate use of the structure.
User Friendly for Teachers	• **New!** Teacher's Edition now contains answers, tests, tape scripts, and complete, **step-by-step teaching suggestions** for every activity.
	• **New!** "Purple Page" activities are now labeled with the skill.
	• **Improved! A tight integration** among the Student Book, the Workbook and the Teacher's Edition make extension activities easy to do.
Flexible	• Instructors can use the units in order or as set by their curriculum.
	• Exercises can be used in order or as needed by the students.
	• "Purple Page" activities can be used at the end of the unit or interspersed throughout the unit.
Effective	Students who learn the form, meaning, and use of each grammar structure will be able to communicate more accurately, meaningfully, and appropriately.

Grammar Dimensions, Platinum Edition

In *Grammar Dimensions, Platinum Edition,* students progress from the sentence level to the discourse level, and learn to communicate appropriately at all levels.

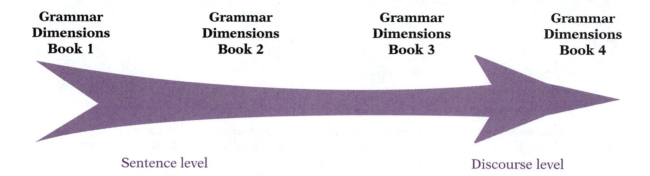

| Grammar Dimensions Book 1 | Grammar Dimensions Book 2 | Grammar Dimensions Book 3 | Grammar Dimensions Book 4 |

Sentence level   Discourse level

	Grammar Dimensions, Book 1	Grammar Dimensions, Book 2	Grammar Dimensions, Book 3	Grammar Dimensions, Book 4
Level	High beginning	Intermediate	High intermediate	Advanced
Grammar level	Sentence and subsentence level	Sentence and subsentence level	Discourse level	Discourse level
Primary language and communication focus	Semantic notions such as *time* and *place*	Social functions, such as *making requests* and *seeking permission*	Cohesion and coherence at the discourse level	Academic and technical discourse
Major skill focus	Listening and speaking	Listening and speaking	Reading and writing	Reading and writing
Outcome	Students form accurate, meaningful, and appropriate structures at the sentence level.	Students form accurate, meaningful, and appropriate structures at the sentence level.	Students learn how accurate, meaningful, and appropriate grammatical structures contribute to the organization of language above the simple sentence.	Students learn how accurate, meaningful, and appropriate grammatical structures contribute to the organization of language above the simple sentence.

Unit Organization

Used with or without the Workbook and the *Grammar 3D* CD-ROM, ***Grammar Dimensions*** Student Book units are designed to be clear, comprehensive, flexible, and communicative.

Goals	• **Focus students' attention** on the learning they will do in each chapter.
Opening Task	• **Contextualizes** the target grammatical structure. • **Enables teachers to diagnose** their students' performance and identify the aspect of the structure with which their students have the most difficulty. • **Provides a roadmap** for the grammar points students need to work on in that chapter.
Focus Boxes	• **Present the form, meaning,** or **use** of a particular grammatical structure. • **Focus students' attention** to a particular feature of the target structure. Each rule or explanation is preceded by examples, so teachers can have students work inductively to try to discover the rule on their own.
Exercises	• Provide a wealth of opportunity to **practice** the form and meaning of the grammar structures. • Help students develop the skill of **"grammaring"**—the ability to use structures accurately, meaningfully, and appropriately. • Are varied, thematically coherent, but purposeful. • Give students many opportunities to personalize and own the language.
Communicative Activities ("The Purple Pages")	• Help students practice **grammar and communication in tandem.** • **Are engaging!** • Encourage students to **use their new language** both inside and outside the classroom. • Provide an opportunity to **practice reading, writing, listening, and speaking skills,** helping students realize the communicative value of the grammar they are learning.

Student Book Supplements

Audiocassettes	• **Provide listening activities for** each unit so students can practice listening to **grammar structures in context.**
Workbooks	• **Provide additional exercises** for each grammar point presented in the student text. • Offer question types found on the **TOEFL**® Test.
CD-ROM	• *Grammar 3D* **provides additional practice** for 34 of the key grammar structures found in the text series. • Offers over **500 activities** for beginning to advanced students. • **Provides an instructional "help page"** that allows students to access grammar explanations at any point. • **Provides feedback** that helps students understand their errors and guides them toward correct answers. • **Free** with each Student Book!
Teacher's Editions	• **Facilitate teaching** by providing in one place notes and examples, answer keys to the Student Book and Workbook, page references to all of the components, the tapescript for the audiocassette activities, and tests with answer keys for each unit. • **Minimize teacher preparation time** by providing step-by-step teaching suggestions for every focus box and activity in the Student Book.

The ***Grammar Dimensions, Platinum Edition*** Student Books and the additional components help teachers teach and students learn to use English grammar structures in communication accurately, meaningfully, and appropriately.

Acknowledgments

Series Director Acknowledgments

This edition would not have come about if it had not been for the enthusiastic response of teachers and students using the previous editions. I am very grateful for the reception **Grammar Dimensions** has been given.

I am also grateful for all the authors' efforts. To be a teacher, and at the same time a writer, is a difficult balance to achieve . . . so is being an innovative creator of materials, and yet, a team player. They have met these challenges exceedingly well in my opinion. Then, too, the Heinle & Heinle team has been impressive. I am grateful for the leadership exercised by Erik Gundersen, formerly of Heinle & Heinle. I also appreciate all the support from Charlotte Sturdy, Mike Burggren, and Marianne Bartow. Deserving special mention are Jean Bernard, and above all, Nancy Jordan, who never lost the vision while they attended to the detail with good humor and professionalism.

I have also benefited from the counsel of Marianne Celce-Murcia, consultant for the first edition this project, and my friend. Finally, I wish to thank my family members, Elliott, Brent, and Gavin, for not once asking the (negative yes–no) question that must have occurred to them countless times: "Haven't you finished yet?"

Author Acknowledgments

This edition represents the extraordinary dedication and ongoing commitment of many, many people: First and foremost, thanks are due to the entire Heinle & Heinle team, whose consistent support, enthusiasm, hard work, and commitment to the series can only be described as an author's dream come true. Most especially I would like to express my appreciation to our patient and long-suffering editors, Diane Larsen-Freeman and Amy Lawler, whose extremely helpful perspectives and perceptive comments (to say nothing of their gentle prodding and consistent good humor) have substantially increased the quality and consistency of the series. Gratitude and appreciation also go to the great web of thoughtful and dedicated teachers whose on-going feedback, wisdom, and involvement with the series have helped us improve, fine-tune, and correct. Their caring professional support and involvement have been crucial to the success of the series.

Finally, to my friends and family, most especially my partner Michael Mercil, whose support, understanding, and gracious relinquishment of vacations, nights, and weekends was (as always) above and beyond, my abiding gratitude and love.

UNIT 1

OVERVIEW OF THE ENGLISH VERB SYSTEM

Time and Tense

UNIT GOALS:

- To review the English verb system
- To keep tenses in the same time frame
- To change the time frame correctly within a passage

▶ OPENING TASK
Comparing Past, Present, and Future

STEP 1 Work with a partner. Student A, look at the following information about Bob Lee, a typical American college student. Student B, look at the information on the next page about Bob's grandfather, Robert Lee. Student A, tell Student B about Bob's life. Student B, tell Student A about Robert's life.

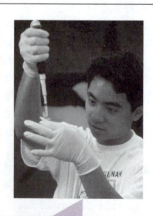

BOB LEE

Born: 1981

Family: Two brothers and one sister, living with mother; parents divorced; Bob lives in a college dorm

Occupation: currently a sophomore, studying biology, plans to be a doctor

Regular activities: school, part-time job in the library, time with girlfriend, visiting family some weekends and during school vacations

Hobbies or favorite sports: basketball, skiing, computers, music, TV

Visits to foreign countries: Mexico (once), Canada (twice)

Special skills or abilities: computers, university chorus

Probable activity at this moment: studying for biology midterm

ROBERT LEE

Born: 1930   **DIED:** 1992

Family: Five brothers, four sisters; only one sister and brother survived childhood; father died of tuberculosis when Robert was fourteen years old

Occupation: factory worker, never finished high school

Regular activities: Job (twelve-hour days); helping mother; family life

Hobbies or favorite sports: radio, baseball (on factory team), church

Visits to foreign countries: none

Special skills or abilities: baseball, harmonica playing

Probable activity when Bob was born: working at the factory

STEP 2   Now work together to create a story for Roberta, Bob's grand-daughter. Fill in some information below and then tell another pair of students about how you think Roberta's life will be.

ROBERTA CHONG-DAVIS

Born: 2035

Family: _____

Occupation: _____

Regular activities: _____

_____

Hobbies or favorite sports: _____

_____

Visits to foreign countries or planets: _____

_____

Special skills or abilities: _____

_____

Probable activity at this moment 100 years from today: _____

▶ **O**verview of the English Verb System

The form of any verb in English is made up of two things: time frame and aspect.

Time frame tells **when** something took place. There are three basic time frames: **present, past,** and **future.**	**Aspect** tells **how** the verb is related to that time, or gives some other information about the quality of the action. (See Unit 2.)

There are four kinds of aspect, and each one has a basic meaning.

ASPECT	MEANING
simple	**at** that time
progressive	**in progress during** that time
perfect	**before** that time
perfect progressive	**in progress during and before** that time

When we combine the three time frames and the four aspects, we get twelve possible combinations of forms. These forms are called *tenses,* and the name of each tense tells which time frame and which aspect are being used. The charts in Appendix 1, on pages A-1 to A-4, show in more detail the three basic time frames and the tenses which are used in each.

ASPECT	SIMPLE	PROGRESSIVE	PERFECT	PERFECT PROGRESSIVE
TIME FRAME			TENSES	
Present	*simple present* study/studies give/gives	*present progressive* is/are studying is/are giving	*present perfect* has/have studied has/have given	*present perfect progressive* has/have been studying has/have been giving
Past	*simple present* ~~past~~ studied gave	*past progressive* was/were studying was/were giving	*past perfect* had studied had given	*past perfect progressive* had been studying had been giving
Future	*simple future* will study will give	*future progressive* will be studying will be giving	*future perfect* will have studied will have given	*future perfect progressive* will have been studying will have been giving

EXERCISE 1

Read the following passages and identify the time frame of each. Is it present time, past time, or future time?

1. (a) Mac had a terrible headache. (b) His tongue was dry, and his eyes were burning. (c) He had been sneezing constantly for nearly an hour. (d) He hated springtime. (e) For most people spring meant flowers and sunshine, but for Mac it meant allergies.

2. (a) I really don't know what to do for vacation. (b) My vacation starts in three weeks, and (c) I'm trying to decide what to do. (d) I've been to Hawaii and New York. (e) It's too early in the year to go camping in the mountains. (f) I've been working hard at the office and I really need a break. (g) I've saved enough money to have a really nice trip. (h) I just can't decide where to go or what to do.

3. (a) The changing world climate will mean changes in food production. (b) Scientists think that summers throughout North America will become much hotter and drier than they are now. (c) Crops that require a lot of water will be less economical to grow. (d) Society will have to develop different energy sources, (e) since fossil fuels, such as coal and oil, may have become depleted by the end of the next century.

4. (a) "Social Darwinism" was a popular theory of the nineteenth century. (b) It compared social and economic development with biological evolution. (c) According to this theory, competition between rich people and poor people was unavoidable. (d) The poor were like dinosaurs who were dying out because they had lost the battle for survival—economic survival.

5. (a) Scientific research often has an important social impact. (b) In recent years scientists have discovered that Vitamin B can prevent certain kinds of childhood blindness. (c) As a result, programs have been established that provide education and dietary supplements to children in developing countries.

EXERCISE 2

Choose three of the passages in Exercise 1, and underline each complete verb phrase (the verb plus any auxiliary—*have, do, is,* etc.—that shows the tense of the verb). Name the tense of each verb phrase you have underlined.

EXERCISE 3

Check your knowledge of irregular verb forms by completing the chart on page 4. You may work with other students. When you finish, check your work using Appendix 6, Irregular Verbs, on page A-10.

Base form	Past tense form	Past participle
become	became	become
begin	began	begun
	bent	
bind		bet
	bit	
blow		bled
	broke	brought
build		
catch	chose	bought
come	cost	
cost		dug
cut	did	
	drew	drunk
do		
drive	ate	fallen
feed	felt	
feel	fought	
fight		
find	fit	
fit		
fly	forgave	frozen
forbid		
forget	gave	
forgive		
get		

Base form	Past tense form	Past participle
go	went	
	grew	ground
hang	had	
hear	hid	
	hit	
	held	known
hurt	kept	
lead	left	let
lend		
make		meant
meet	put	
		quit
read	rode	
		rung
rise	ran	
	saw	said
see	sought	saw
sell	sold	sold
send	set	
		shaken
shine	shot	
		shut

Base form	Past tense form	Past participle
sing	sank	
		sat
sleep	slid	
		spoken
speed	spent	split
spread	sprang	stood
steal		
strike	stuck	stung
swear		
	swept	swung
	swam	
take	taught	torn / talk
tell	talk	
	thought	thrown
understand		
	woke	worn
weave		
	wept	won
wind	wrote	

▶ # Keeping Tenses in the Same Time Frame

In general, we choose a particular time frame and then choose from among the tenses within that time frame in order to describe events.

EXAMPLES	EXPLANATIONS
(a) My roommate **had** a dance party last Friday night. I **was working** that night, so I **didn't get** home until 10:00, and everyone **had** already **started** dancing.	Use past tenses to describe things that happened at a specific time in the past.
(b) My roommate **has** a dance party every Friday night. I **work** on Friday nights, so I **don't get** home until 10:00, and everyone **has** already **started** dancing.	Use present tenses to describe things that are happening now, are related to now, or happen again and again.
(c) My roommate **is going to have** a dance party next Friday night. I **will be working** next Friday night, so I **won't get** home until 10:00, and everyone **will** already **have started** dancing.	Use future tenses to describe events that are going to happen at some time in the future.

EXERCISE 4
Decide what time frame each of these passages should be written in, and then write the appropriate verb form in the blanks.

1. I hear we (a) _____ (be playing) games at Mike's party next week. I hope there (b) _____ (be) dancing as well! I (c) _____ (have completed) my dance class by then.

2. I (a) _____ (have) an interesting experience yesterday afternoon. As I (b) _____ (be walking) from my house to the grocery store, I (c) _____ (see) someone I (d) _____ (have gone) to high school with.

3. Steve (a) _____ (have) a terrible time getting to work every day. When he (b) _____ (be driving) to work he often (c) _____ (get) caught in terrible traffic jams. Even though he only (d) _____ (live) a few miles from the office, it sometimes (e) _____ (take) nearly an hour to get to work.

4. The Imperial City of Rome (a) _____ (be) badly damaged by fire during the First Century A.D. At the time it (b) _____ (be believed) that the Emperor Nero (c) _____ (be playing) a violin while the city (d) _____ (burn) to the ground.

5. Scientists (a) _____ (be) worried that the world climate (b) _____ (be changing). They (c) _____ (believe) this change (d) _____ (have resulted) from an increase in the amount of carbon dioxide (CO_2) in the earth's atmosphere. Whenever "fossil fuels" such as coal or oil (e) _____ (be burned), the amount of CO_2 (f) _____ (increase). This (g) _____ (cause) the atmosphere to retain more heat. There (h) _____ (be) proof that this process already (i) _____ (have begun). Scientists (j) _____ (have discovered) that the average temperature of the world's oceans (k) _____ (have risen) by one degree in the last twenty years.

6. John (a) _____ (leave) for Paris on Tuesday. He (b) _____ (be staying) with a local family for the first few weeks. After that, he probably (c) _____ (find) a small apartment of his own.

Changing the Time Frame Within a Passage

USE

Although the time frame often stays the same within a passage, an author sometimes changes the time frame.

EXAMPLES	EXPLANATIONS
(a) There **are** many examples in history of increasing military power causing a decreasing standard of living. Rome **was** unable to feed both its army and its population. Great Britain **declined** steadily from its economic position in the early part of this century.	• to move from a general statement to specific examples
(b) **One hundred years ago** the life expectancy in the United States **was** about sixty-five. **Nowadays,** it **has increased** by an average of ten years. **In the next century,** if current trends continue, people **should be able to live** until their nineties. Interestingly enough, however, **a hundred years ago** the number of people who were over one hundred **was** less than one percent of the population. That figure **has not changed** substantially, even **today.**	• to show contrast between one time and another
(c) I saw an elderly lady yesterday. **You don't see her kind much anymore.** She was wearing a black dress and she was carrying an umbrella. **Most elderly ladies I know don't carry umbrellas, and pants are more common than dresses.** As she walked down the street, I thought about how much life has changed since she was my age.	• to make a statement of general truth

EXERCISE 5

Mark the following passages with a vertical line (/) to show where the time frame changes. The first one has been done for you as an example.

1. My brother called me up yesterday. / I always know he needs to borrow money when he calls, because I never hear from him at any other time. / We spoke about this and that for a few minutes. He asked about my job and my family. We talked about his problems with his boss. / These are typical topics before he finally asks for a loan. / This phone call was no exception. He needed fifty dollars "until pay day." / Somehow, when pay-day comes he never remembers to pay back the loan.

2. I'll be really happy when the summer is over. / I don't like hot weather,

and I can't stand mosquitoes. There's a lot of both of those things in the summer. Last summer I tried to escape by going on a trip to Alaska. The heat wasn't bad, but the mosquitoes were terrible! Next year I think I'll consider a vacation in Antarctica. I understand it's really cold there in July.

2. For more than fifty years scientists around the world have all used a single system to measure the strength (or "magnitude") of earthquakes. The Richter Scale was developed by Charles Richter in 1935. It was designed so scientists could compare the strength of earthquakes in different parts of the world. It was not designed to measure damage in earthquakes, but only intensity. This is because a less powerful earthquake in a heavily populated area can cause more damage than a stronger earthquake in an unpopulated area.

EXERCISE 6

Discuss each change of time frame that you found in Exercise 5 with a partner. Why did the author change the time frame? There may be more than one reason. Share your explanation with the rest of the class.

EXERCISE 7

Underline the complete verb phrases (verb plus auxiliaries) in the passages in Exercise 5 and name the tense of each verb phrase.

Use Your English

ACTIVITY 1: SPEAKING/WRITING

STEP 1 Work with a partner. Describe a typical day in your life. Tell your partner about the things you do, where you go, and how you typically spend your time. Mention at least five regular activities.

STEP 2 Next, describe a typical day in your life five years ago. Mention at least five activities that you did on a regular basis.

STEP 3 Your partner should use this information to decide what three things in your life have changed the most in the last five years, and report this information to the rest of the class. Make a similar report to the class about the changes in your partner's life.

ACTIVITY 2: LISTENING

Listen to these descriptions about two people—one who is no longer living and one who is still alive. Based on the time frame and verb tenses used in the descriptions, decide which person is still living and which person is deceased.

ACTIVITY 3: SPEAKING/WRITING

Congratulations! You've just won a million dollars in a contest. BUT . . . you have to spend all the money in a single week. AND . . . you can't spend more than $50,000 for any single purchase. (In other words, you can't just buy a million dollar house. You have to make at least twenty separate purchases.) If you don't spend it all, you won't get any of it.

STEP 1 What are your plans? In a brief essay, or in an oral presentation, answer this question: **How you will spend the money?**

STEP 2 It's the end of the week. How did you spend your money? Change the verb tenses of your essay or presentation to answer to this question: **How did you spend the money?**

ACTIVITY 4: WRITING/SPEAKING

Newspaper headlines represent a special kind of English. They usually omit a lot of important grammatical information. Test how well you know the basic sentence elements of English by "translating" these headlines into complete sentences. Compare your "translations" to those of another student.

▶ **EXAMPLES:** BABY FOUND IN BUS STATION

A baby has been found in the bus station.

- STOCK MARKET CRASHES
- U.S. POPULATION MOVING WEST
- NEW BUDGET TERMED "DISASTER"
- U.S. TO PROTEST NUCLEAR TESTING
- PRESIDENT TO VISIT CHINA
- DROUGHT EXPECTED TO WORSEN
- BIG WHITE HOUSE SHAKE-UP
- NEW PLAN TO IMPROVE BUS SERVICES

- TEST SCORES IMPROVING IN PUBLIC SCHOOLS
- LINK FOUND BETWEEN DIET AND HEART DISEASE
- CANCER REPORTED INCREASING
- MAJOR GROWTH IN INTERNATIONAL STUDENTS IN U.S.

ACTIVITY 5: SPEAKING/WRITING

How are you progressing in English? Fill in this chart, following the steps listed below.

ACCOMPLISHMENTS	GOALS	STRATEGIES
1.	1.	1.
2.	2.	2.
3.	3.	3.

STEP 1 Describe how your ability to communicate in English has changed since you began your studies. What kinds of things were you able to accomplish a year ago, and what can yo do now that is different?

▶ **EXAMPLES:**
1. A year ago, I couldn't understand spoken English very well. My listening comprehension has improved a lot. I understand most things people say to me.

2. A year ago I needed to use a dictionary for almost every word. Now my vocabulary is much larger.

Think of three areas where your skills have improved. Write sentences describing those things under the column marked **Accomplishments.**

STEP 2 Next, describe some things that you still can't do, but you want to be able to do. Think of at least three things you can't or don't do now, but want to be able to do by the end of this course

▶ **EXAMPLES:**
1. I don't talk to my friends on the telephone because I have a hard time understanding them. I want to be able to talk on the telephone.

2. I can't pass the TOEFL. My scores on Part 2 are a little low. I want to get a good score on the TOEFL.

Write sentences describing those skills under the column marked **Goals.**

STEP 3 Compare your accomplishments and goals to those of other people in the class. As a group, think of three strategies for increasing your language abilities and achieving your goals, and write them under the column marked **Strategies.** Present your list of strategies to the rest of the class.

ACTIVITY 6: READING/WRITING

Now that you have finished this first unit and have some ideas about your areas of strength and weakness, look briefly through all the units of this book and the Table of Contents on pp. iv–xii in order to identify:

- one unit you would like the whole class to study
- one unit you would enjoy studying by yourself
- one unit you think you could study together with another student in the class
- one unit you feel you already understand well enough to explain to another student.

ACTIVITY 7: WRITING

Language teachers recommend that students keep a journal or language learning log to record their progress, goals, and questions. Studies have proven that students who do this learn more quickly and effectively. Here is one example of a language learning log format. Fill out this log at least once a week during this course and turn it in or discuss it with your teacher or with another student in the class.

LANGUAGE LEARNING LOG

Section 1. MISTAKES, CORRECTIONS, AND EXPLANATIONS

Write down **five mistakes** that you made in either writing or speaking in the last week. For each mistake write the correct form. In your own words, explain what was wrong with your original sentence.

▶ **EXAMPLES:** Mistake: I *enjoy to shop* in my free time.
Correction: I *enjoy shopping* in my free time.
Explanation: *enjoy* must take a gerund . . . not an infinitive.

Section 2. QUESTIONS

Write **three question**s you have about any aspect of grammar that you have read, heard, or studied in the last week. Your teacher will return your journal with an explanation of your questions.

▶ **EXAMPLES:** I don't understand the difference between <u>interesting/interested.</u>

I hear my friend say "If I <u>was</u> rich . . . " But we learned that <u>were</u> is correct. How can he say that?

OVERVIEW OF THE ENGLISH VERB SYSTEM

Aspect

UNIT GOALS:

- To review aspect in English verbs
- To review the simple tenses
- To use progressive, perfect, and perfect progressive aspect appropriately

▶ **OPENING TASK**
A Picture Is Worth a Thousand Words

STEP 1 With a partner, discuss each of these photographs and together write sentences about them. Your sentences should answer these questions.

- What has just happened? Why do you think so?
- What is happening now? Why do you think so?
- What is going to happen next? Why do you think so?

STEP 2 Once you have described all the pictures, compare your descriptions with two other pairs of students. Do you all agree? Did you use the same verb tenses in your descriptions?

STEP 3 Report any interesting similarities and differences to the rest of the class.

▶ **O**verview of Aspect

In addition to the basic aspect meanings listed in Unit 1, aspect can also be used to describe the quality of an action or situation.

EXAMPLES	EXPLANATIONS
(a) The protester **disrupted** the politician's speech.	• action happens just once
(b) Protesters **have been disrupting** politician's speeches as long as politicians **have been making** them.	• action happens continuously or repeatedly
(c) The police **are arresting** the protester, but perhaps he'll escape.	• action is still happening
(d) The police **have arrested** the protester, so he won't be able to escape.	• action is completed
(e) Shopkeepers **are storing** some of their breakable items on the floor until the threat of earthquake aftershocks has passed.	• situation is temporary
(f) Shopkeepers in earthquake areas **store** expensive, breakable items on the lower shelves in order to lessen the possibility of damage.	• situation is permanent

EXERCISE 1

Analyze one of these paragraphs with a partner. Identify the basic time frame. Then say what meaning is contributed by the aspect in the underlined verb phrases.

1. By the time John gets on Flight 53 to Paris the day after tomorrow, he will have accomplished a great deal in a short period of time. He <u>will have moved out</u> of the apartment where he <u>has been living</u> for the last couple of years. He will have said some long, sad good-byes. He <u>will certainly be thinking</u> about all the friends he will no longer see every day.

2. When the earthquake hit San Francisco in 1989, Jeff was still at his office. He had been trying to finish a project. He <u>had been working</u> on it for over a week, and he was almost done. He <u>was just making</u> some final changes when the building started to move. When the quake started, he quickly got under his desk. He was glad that he had once read an article on what to do in earthquakes. He <u>had studied</u> the article carefully, so he knew exactly what to do.

3. Nancy is quite a stylish dresser. She thinks that it is important to be neat and well-dressed, and she always <u>wants</u> to look her best. Every morning before she leaves for work, she looks at herself in the mirror. She checks to make sure that she has combed her hair and hasn't put her makeup on too heavily. She makes sure that she <u>is wearing</u> colors that go nicely with the clothes she is wearing. She checks to see that her slip isn't showing, and if her stockings are straight. She makes sure that the shoes she <u>has chosen</u> match the color of her dress and her coat. She likes feeling confident and attractive, and feels that taking an extra minute in front of the mirror is worth the time.

FOCUS **2**

▶ **Simple Tenses**

USE

EXAMPLES	EXPLANATIONS
(a) Social psychology **is** the study of the factors that **influence** group behavior.	Use simple tenses:
(b) The people of ancient Rome **spoke** Latin.	• to express general ideas, relationships, and truths
(c) A criminal **will** always **return** to the scene of the crime.	
(d) Denise always **checks** her appearance in the mirror before she leaves for work.	• to describe habitual or recurrent actions
(e) James Fenimore Cooper **wrote** for three hours every day except Sunday.	
(f) People **will commute** to the moon by spaceship at the end of the next century.	
(g) Scientists **report** that they have identified the cause of AIDS.	• to identify time frame
(h) When Alexander the Great **decided** to conquer Asia, he had already heard many stories about the great riches there.	
(i) Mary **will visit** John while he is studying in France.	
(j) Bambang **worries** that he won't pass the TOEFL.	• to describe mental perceptions or emotions
(k) One hundred years ago people **felt** that a woman's place was in the home.	
(l) If we're late for dinner, Mom **will worry** about us.	
(m) Bob **has** two brothers and a sister.	• to express possession or logical relationship
(n) Robert's hobbies **consisted** of playing baseball and the harmonica.	
(o) Roberta's job **will require** regular travel to the moon.	

EXERCISE 2

Work with the same partner that you did for the Opening Task of Unit 1. But instead of describing Bob Lee and his family, describe your own lives, and those of your grandfathers and what may be true for your granddaughters. Each of you should write at least two sentences that describe the lives of each generation.

▶ **Progressive Aspect**

Progressive tenses (present progressive, past progressive, and future progressive) are made by using forms of

$$\text{BE} + \text{VERB} + \text{-ING}$$

EXAMPLES	EXPLANATIONS
(a) Other people **are** always **waiting** when Jeff **gets** to the bus stop. (They're already waiting **before** he gets there.)	Use progressive aspect instead of simple aspect to describe: • actions already in progress versus actions that happen afterwards.
(b) Jeff **reads** the morning paper when he **gets** to the bus stop. (He reads his paper **after** he gets there.)	
(c) When I **entered** the room, the students **were studying,** but when I left the room, they **laughed.** (They were studying **before** I entered, but they laughed **after** I left.)	
(d) I **teach** French, but I**'m not teaching** at the moment.	• actions at a specific time (**now** or **then**) versus habitual or recurring actions
(e) John **studied** in France for a year, but he certainly **wasn't studying** last Bastille Day.	
(f) Mary still **lives** with her parents, but she**'s staying** with friends while her parents are away.	• temporary situations versus permanent states
(g) Those students **are** always **asking** questions.	• repeated actions
(h) John **is** still **working** to perfect his French accent.	• uncompleted actions
(i) Those children **are being** very noisy, but they **are** young, so I guess it's understandable.	• actions rather than states

EXERCISE 3

Why is progressive aspect used in these sentences? There may be more than one possible reason.

▶ **EXAMPLE:**   He is studying for an examination now.

   action in progress now, uncompleted action

1. John was reading a book when I saw him.
2. Don't call him after 10:00 because he will be sleeping.
3. They were selling candy from house to house yesterday afternoon.
4. Whenever I see John, he is always reading a book.
5. I will be visiting friends all over the country during the summer.
6. John was thinking about a solution to his problem, so I didn't interrupt him.
7. He was living with his cousin for a while.
8. I am having trouble with this assignment.
9. I will be staying at the Bates Motel during the conference.
10. I am trying to explain this, so please pay attention.

EXERCISE 4

Decide whether simple or progressive aspect should be used in these sentences. Both choices may be correct.

1. Please turn down the radio. I _____ (study) for a test.
2. Lilik _____ (read) the newspaper when the phone rang.
3. I'm afraid those students might (a) _____ (get) in trouble with Immigration because they (b) _____ (work) without official permission.
4. I still _____ (not study) as much as my parents want me to.
5. Rebecca _____ (speak) Russian. I wonder where she learned it?
6. Columbus (a) _____ (look) for a shorter route to Asia when he (b) _____ (discover) the New World by mistake.
7. When Columbus (a) _____ (reach) Cuba, he (b) _____ (think) it was India.
8. I _____ (try) to help you. Please listen carefully.
9. I (a) _____ (study) in the library, when I (b) _____ (hear) the news about Yitzhak Rabin's assassination.
10. Paolo will probably _____ (sleep) if you wait until midnight to try to call him.

▶ **Perfect Aspect**

Perfect Tenses (present, perfect, past perfect, and future perfect) are made by using forms of:

HAVE + VERB-EN (past participle)

The basic meaning of the perfect aspect is this: the action described using the perfect aspect began before other action or another point in time, and it continues to have influence. We do **not** use perfect aspect to connect unrelated events.

EXAMPLES	EXPLANATIONS
(a) He **had finished** the project when I **talked** to him. (The project was finished before I talked to him.) (b) He **finished** the project when I **talked** to him. (I talked to him first, and then he finished the project.)	Use perfect aspect instead of simple aspect to describe actions: • that happen before another action
(c) We have an English test tomorrow. I **have reviewed** the vocabulary words, but I **haven't studied** the grammar yet.	• that focus on whether they are completed or uncompleted
(d) I **have finished** my homework so now I'm watching TV. (e) Anna **has** just **had** a snack, so she doesn't want dinner.	• that are related to the present moment
(f) Robert Lee **has worked** in a factory for thirty-five years. (He still works there.). (g) Robert Lee **worked** in a factory for thirty-five years. (He doesn't work there anymore.)	• that began in the past but still continue until now

EXERCISE 5

Why is perfect aspect used in these sentences? There may be more than one reason.

1. Please don't take my plate. I haven't finished my dessert.
2. You are too late; the doctor has just left the office.
3. He had forgotten to leave a key, so we couldn't get into the office.
4. She will already have left before you receive her farewell letter.
5. I've done my homework for tomorrow.
6. Biff hadn't even finished high school when he joined the Army.
7. The teacher has canceled the test, so you won't need to study tonight.
8. It has rained every January for the last ten years, so I don't think it's a good idea to plan a picnic.

EXERCISE 6

Decide whether perfect or simple aspect should be used in these sentences.

1. John _____ (say) goodbye to his classmates at school when he started packing for his trip.
2. Jonas Salk _____ (conduct) many unsuccessful experiments when his efforts finally resulted in the discovery of a vaccine for polio.
3. The United States _____ (have) the same form of government for more than two hundred years.
4. Bob _____ (visit) Mexico five times so far. He really likes travel-ing there.
5. When Bambang (a) _____ (come) to the United States, he (b) _____ (not be) away from his parents for more than a few days.
6. By the time Roberta Chong-Davis is fifty years old, she will probably _____ (travel) to the moon several times.
7. I _____ (not sleep) well since those noisy people moved into the apartment next door.
8. Columbus (a) _has_ (complete) three voyages to islands in the Caribbean when he (b) _____ (realize) that the islands (c) _were not_ (not be) part of India.
9. We _have live_ (live) in this house since 1968.
10. Lucy _has_ (study) very hard for the TOEFL, so I hope she passes!

studing

▶ **P**erfect **P**rogressive **A**spect

USE

Perfect progressive tenses (present perfect progressive, past perfect progressive, and future perfect progressive) are made by using forms of:

HAVE + BEEN + VERB + -ING

EXAMPLES	EXPLANATIONS
(a) Jeff **has been working** on that project all day. He still hasn't finished it.	Use perfect progressive aspect instead of perfect aspect to describe:
(b) Jeff **has worked** on that project for three hours. Now he can do something else.	• actions that are uncompleted (a) instead of completed (b)
(c) You **have been talking** for the last hour. Please give someone else a chance to use the phone.	• actions that are continuous (c) instead of repeated (d)
(d) I **have talked** to that student several times about his lack of effort.	

EXERCISE 7

Decide whether perfect or perfect progressive aspect should be used in these sentences. More than one answer may be correct.

1. It _____ (rain) ever since we got here. I wish it would stop.

2. He _____ (work) on that computer virus for nearly a year before he realized that nothing could destroy it.

3. I'm very pleased. I _____ (find) the article you mentioned in your paper.

4. Lately John _____ (find) life without Mary more and more difficult.

5. Joyce _____ (cook) all afternoon. I hope the food will be as delicious as it smells.

6. Omar (a) _____ (look) for his car keys for over an hour, when he realized that he (b) _____ (leave) them in the car.

7. I _____ (try) to solve the problem for over an hour. I give up!

8. Next January 31, Jeff and Matt _____ (live) together as roommates for five years.

9. The Girl Scouts (a) _____ (come) to the house to sell cookies
once a year ever since I (b) _____ (move) here.

10. I _____ (try) to reach him several times by phone, without success.

EXERCISE 8

Write the appropriate form for the verbs in the following paragraph. The first
three have been done for you as examples.

My roommate (1) __had__ (have) a dance party last Friday night. I
(2) __was working__ (work) that Friday night, so I (3) __didn't get__ (not get)
home until 10:00. By the time I (4) ___go___ (get) there, everyone ~~walked~~
(5) __had started__ (start) dancing. When I (6) __was walked walker__ (walk) into the room
everybody (7) __shouted__ (shout) "welcome home!" because I (8) __had__ (just
arrive), and they (9) __keeped keped__ (keep) dancing. I (10) __went__ (go)
into the kitchen to find something to eat. There (11) __were__ (be) several
other people in the kitchen. They (12) __were ing__ (sit) by an open window.
We (13) __talked__ (talk) and (14) __laughed__ (laugh) for a while.
Just when I (15) __was__ (be) ready to start dancing myself, there
(16) __was__ (be) a knock at the door. I (17) __went__ (go) to answer
it, and (18) __discovered__ (discover) our neighbor, who (19) __was__ (complain ing) about the noise. He (20) __asked__ (ask) us to turn the music
down. We (21) __obeyed__ (obey), of course. And although the party
(22) __got__ (get) a little quieter, we still (23) __had__ (have) fun.

EXERCISE 9

Rewrite the paragraph in Exercise 8 in a present time frame. Keep the time relations between the verbs the same by maintaining the same aspect differences as in the paragraph in Exercise 8.

My roommate (1) __has__ (have) a dance party every Friday night. I (2) __am working__ (work) Friday night these days, so I (3) __don't get__ (not get) home until 10:00. On most Fridays, by the time I (4) __get__ (get) there, everyone (5) __starts__ (start) dancing. When I (6) __walk__ (walk) into the room everybody (7) __shouts__ (shout) "welcome home!" because I (8) __have__ (just arrive), and they (9) __keep__ (keep) dancing. I generally (10) __go__ (go) into the kitchen to find something to eat. Usually, there (11) __are__ (be) several other people in the kitchen. They (12 __sit__ (sit) by an open window. We (13) __talk__ (talk) and (14) __laugh__ (laugh) for a while. Just when I (15) __am__ (be) ready to start dancing myself, there (16) __is__ (be) almost always a knock at the door. I (17) __go__ (go) to answer it, and (18) __discover__ (discover) our neighbor, who (19) __plains__ (complain) about the noise. He (20) __ask__ (ask) us to turn the music down. We (21) __obey__ (obey), of course. And although the party (22) __gets__ (get) a little quieter, we generally still (23) __have__ (have) fun.

EXERCISE 10

Rewrite the paragraph in Exercise 8 in a future time frame. Keep the time relations between the verbs the same by maintaining the same aspect differences as in the paragraph in Exercise 8.

My roommate (1) **is going to have** (have) a dance party next Friday night. He has done this so often that I think I know exactly what's going to happen. I (2) **will be working** (work) next Friday night, so I (3) **won't get** (not get) home until 10:00. By the time I (4) _get_ (get) there, I'm sure that everyone (5) _will have started_ (start) dancing already. When I (6) _walked_ (walk) into the room everybody (7) _will shout_ (shout) "welcome home!" because I (8) _just arrive_ (just arrive), but they probably (9) _keep_ (keep) dancing. I probably (10) _will go_ (go) into the kitchen to find something to eat, and undoubtedly there (11) _will be_ (be) several other people in the kitchen. They (12) _will be sitting_ (sit) by an open window. If next Friday is like most of these parties, we (13) _will talk_ (talk) and (14) _laugh_ (laugh) for a while, and just when I (15) _am be_ (be) ready to start dancing myself, there most likely (16) _will be_ (be) a knock at the door. I (17) _will go_ (go) to answer it, and (18) _discover_ (discover) our neighbor. He (19) _will_ (complain) about the noise, and (20) _aske_ (ask) us to turn the music down. We (21) _will obey_ (obey), of course. And although the party (22) _will get_ (get) a little quieter, we undoubtedly still (23) _will have_ (have) fun.

EXERCISE 11

Work with a partner. Compare the tenses you used in Exercises 8, 9, and 10. Did you use the same aspect for each verb in all three exercises? What does this tell you about how tenses work together in a particular time frame? Discuss these questions with your partner, and report your ideas to the rest of the class.

EXERCISE 12

Complete these sentences with information about yourself. Compare your answers with other students. Did you use the same verb forms?

1. Until I came to this country I . . .
2. I often think about my problems when . . .
3. I had never seen . . . before I . . .
4. The next time I see my family they . . .
5. I am usually unhappy if . . .
6. When I was growing up, I . . .
7. I have been studying English since I . . .
8. Lately I . . .
9. Once I have completed my education, I . . .
10. I have never . . . , but I plan to do it someday.

Use Your English

ACTIVITY 1: LISTENING

Listen to the following conversations and put a check next to the statements which can be correctly inferred from each conversation.

Conversation 1

_____✓_ (a) Mary doesn't want a roommate.

_____ (b) Mary doesn't have a roommate at the moment, but she's looking for one.

_____ (c) John doesn't want a roommate.

___✓_ (d) John doesn't have a roommate at the moment, but he's looking for one.

Conversation 2

_____ (a) Peter is looking the contract over at this moment.

___✓_ (b) Peter is not looking the contract over at this moment.

___✓_ (c) Denise is looking the contract over at this moment.

_____ (d) Denise is not looking the contract over at this moment.

Conversation 3

_____ (a) The janitor finished washing the floors before Angela's arrival.

___✓_ (b) He finished washing the floors after Angela's arrival.

_____ (c) The janitor emptied the trash before Angela's arrival.

___✓_ (d) He emptied the trash after Angela's arrival.

___✓_ (e) The janitor finished the windows before Angela's arrival.

_____ (f) He finished the windows after Angela's arrival.

Conversation 4

___✓_ (a) Bob works at the steel mill now.

_____ (b) Bob doesn't work at the steel mill now.

_____ (c) Dave works at the steel mill now.

___✓_ (d) Dave doesn't work at the steel mill now.

ACTIVITY 2: WRITING

Revise your descriptions of the photographs in the Opening Task on pages 12 and 13 by using the past time frame. Start your descriptions like this: *When this picture was taken . . .*

ACTIVITY 3: READING

Look at the front page of a newspaper. Find three examples of each of the three time frames (present, past, and future). They may be in the same article or three different articles.

ACTIVITY 4: SPEAKING

Bring in three interesting photographs from a newspaper. Make a brief presentation about these photos to the class. Describe what is happening, what has happened, and what is going to happen. Then give three reasons why you think the photo is interesting.

ACTIVITY 5: WRITING/SPEAKING

Describe a routine that you typically follow. Then describe one time when you did not follow that routine, and tell what happened. For example, perhaps you usually take the bus to school. What time do you get there? What are people on the bus doing when you get on? What happened on the day when you decided to walk to school because the bus was late, or on the day when your classmate offered to take you for a ride in his cousin's brand-new car?

UNIT 3

ADVERBIAL PHRASES AND CLAUSES

Adverbial Phrases and Clauses

UNIT GOALS:

- To identify phrases and clauses
- To correctly position adverbs
- To correctly position adverbial phrases and clauses

adverbial

▶ OPENING TASK
Who? What? Which? Where? When? Why? How?

Ski Mask Bank Robber Strikes Again

VANCOUVER, BC

Columbia Savings and Loan was struck by a bank robber for the third time this year. An unidentified man in a blue ski mask entered the bank during the busiest time of the day and demanded money from the cashier.

Although three security officers were on duty, the thief was able to escape on foot. Bank officials estimate total losses of over ten thousand dollars. Police have been interviewing witnesses in hopes of getting a more complete description of the thief.

Similar robberies in other parts of the city have led police to suspect that the same person might be responsible for all three robberies. Authorities are concerned about the fact that robberies have increased a great deal in the last three months. As a result, bank officials say, they will begin to install metal detectors in order to prevent people from entering banks with guns.

STEP 1   Newspaper reporters say that all basic news information about people and events can be summarized by asking and answering only the seven "Universal Questions" (Who? What? Which? Where? When? Why? How?). Summarize this newspaper article by writing W*h*-questions. Write as many questions as you need to in order to summarize all the important information.

STEP 2   Give your questions to a partner. Your partner should try to reconstruct the article by writing answers to your questions. Do the same with your partner's list of questions.

STEP 3   Compare your partner's answers with your questions and with the article. Your partner should do the same with your answers. Is any important information missing from your answers? Was there anything that you did not know how to ask about? Were there questions that you could not answer?

FORM

▶ **Identifying Phrases and Clauses**

Phrases are groups of related words.

EXAMPLES	EXPLANATIONS
(a) **An unidentified man** in a blue ski mask has been robbing **city banks** for several months.	**Noun phrases:** noun + determiner and modifiers *Who, whom,* and *what,* ask about noun phrases.
(b) An unidentified man in a blue ski mask **has been robbing** city banks for several months.	**Verb phrases:** auxiliaries + verb *What . . . do . . .* asks about verb phrases.
(c) An unidentified man **in a blue ski mask** has been robbing city banks for several months.	**Prepositional phrases** preposition + noun phrase Adjective prepositional phrases give more information about nouns. *Which* asks about adjective phrases.
(d) An unidentified man in a blue ski mask has been robbing city banks **for several months.**	Adverbial prepositional phrases give more information about verbs. *Where, when, how,* and *why* ask about adverbial phrases.

Clauses are groups of related words that contain both a noun and a verb.

EXAMPLES	EXPLANATIONS
(e) **A man robbed the bank.** IC	Independent clauses can function as sentences.
(f) Have you heard **that a man robbed the bank?** DC	Dependent clauses cannot function as independent sentences.
(g) A man robbed the bank **that we visited yesterday.**	Adjective clauses (also called relative clauses) give more information about noun phrases.
(h) A man robbed the bank **before the police could arrive to catch him.** adv. c	Adverbial clauses give more information about verb phrases.

The following chart shows how different kinds of *Wh*-questions focus on different parts of the sentences and can be answered with either phrases or clauses.

WH-QUESTIONS		PHRASES	CLAUSES
WHO/WHOM	**Who** reported the crime to the police?	**The security manager** did.	**Whoever is responsible for security** reported it.
	Who(m) did the police arrest?	They arrested **the old man.**	They arrested the man **who they found hiding in the alley.**
WHAT	**What** have you told the reporters?	I told them **my experience.**	I told them **that the investigation is still not finished.**
WHAT . . . DO	**What did** the police **do?**	They **tried to catch the thief.**	They hoped **that they would find the criminal.**
WHICH	**Which teller** was robbed?	The teller **with the blonde hair** was.	The teller **who was interviewed by the police** was.
WHERE	**Where** did the thief go?	He went **down the street, towards the park.**	The thief went **where the police couldn't find him.**
WHEN	**When** did they finish the investigation?	They finished it **on Tuesday at 3:00.**	They finished it **when they had collected all the evidence.**
HOW	**How** did the thief get away?	He got away **on foot.**	The thief disappeared **as if he had become invisible.**
HOW _____	**How** busy was the bank yesterday?	It was **busier than usual.**	It was **so busy that nobody noticed the thief.**
HOW LONG	**How long** has that officer been on the police force?	He's been a policeman **for a long time.**	He has been a policeman **since he first moved to the city.**
HOW OFTEN	**How often** has this bank been robbed?	It's been robbed **from time to time.**	It's been robbed **as often as any other bank has been robbed.**
HOW MUCH	**How much** money did the thief take?	He took **too much to count.**	He took **so much that they haven't determined the entire amount.**
WHY	**Why** did you go to the bank?	I went **for some money.** I went to the bank **to cash a check.**	I went to the bank **because I needed money.** I went to the bank **so that I could cash a check.**

EXERCISE 1

There is a popular American TV quiz show called "Jeopardy." Contestants are given answers, and they must provide a question for each answer. Play Jeopardy with a partner. Here are some answers. For each answer, decide what form it is (phrase or clause) and make up a suitable question.

▶ **EXAMPLES:** by studying (phrase): *How can I get a good score on* the TOEFL?

once I get 550 on TOEFL (clause): *When will you begin your university studies?*

1. the president
2. He went to the movies.
3. I am.
4. in 1997
5. at noon
6. from Japan
7. for fun
8. after I finish school
9. because he needs money
10. because of the TOEFL
11. by studying
12. My sister can.
13. in order to learn English
14. to find a good job
15. the old man
16. until he passes the TOEFL
17. to my brother
18. a book and a pen
19. too expensive
20. as long as I am a student
21. so he can buy books

EXERCISE 2

Each of these sentences consists of two or more clauses. Put brackets around each clause, as shown in the example.

▶ **EXAMPLE:** [Although John is a little homesick], [he still plans to stay in France for at least a year].

1. Ali likes to get up early most days, but prefers to sleep late on weekends.
2. Denise has a lot of work that has to get done, so she won't consider taking a vacation.
3. Because they feel war is too destructive, many people are opposed to military solutions for international problems.
4. I once met a man who looked just like a friend of mine.
5. Bob is looking for an additional job that he can do in his spare time because he needs some extra money.
6. I know an old lady who swallowed a fly.
7. Although I have many friends, I still enjoy meeting people that I've never met before.
8. Last night after dinner I wrote to an old friend who went to school with me.

Basic Adverbial Position

Adverbials are words, phrases, and clauses that answer questions like *when, where, why, how much,* and *how often.*

EXAMPLES	EXPLANATIONS
(a) Biff **never** goes **downtown anymore.**	adverbs
(b) Biff exercises **as often as possible at the gym on Saturdays.**	adverbial phrases
(c) Biff works out **because he wants to improve his physique.**	adverbial clauses

Most adverbial information follows the verb phrase (verb + object) and usually appears in a basic order (some other variations are possible).

Verb phrase	Manner	Place	Frequency	Time	Purpose or reason
what . . . do	**how**	**where**	**how often**	**when**	**why**
(d) *Biff lifts weights*	*vigorously*	*at the gym*	*every day*	*after work*	*to fight stress.*

Some adverbs can come before the verb or between the auxiliary and the main verb.

EXAMPLES	EXPLANATIONS
(e) Gladstone **often** goes on strange diets. (f) He has **never** lost more than a few pounds.	**Adverbs of frequency:** affirmative: *always, often, usually, sometimes* negative: *seldom, rarely, hardly ever, never*
(g) He has **rigorously** avoided sweets for more than a year.	**Adverbs of manner:** *rigorously, quickly, completely,* etc.
(h) He **recently** lost fifty pounds.	**Indefinite adverbs of time:** *recently, typically, previously, finally,* etc.

EXERCISE 3

Read the following passage.

1. Circle the verb phrase in every sentence.

2. Underline the adverbs and adverbial phrases.

3. Decide whether the meaning of each adverbial is frequency, manner, place, time, or reason/purpose.

The first paragraph has been done for you as an example.

Biff Bicep

Gladstone Gulp

Biff Bicep and Gladstone Gulp are close friends. (1) They are always trying to change the way they look because neither one is very pleased with his appearance, (2) but they do it differently.

frequency

manner

Biff Bicep is a serious body-builder. (3) He tries to increase the size of his muscles by lifting weights at a gym near his house. (4) He usually goes there at the same time every day. (5) He drinks special vitamin supplements to gain weight, and (6) works out vigorously twice a day—in the morning and in the afternoon. (7) He usually starts out on an exercise bike to warm up his muscles. Then he moves on to his exercises. (8) He exercises his upper body on Mondays, Wednesdays, and Fridays. (9) On Tuesdays, Thursdays, and Saturdays, he does exercises to develop the muscles of his lower body. (10) He never works out on Sundays, so his muscles can have a chance to rest.

manner

Rison

Gladstone Gulp is a serious dieter. (11) He always seems to be trying to lose weight by going on special weight-reducing diets whenever he feels too heavy. (12) He usually drinks a special diet drink at breakfast and lunch. (13) Sometimes he doesn't eat anything after breakfast in order to save a few calories. (14) He also tries not to snack in between meals. (15) As a result, he is usually really hungry when he gets home and (16) so he often goes directly to the kitchen to find something to eat. Although he is a serious dieter, he's not a terribly successful one. (17) He has never permanently lost more than a few pounds. (18) He's always looking for a magic way to lose weight without having to diet or exercise.

EXERCISE 4

Add the adverbials in parentheses to each sentence. There may be more than one possible position.

▶ **EXAMPLE:** He gains back the lost weight. (quickly) (usually)

  He usually gains the lost weight back quickly.

  Usually he quickly gains back the lost weight.

1. Gladstone Gulp goes on a new diet. (because he feels heavy) (every few months)
2. He uses diet pills (to increase his metabolism) (regularly)
3. He rides an exercise bicycle (occasionally) (to use up calories) (very hard)
4. He trades diet plans. (with his friend Biff) (sometimes)
5. He reads about every new diet. (in magazines) (carefully) (whenever he can)
6. He doesn't follow their directions (carefully) (always)
7. He drinks a special vitamin supplement (usually) (to make sure he gets proper nutrition)

EXERCISE 5

Interview a classmate and find out something that he or she does:

1. every day
2. for his or her health
3. very well
4. before bedtime
5. outdoors
6. occasionally
7. better than anyone else in his or her family
8. automatically
9. with considerable difficulty
10. after class

Write complete sentences about these activities and report them to the class.

adverbials

— long adverbials go last

— more specific adverbials go first

ex. I study English at Perimeter every week.
     more specific

— when are many adverbials, move one to the front of the sentence

▶ **P**osition and Order of Adverbial Phrases

When there is more than one adverbal phrase in a clause, the order usually follows these guidelines.

EXAMPLES	EXPLANATIONS
(a) AWKWARD: He exercise vigorously at the gym **every Monday, Wednesday, and Friday after work.** **(b)** BETTER: He exercises vigorously at the gym **after work every Monday, Wednesday, and Friday.**	Shorter adverbial phrases usually come before longer adverbial phrases. Since the frequency phrase is long, it is better to have it follow the time phrase.
(c) Many people frequently eat dinner **in neighborhood restaurants in Toronto.** **(d)** NOT: Many people frequently eat dinner **in Toronto in neighborhood restaurants.**	When there are two adverbial phrases of the same kind (place, time, etc.), the more specific adverbial phrase always comes first.
(e) AWKWARD: He washes his car **carefully in the driveway with a special soap once a week.** **(f)** BETTER: **Once a week,** he carefully washes his car **in the driveway with a special soap.**	It is not common to have more than two or three adverbials after the verb phrase. If there are several adverbials, then one is usually moved to the beginning of the sentence.

EXERCISE 6

Identify the meaning (place, frequency, reason, time, etc.) and form (adverb, adverb phrase, adverbial clause) of the underlined adverbials in the numbered sentences in this article. Tell why you think they appear in the order that they do. There may be several possible reasons, so discuss your ideas with a partner. The first sentence has been done for you as an example.

▶ **EXAMPLE:** (a) manner, adverb, (b) place, adverbial prepositional phrase, (c) time, adverbial clause. **Reasons:** adverbials follow general manner, place, and time order.

Bizarre Attack by Wild Pigs on Rampage

Buttonwillow, GA

Mary Morris is a lucky woman tonight. (1) She is resting (a) <u>comfortably</u> (b) <u>at her Buttonwillow home</u> (c) <u>after doctors released her from Button-willow Hospital</u> (d) <u>earlier this afternoon.</u> Early this morning she was involved in one of the strangest automobile accidents in local history. Her car was attacked by a herd of wild pigs.

(2) "I was driving (a) <u>on a dirt road</u> (b) <u>along the river,</u> (c) <u>just like I always do,</u>" she told reporters in an impromptu news conference at the hospital, (d) "<u>when I hit a muddy patch of road</u>. I got out of the car to try to push it out of the mud. (3) (a) <u>While I was doing that</u> a herd of pigs (b) <u>suddenly</u> came (c) <u>out of the bushes</u> (d) <u>to attack me.</u> There were so many of them that I was completely surrounded, but I was able to get back into the car. (4) I (a) <u>finally</u> scared them (b) <u>back into the bushes</u> (c) <u>by blowing the horn.</u> (5) Then I sat (a) <u>there</u> (b) <u>for several hours</u> (c) <u>before I felt safe enough to leave the car</u> and (d) <u>could look for some help.</u>" Ms. Morris was treated for gashes on her legs and shock. She was given a tetanus shot, and released later in the day.

Scientists are a little puzzled as to why the pigs might have attacked in the first place. Animal psychologist Dr. Lassie Kumholm suggested that it may have been because one of the females in the herd could have just given birth near where the car got stuck. (6) (a) <u>Sometimes</u> pigs can (b) <u>suddenly</u> become aggressive (c) <u>quite quickly</u> (d) <u>if their young are threatened</u>. This herd of pigs is a well-known nuisance. (7) They have (a) <u>repeatedly</u> caused minor damage (b) <u>in the area</u> (c) <u>for the last several years,</u> but this is the first time they have been known to actually attack humans. (8) (a) <u>On several occasions</u> local property owners have sent petitions (b) <u>to county offices</u> (c) <u>to complain about the problem.</u>

▶ Putting Adverbial Phrases at the Beginning of a Sentence

EXAMPLES	EXPLANATIONS
(a) **Once a week,** he carefully washes his car in the driveway with a special soap. **(b)** **In the suitcase,** he found an extra wool sweater that had been knitted by his grandmother. **(c)** NOT: He found an extra wool sweater that had been knitted by his grand-mother **in the suitcase.**	Most adverbials can also appear at the beginning of a clause or sentence for the following reasons. • if there are several other adverbs or adverbial phrases, or if the object of the verb phrase is very long
(d) **Carefully and slowly,** John carried the heavy tray of fragile glasses to the table.	• in order to emphasize adverbial information
(e) Berta has a beautiful apartment. **Along one wall,** there are big windows with a marvelous view. **(f)** Matt was born in 1965. **In 1980,** he moved to San Francisco. **(g)** John became quite fluent in French. **As a result,** he was able to get a job with a company that exports computer parts to West Africa.	• to show logical relationships between sentences.

Most adverbials can be placed at the beginning of the sentence without making other changes in word order, but some require a question word order when they are put at the beginning of the sentence.

EXAMPLES	EXPLANATIONS
Normal Position: **(h)** Gladstone **seldom loses** more than a few pounds. **Emphatic Position:** **(i)** **Seldom does** Gladstone **lose** more than a few pounds.	negative adverbs of frequency (*never, seldom, rarely*)

make a strong statement

EXERCISE 7

Make these sentences more emphatic by moving the adverbial to the beginning of the sentence. Be sure to change the word order if necessary.

1. I have rarely seen such a mess.
2. Gladstone is often so hungry that he eats an entire cake.
3. He usually doesn't lose control.
4. We will never finish this project.
5. Steve seldom feels unhappy for very long.
6. Alice typed the letter quickly and efficiently, and sent it special delivery

FOCUS **5**

Position of Adverbial Clauses

USE

Most adverbial clauses appear after the main clause, but many can also come before the main clause.

EXAMPLES	EXPLANATIONS
(a) **As if it were the easiest thing in the world,** Mary did a triple spin and sailed off across the ice. **(b)** **As soon as John got to the airport,** he began to have second thoughts about going to France.	• to emphasize the adverbial clause
(c) **Until Jeff moved to San Francisco,** he had never seen the ocean. He had never been to a disco or eaten Chinese food. He had never even fallen in love. **(d)** **Whenever John thought about Mary** he began to feel guilty. He would imagine her sitting sadly at home alone, writing him long letters. He felt that he wasn't missing her as much as she was missing him.	• to establish a context that applies to several sentences
(e) I usually read the paper **before** I take a shower. **(f)** **After** I read the paper, I usually take a shower. **(g)** **If** you wash the dishes, **then** I'll dry them and put them away.	• to show sequence

Certain adverbial clauses almost always appear after the main clause.

EXAMPLES	EXPLANATIONS
(h) I shop **where** Juan shops. **(i)** AWKWARD: **Where** Juan shops, I shop. **(j)** **Wherever** he goes, Juan makes new friends and has wonderful adventures.	• adverbial clauses of place except those that begin with *wherever* or *everywhere*
(k) Dalia worked all summer **so (that) she would have enough money.** **(l)** AWKWARD: **So that she would have enough money,** Dalia worked all summer.	• adverbial clauses of result with *so that*
(m) I visited my grandmother **for I knew she had been sick.** **(n)** NOT: **For I knew she had been sick,** I visited my grandmother.	• adverbial clauses of reason with *for*

Punctuation of adverbial clauses depends on their position in a sentence.

EXAMPLES	EXPLANATIONS
(o) **After I took the examination,** I ate lunch. **(p)** I ate lunch **after I took the examination.**	Adverbial clauses before the main clause are followed by a comma. No extra punctuation is necessary if they appear after the main clause.
(q) **Since you don't have much money,** I'll pay for dinner. **(r)** I'll pay for dinner **since you don't have much money.**	

EXERCISE 8

Work with a partner to answer these questions about the sentences below. The first sentence has been done as an example.

(a) Does the adverbial clause in these sentences appear before or after the main clause? *before*

(b) Decide which of the reasons listed in Focus 5 can be used to explain why the author chose to put the adverbial clauses in this order. *to emphasize the adverbial clause*

1. Because Biff enjoys vigorous exercise, he tends to pursue sports that build up his muscles.

2. On the other hand, Gladstone practices sports like yoga because for him exercise is a means of relaxation.

3. Both Biff and Gladstone want to lose weight because they want to feel and look better.

4. Because Mary Morris may have stopped her car too close to a newborn piglet, she became the victim of a bizarre attack.

5. When the ski-mask robber entered the bank, he showed the teller a gun and demanded money.

6. Columbia Savings and Loan had already been robbed three times when the ski-mask robber appeared yesterday.

7. The bank manager told the press about the robbery so that the public would become aware of the need for more security.

8. Since he first agreed to work on the project in 1985, he has spent more than ten years trying to educate people about grammar.

Use Your English

ACTIVITY 1: SPEAKING/WRITING

STEP 1 Find out some basic information about another student in the class by asking some of the "Universal Questions" that were described in the Opening Task. Here are some suggested topics.

WHO:	name, family background
WHAT:	hobbies, special interests, plans for the future
WHERE:	home town, current living situation
WHEN:	date of birth, date of arrival in this country, date of expected completion of English studies
HOW LONG:	length of time in this country, amount of previous English study
HOW OFTEN:	regular activities, hobbies
HOW MUCH:	special skills, abilities, and interests
WHY:	reasons and goals for studying English, joining this class, leaving home

STEP 2 Report the information to the rest of the class in a short paragraph or oral presentation.

ACTIVITY 2: SPEAKING

An "ulterior motive" is a bad reason for doing a good thing. For example, helping a friend who is in trouble is a good thing to do, but if your real reason for doing it is because you want that person to lend you money later, your motive may make your action a bad one.

STEP 1 In a small group discuss the following situations. For each situation identify some "pure motives"—reasons for doing the action that would make it a good or generous act—and some "ulterior motives"—reasons that would make the act a bad or selfish one.

- loaning someone money
- not telling a friend some bad news
- being friendly and obedient to a rich relative
- working harder than anyone else at your job

STEP 2 Based on your discussion decide whether people's actions should be judged by what they do (their actions) or why they do it (their motivations). Present your opinion and your reasons to the rest of the class.

ACTIVITY 3: WRITING/SPEAKING

Which form of motivation is more common in your day-to-day activities: extrinsic motivation or intrinsic motivation?

Extrinsic motivation is **purpose.** You do something in order to achieve something else, such as studying business in order to get a high-paying job in the future.	Intrinsic motivation is **cause.** You do something because you like the activity itself, such as studying business because you love being a student and enjoy economic theory.

STEP 1 Decide whether your basic motivation for each of these activities is extrinsic or intrinsic, and identify two additional things you do because of intrinsic motivation. Then, in the first column in the following chart, write three things you do because of intrinsic motivation.

studying English	watching TV	cleaning the house
driving a car	reading newspapers	doing homework
cooking	exercise	shopping

STEP 2 Interview three other students in the class to find out things they do because of intrinsic motivation. Write the information in the chart below.

Your activities	Classmate 1	Classmate 2	Classmate 3
1) _____ _____	1) _____ _____	1) _____ _____	1) _____ _____
2) _____ _____	2) _____ _____	2) _____ _____	2) _____ _____
3) _____ _____	3) _____ _____	3) _____ _____	3) _____ _____

STEP 3 Form a group with two or three other students whom you did not interview and compare all the information you have gathered. As a group, decide on answers to the following question and present your ideas to the rest of the class.

What are the three most common characteristics shared by all things that people do because of intrinsic motivation? For example, do intrinsically motivated activities result in self-improvement? Are they pleasurable? Do people feel unhappy if they don't have an opportunity to pursue these activities?

ACTIVITY 4: SPEAKING

In a small group discuss the following situations. For each situation decide whether there are ever any justifiable reasons or purposes for the following actions:

• leaving your family forever
• getting married to someone against your family's wishes
• not reporting a criminal to the police
• falling in love with someone other than your spouse
• taking something that doesn't belong to you

Based on your discussion decide whether a person's actions should be determined by his or her motivations or merely by the actions themselves. Present your opinions and your reasons to the rest of the class.

ACTIVITY 5: SPEAKING

The world seems to be divided into two kinds of people: morning people (who do their best work early in the day) and night people (who are sleepy in the morning, and most productive in the late afternoon or even late at night). Which kind are you? Interview a partner to find out which kind of person he or she is.

STEP 1 Find out **how** your partner does each activity in the chart below at the time of day listed. (Some examples have been provided.) Ask about two additional activities.

STEP 2 Decide on whether your partner is a morning person or a night person, and report your findings to the rest of the class.

WHEN? WHAT?	Early morning HOW?	After lunch HOW?	Late at night HOW?
vigorous exercise	slowly	well, but not if he's hungry	easily, but it keeps him awake
balancing your checkbook			
thinking up original ideas			
relaxed reading for pleasure			
concentrated reading for work or school			
social activity and conversation			

ACTIVITY 6: LISTENING

STEP 1   Listen to the following news broadcasts. Based on what you hear write as many questions as you can with *Who, What, Where, When Why, How* about each broadcast and give them to a partner to answer. You may need to listen to the broadcasts more than once in order to ask and answer the questions.

STEP 2   Compare your questions and answers with those of another pair of students. As a group try to write a summary of one of the news stories.

Pᴀssɪᴠᴇ Vᴇʀʙs

UNIT GOALS:

- To review passive form and meaning
- To know when to include the agent
- To use *get* passives
- To choose between passive and active

▶ Oᴘᴇɴɪɴɢ ᴛᴀsᴋ
Mysterious Places

Stonehenge is a circle of giant stones. It is located far away from anything else in the middle of a plain in southern England.

The Nazca Lines are a group of huge pictures drawn in the desert of western Peru that can only be seen from an airplane.

STEP 1   Some people believe that these places prove that beings from other planets have visited the Earth because no one can explain exactly how or why they were constructed. Read about either Stonehenge or the Nazca Lines. Develop at least one possible explanation for each of the three unanswered questions.

How were they constructed? Here are some clues.

STONEHENGE	THE NAZCA LINES
• The giant stones were transported from a great distance from an unknown place. • The stones are too heavy to be lifted upright or to be placed on top of each other. • A large number of people would probably be required to construct such a large structure, more people than were probably living in prehistoric Britain. • The distances between the stones are very precise, accurate to the millimeter	• The pictures can only be seen from the air. The people who built the designs could not actually see them. • A large number of people would be required to construct such large pictures. There definitely isn't enough water for so many people there, because it is one of the driest places on earth. • The designs are very precise. One image is a perfect spiral, accurate to the millimeter.

Why were they constructed? Here are some clues.

STONEHENGE	THE NAZCA LINES
• Some stones seem to point to certain stars. • Some stones seem to have some connection with the position of the sun at certain times of year. • Some stones may have had some connection with human sacrifices.	• Some pictures seem to have some mathematical or geometrical meaning. • Some pictures represent flowers and animals that are not found anywhere near the location of the lines. • Some designs look like symbols that are used to direct modern-day aircraft.

When were they constructed? Here are some clues.

STONEHENGE	THE NAZCA LINES
• It was already considered to be a mysterious place when Britain was occupied by the Romans in the first century B.C. • There is no historical record of its construction.	• They weren't discovered until people started flying over the area in airplanes. • They predate Inca civilization by at least 2,000 years.

STEP 2   Form a group with one student who read about the same mysterious place as you, and two students who read about the other mysterious place. Compare your answers.

STEP 3   In your group discuss this question: Are these structures proof that the Earth has been visited by beings from some other planet? Why or why not? Share your ideas with the rest of the class.

optional

▶ **Review of Passive Forms**

EXAMPLES	EXPLANATIONS
(a) The Nazca Lines **were discovered** by airplane pilots. **(b)** They **weren't discovered** until the 1930s. **(c)** How **were** such huge designs **built?**	***be* + past participle (+ *by* phrase)** Form all passive verbs in the same way. Only the *be* auxiliary changes form. There is often no information about who or what performed the action, but when there is, it appears as a *by* phrase.
(d) Stonehenge **was** constructed of rocks that came from many miles away. **(e)** The Nazca Lines **were** made by removing soil and rocks to expose the different-colored soil underneath.	**Change *be* to indicate:** • singular or plural
(f) Stonehenge **was** constructed long before Britain **was** invaded by the armies of Rome. **(g)** The Nazca Lines **weren't** discovered until the 1930s because they **weren't** seen by people on the ground.	• affirmative or negative
(h) Mysterious structures **are** found in a number of places in the world. **(i)** Some **were discovered** this century. **(j)** Perhaps the reasons for their existence **will be** discovered with further research. **(k)** While they **were being** built, civilization was still very young. **(l)** Many theories explaining their existence **have been** proposed.	• time frame (*present, past, future*) and aspect (*simple, perfect, progressive*)
(m) The Nazca Lines **may be** destroyed, if further protection **can't be** provided. **(n)** Preservation efforts for all such mysterious structures **ought to be** started without delay. **(o)** Both Stonehenge and the Nazca Lines **might have been** used to predict astronomical events.	• modal information (*prediction, advisability, possibility,* etc.)

EXERCISE 1

Find ten examples of passive verb forms in the information provided on page 47 and underline them. Tell whether each form is:

a) singular or plural

b) affirmative or negative

c) present, past, or future time frame

d) simple, perfect, or progressive aspect

EXERCISE 2

Write the passive forms for the verbs provided below.

▶ **EXAMPLE:**   construct (singular, present progressive) *is being constructed*

1. I forget (plural, past perfect)

2. establish (singular, simple past)

3. manufacture (singular, simple present)

4. obtain (singular, simple present)

5. require (plural, simple future)

6. discover (plural, present perfect)

7. make (singular, present progressive)

8. leave (plural, past perfect)

9. build (singular, simple past)

10. produce (singular, simple present)

11. send (singular, future perfect)

12. notice (plural, past progressive)

13. need (singular, simple future)

14. forget (plural, present perfect)

15. study (plural, present progressive)

EXERCISE 3

Use the information provided below to construct passive sentences.

▶ **EXAMPLE:**   The Chinese invented gunpowder.

Gunpowder ___was invented___ in China.

1. Pakistanis speak Urdu, Punjabi, Sindhi, Baluchi, Pashtu, and English.

   Urdu, Punjabi, Sindhi, Baluchi, Pashtu, and English __are spoken__ in Pakistan.

2. The people of Sri Lanka have mined gems for centuries.

   For centuries gems __have been mined__ in Sri Lanka.

3. The French consider snails a great delicacy.

   Snails __are consider__ a great delicacy in France.

4. People throughout Asia eat rice.

   Rice __is eating__ throughout Asia.

5. Argentineans consume more beef per capita than in any other country.

   More beef __is consumed__ per capita in Argentina than in any other country.

6. Ancient Egyptians worshiped cats.

   Cats __were worshiped__ in ancient Egypt.

7. The Japanese have developed a new system of high-resolution television.

   A new system of high-resolution television __has been developed__ in Japan.

8. Americans invented the games of baseball and basketball.

   The games of baseball and basketball both __were invented__ in America.

EXERCISE 4

Working with a partner, make up five additional passive sentences about products or accomplishments of a national or cultural group that you are familiar with.

EXERCISE 5

Choose eight verbs from Exercise 2. Make an original sentence for each verb.

FOCUS **2**

▶ **Passive Meaning:**
Agent Versus Receiver

Agent and Receiver in Active Sentences

subject	active verb	object	
agent	**action**	**receiver**	The **agent** is the **doer** of an action. The **receiver** is the person or thing that is affected by the action. In active sentences the agent is the subject of the sentence. The receiver is the object.
(a) An employee	found	a wallet out-side the office.	

Agent and Receiver in Passive Sentences

subject	passive verb	(*by* + noun phrase)	
receiver	**action**	**(agent)**	In passive sentences the receiver is the subject and the agent is often not mentioned. When it is included, it occurs as a prepositional phrase with *by*.
(b) A wallet	was found outside the office.		
(c) The wallet	was found	by an employee.	

EXERCISE 6

Read this article about the Nazca Lines. Underline all the passive constructions that you find. For each example of the passive that you can find, circle the **receiver.** If the **agent** is mentioned, draw a square around it. The first sentence of each paragraph has been done as an example.

THE MYSTERY OF THE NAZCA LINES

(1) The Nazca Lines were not discovered until the 1930s, when they were first noticed by airplane pilots flying over Peru's Atacama Desert. (2) They consist of huge pictures, several kilometers in size, that were drawn in the desert. (3) They portray such things as birds, spiders, and abstract geometrical designs. (4) These pictures were made more than three thousand years ago by removing stones and dirt over large areas to expose the differently-colored soil beneath.

(5) The amazing thing about the Nazca Lines is that none of these pictures can be seen by people on the ground. (6) They are so huge that they can only be seen from a great height. (7) The pictures were constructed with amazing precision. (8) How such measurements were made still hasn't been satisfactorily explained. (9) It seems impossible that the primitive construction techniques that existed three thousand years ago could have been used to create such gigantic, perfectly-constructed designs.

(10) Why were these gigantic pictures made? (11) Were they intended as gifts for the gods, as some people have suggested? (12) Or, as others believe, were they created as "direction signs" for visitors from other planets? (13) No one knows. (14) One thing is known: The reasons and methods of their construction have been destroyed by time, but the pictures have been preserved for at least two thousand—and maybe even three thousand—years!

EXERCISE 7

Write one active sentence and one passive sentence for each set of agent, receiver, and verb.

▶ **EXAMPLE:** **Agent:** the maid; **Receiver:** the money; **Verb:** find

active: The maid found the money.
passive: The money was found by the maid.

1. **Agent:** pilots; **Receiver:** the Nazca Lines; **Verb:** discover
2. **Agent:** Ancient Romans; **Receiver:** Stonehenge; **Verb:** can not explain
3. **Agent:** Lee Harvey Oswald; **Receiver:** John F. Kennedy; **Verb:** assassinate
4. **Agent:** beings from outer space; **Receiver:** the Earth; **Verb:** visit
5. **Agent:** parents; **Receiver:** their children; **Verb:** teach good manners
6. **Agent:** society; **Receiver:** social minorities; **Verb:** discriminate against

Pilots discover the Nazca Lines A.
The Nazca lines were discover by the piots A.

USE

▶ ## **W**hen to Include the Agent

Because we most often use passive verbs to describe situations when the agent is unknown or unimportant, we usually do not include agents (*by* + noun phrase) in passive sentences. However, sometimes it is necessary to include the agent.

EXAMPLES	EXPLANATIONS
	Include the agents:
(a) Many important scientific discoveries have been made **by women.**	• when the agent gives us additional new information.
(b) Radioactivity, for example, was discovered **by Marie Curie** in 1903.	• when information about the agent is too important to omit.
(c) This music was written **by a computer.** **(d)** That picture was painted **by a monkey.**	• when the agent is surprising or unexpected

EXERCISE 8

Identify the agent in each of these sentences and decide if it is necessary. Correct any sentences by omitting unnecessary *by* phrases.

▶ **EXAMPLE:** That symphony was written by a composer in the 19th century

Not necessary. (That symphony was written in the 19th century.)

1. The Nazca Lines were constructed by an unknown civilization approximately two thousand years ago.
2. The lesson was assigned by the teacher for next week.
3. This picture was painted by Picasso when Picasso was twelve years old.
4. My briefcase was taken by someone, but it was found and turned in to the Lost and Found Office by someone in my English class.
5. Many foreign students don't need scholarships because they are being supported by friends or relatives.
6. I would never guess that these poems were translated by children.

▶ # **T**he *Get* Passive

Forming the *Get* Passive

EXAMPLES	EXPLANATIONS
(a) John rides to work with a neighbor who works nearby. He **gets picked up** at the bus stop every morning. **(b)** John **gets dropped off** in front of his office. **(c)** He **should be getting picked up** in a few minutes.	In spoken or informal English, we can use *get* instead of *be* as the passive auxiliary
(d) **Did** John **get** picked up yesterday? **(e)** He **didn't get** dropped off at the usual place. **(f)** He **might not have gotten picked up** by the usual person.	Questions and negatives require *do* if the verb phrase does not contain a form of *be* or a model auxiliary.

Using *Get* Passive Sentences

EXAMPLES	EXPLANATIONS
(g) Kennedy **was** elected president in 1960. **(h)** He **got** elected by a very small majority. **(i)** The hospital **was built** in the 1930s. **(j)** NOT: The hospital **got built** in the 1930s.	The *get* passive is more common with animate (living) subjects, than with inanimate (nonliving) ones.
(k) Mariko **got married** last Saturday. **(l)** She **has** never **been married** before.	It emphasizes the action rather than the state.

EXERCISE 9

Decide whether *be* or *get* is more appropriate in these sentences. Sometimes either form could be correct.

▶ **EXAMPLES:** North America _was_____ settled by several European countries.

John's car __got/was_____ damaged, so he had to take public transportation.

1. The Nazca Lines _____ discovered in the 1930s.
2. Scott _____ arrested on his way home from the football game.
3. New medicines are _____ developed that seem effective in fighting cancer.
4. That's really dangerous. If your leg _____ broken, don't blame me.
5. I don't think Luis and Karin will ever _____ married. They're too different.
6. Don't put that fish in the same aquarium with the others. It might _____ eaten by the larger ones.

FOCUS **5**

▶ **S**pecial Cases: Verbs
with No Passive Forms
and Other Verbs
with No Active Forms

EXAMPLES	EXPLANATIONS
(a) Few changes **have occurred** at Stonehenge over the years. **(b)** The discovery of the Nazca Lines **happened** in the 1930s. **(c)** Some Nazca lines **seem** to be in the shape of flowers. **(d)** The purpose of the Nazca lines **has disappeared** under the sands of the Atacama Desert.	Some verbs don't have a passive form because they do not take direct objects. This category includes verbs such as: *collide, occur, happen, take place . . .* *appear, resemble, seem, look . . .* *emerge, disappear, appear . . .*
(e) **NOT:** A ceremonial function was had by these pictures. **(f)** NOT: Some animals are resembled by the pictures.	Even verbs that take objects, when they describe states, do not occur in the passive.
(g) The drawing of the Nazca lines $\begin{Bmatrix} \text{began} \\ \text{was begun} \end{Bmatrix}$ more than 2000 years ago.	Some verbs describe changes of state and can occur in the active with a passive meaning.
(h) Jeff **was born** in Kansas. **(i)** NOT: Jeff's mother **bore** him in Kansas.	A few passive verbs do not have active forms.
(j) The Nazca Lines **are located** (exist) in the Atacama Desert of Peru. **(k)** They **located** (found) the Atacama Desert on a map.	Some passive verbs have different meanings in passive and active.

EXERCISE 10

Here is a list of some verbs that do not have passive forms. Choose five verbs and write a sentence for each one. Compare your sentences with those of other students.

appear	*consist of*	*seem*	*look*	*occur*
take place	*resemble*	*happen*	*have*	*emerge*
disappear	*vanish*	*collide*		

▶ Choosing Passive Versus Active

As a general rule, it is usually better style to use active forms. But in some situations the passive form is preferred.

EXAMPLES	EXPLANATIONS
(a) Jan's purse **was stolen** from her locker at school.	Use passive instead of active: • if the agent is unknown
(b) The new library **was finished** about a year ago.	• if the agent is unimportant
(c) I had an accident yesterday. This other car went through a red light and hit me. My car **was** completely **destroyed.**	• if the agent is obvious from context
(d) Did you hear the news? Matt **was injured** slightly in the earthquake, but Jeff was O.K.	• to emphasize the receiver
(e) Passengers **are asked** to refrain from smoking. **(f)** The audience **will be encouraged** to participate. **(g)** Something **should be done** about the drug problem.. **(h)** The present perfect tense **is used** to describe actions in the past that are related to the present in some way. **(i)** Water **is formed** by combining hydrogen and oxygen.	• to make general explanations, statements and announcements, or in scientific and technical writing.

EXERCISE 11

Why do you think the author used passive verbs in these sentences? There may be more than one possible reason.

▶ **EXAMPLE:** No one is permitted to enter the laboratory while the experiment is being conducted. *general announcement*

1. Reagan was first elected president of the United States in 1980.

2. There is a lot of controversy about the Nazca Lines, especially about why they were built and how they were constructed.

3. They weren't even noticed until people started flying over the area in planes.

4. Was it John's brother who got arrested at the demonstration?

5. The house was broken into while the family was away.

EXERCISE 12

Read this excerpt from an introductory sociology textbook. Choose one paragraph, and underline all the passive constructions that you find. With a partner, decide why the author chose to use passive constructions.

CHAPTER 3: SOCIAL MINORITIES AND DISCRIMINATION

INTRODUCTION

(1) In most societies, certain **social minorities** are sometimes discriminated against by society as a whole. (2) Discrimination may occur because of a group's race, religion, ethnic or cultural background, sexual preference, or even the language that they speak in their homes. (3) Such groups are sometimes denied basic rights, legal protections, or access to the same facilities as the general public. (4) In many societies, discrimination is slowly being eliminated—at least in terms of legal and governmental policies. (5) But these changes have not come quickly or easily.

(6) The United States, for example, has made a great deal of progress in eliminating discrimination against some of its social minorities. (7) As recently as the 1950s blacks and whites were not allowed to get married in many southern states. (8) They were forced to use separate drinking fountains, rest rooms, and even schools and libraries. (9) However, as a result of active protest and political demonstration such discriminatory laws were changed, and segregation based on race is no longer permitted.

(10) But other groups have been less successful. (11) Women have made many gains in American society, but they are still paid less than men for the same kinds of work. (12) Gay people still face enormous legal and social discrimination. (13) They are not allowed to serve in the army or join organizations like the Boy Scouts; in many states they can be fired from their jobs if employers learn of their sexual orientation. (14) They do not have the same kind of basic legal protection for family relationships and property that the rest of society takes for granted. (15) Courts may still take children away from homosexual parents, or deny inheritance rights to lifelong partners when one partner dies.

(16) Conditions for all minorities in the United States seem to be improving, although it will be a long time before social attitudes catch up with the progress that has been made in legal protections.

EXERCISE 13

Decide whether active or passive forms should be used in these sentences, and write the correct form in the blank. There may be more than one correct choice.

The age of pyramid-building in Egypt (1) _____ (begin) about
2900 B.C. The great pyramids (2) _____ (intend) to serve as burial
places for the Pharaohs, as the kings of Egypt (3) _____ (call).
Construction on the largest pyramid (4) _____ (start) around
2800 B.C. for Khufu, the King of the Fourth Dynasty, or Cheops, as he
(5) _____ (refer to) by Greek historians. It (6) _____ (be)
482 feet high and 755 feet long. The Pyramids as a group (7) _____
(comprise) one of the Seven Wonders of the Ancient World. The other Six
Wonders no longer (8) _____ (stand), and modern archaeologists
(9) _____ (know) of them only through the descriptions that
(10) _____ (write) at the time they still (11) _____ (exist).

EXERCISE 14

Decide whether active or passive forms should be used in these sentences, and write the correct form in the blank. There may be more than one correct choice.

The Taj Mahal in Agra, India, (1) _____ (build) for the Moghul
Emperor Shah Jahan. It (2) _____ (design) to (3) _____

(serve) as a tomb for his beloved wife. Many people (4) _considered_
(consider) the Taj to be the most beautiful building in the world. The entire
structure (5) _was maked_ (make) of white marble and semiprecious
stones. Shah Jahan originally (6) _intended_ (intend) for a second Taj
to (7) _located_ (locate) across the river from the first one. The second
Taj was supposed to (8) _copy_ (copy) the original Taj in every detail
except one: The seconed Taj, which Shah Jahan (9) _planed_ (plan) as his
own tomb, was supposed to (10) _consisted_ (consist) of black marble and
semiprecious stones, instead of the same white marble that (11) _was used_
(use) for the first Taj. Shah Jahan (12) _was im prison_ (imprison) by his own son ✗
and (13) _died_ (die) before he (14) _got_ (get) a chance
to (15) _implemented_ (implement) his plan. His vision of two twin Taj Mahals,
one white and one black, never (16) _was_ (accomplish). _by the shao_
accomplished.

Use Your English

ACTIVITY 1: READING/SPEAKING

The article in Exercise 12 discussed discrimination against social minorities in the United States. Share your ideas and opinions about discrimination with other students.

STEP 1 Read the article and discuss these questions with a partner or in a small group:

1. What is the main idea of this article?
2. What are some common reasons for discrimination mentioned in the article?
3. What examples does the article give of successful progress in eliminating discrimination in the United States?
4. What examples does the article provide about discrimination against women? Can you think of other examples?
5. The article discusses legalized discrimination and social discrimination. Name one example of each kind of discrimination against gay people.

STEP 2 Listed below are examples of some other social groups that sometimes face discrimination. Identify one example that you are familiar with and describe that discrimination to another student.

Koreans in Japan Turks in Germany Arabs in France Chinese in Southeast Asia Jews in Eastern Europe Hindus in Sri Lanka	Catholics in Northern Ireland people with physical disabilities people with certain political beliefs people with certain physical characteristics (fat people, short people, left-handed people)

STEP 3 With your partner think of one additional example and describe the discrimination that this group faces to the rest of the class.

STEP 4 Discuss whether there are situations in which legal or social discrimination can ever be justified. Report the results of your discussion to the rest of the class.

ACTIVITY 2: WRITING

Write a report on the history of a famous structure or public monument. Include facts about its design, construction, and function, and why it is famous. Pick one of these examples, or choose one of your own.

The Eiffel Tower (Paris)
The Golden Gate Bridge (San Francisco)
The Statue of Liberty (New York)
Angkor Wat (Cambodia)
The Parthenon (Athens)

Latin American Tower (Mexico City)
The Imperial Palace (Tokyo)
The Temple of Heaven (Beijing)
The Chunnel (between England and France)
The Sydney Opera House (Australia)

ACTIVITY 3: WRITING

Have you ever had a day that was so unlucky that it made you wish that you had never even gotten out of bed? What happened? Was it unlucky because of what happened to you or because of something you did? Were you the "agent" or the "receiver" of your unlucky events? Write a paragraph that describes what happened on that day.

ACTIVITY 4: READING/ SPEAKING/WRITING

Find out how one or more of the common items listed below are manufactured. If you prefer, you can talk about some other item you are familiar with. Report your findings to the rest of the class.

glass   molasses   silicon chips   rope   porcelain   paper

ACTIVITY 5: SPEAKING

Do you personally believe in flying saucers, UFOs, and visitors from outer space? Prepare a debate between people who believe that such things are possible and people who don't. Each side should present reasons and specific examples to support their opinions.

ACTIVITY 6: LISTENING

STEP 1 Listen to the following news broadcast and write a one-sentence summary of what the news broadcast is about.

_____

_____

_____

STEP 2 Read the questions below and then listen to the news broadcast again. Answer the questions in complete sentences.

1. What was announced today?

_____

2. When did Velasquez probably paint the portrait?

_____

3. How did the painting get into the closet?

_____

4. Why didn't officials know about the painting's existence?

_____

5. Who authenticated the painting?

_____

6. What is being done now, as a result of this discovery?

_____

7. How much is the painting worth?

_____

STEP 3 Compare your answers with a partner's. Listen to the news broadcast a third time to check answers that you disagree on or are unsure about. Share your final answers with the rest of the class.

ACTIVITY 7: LISTENING

Listen to a national TV or radio news broadcast in English and write down five examples of passive verbs that you hear. Try to identify the receiver and the agent, if it is stated, and suggest why the passive form was used. If possible, have a partner listen independently to the same broadcast and then compare your answers.

UNIT 5

ONE-WORD AND PHRASAL MODALS

UNIT GOALS:

- To review modal forms and uses
- To identify and use one-word and phrasal modals
- To understand formal and informal uses of modals

▶ **OPENING TASK**

Identifying the Pros and Cons of Immigration

Each year about 600,000 immigrants become new citizens of the United States. In addition to legal immigration, several thousand people enter or remain in the country illegally. For all immigrants, both legal and illegal, the move to their new country often involves a lot of difficulties.

STEP 1   Below is a list of reasons why people immigrate to a new country and a list of difficulties people sometimes face after they immigrate. Check reasons why you might immigrate to another country. Then try to add one more reason to the list.

REASONS	DIFFICULTIES
_____ People can't make enough money to feed their families.	_____ People have to learn a new language.
_____ People aren't allowed to practice their religion.	_____ People aren't able to forget their old customs.
_____ People have to serve in the army for a long time.	_____ Their children won't grow up the way they did.
_____ People are supposed to do what their parents want them to do.	_____ People have to take low-paying jobs because they can't speak the language well.
_____	_____
_____	_____

STEP 2   Check difficulties that you think you would face if you moved permanently to a new county. Then try to add one more reason to the list.

STEP 3   Discuss your responses with several classmates. Are there reasons or difficulties that everyone mentioned? Are there reasons or difficulties which apply to one particular country but not others?

FOCUS **1**

▶ **REVIEW OF MODAL FORMS**

Many one-word modals correspond to one or more phrasal modals with a similar meaning.

One-Word Modals		Phrasal Modals	
can/could *will/would* *must*	*may/might* *shall/should*	*be able to* *be going to* *ought to, be supposed to, had better*	*be allowed to* *have to, have got to*

MODAL	AFFIRMATIVE STATEMENTS	NEGATIVE STATEMENTS	QUESTIONS/ SHORT ANSWERS
ONE-WORD MODALS *can/could* *may/might* *will/would* *shall/should* *must*	**(a)** Victor **can** speak Spanish. **(e)** Victor **should** speak English at school.	**(b)** He **cannot** speak it at school. **(f)** He **shouldn't** speak Spanish at school.	**(c)** Where **can** he speak it? **(d) Can** he speak it at home? Yes, he probably **can.** **(g) Should** he speak Spanish in school? No, he **shouldn't.**
PHRASAL MODALS WITH *BE* *be able to* *be going to* *be about to* *be supposed to* *be allowed to*	**(h)** Victor **is able to** speak Spanish. **(k)** Victor **was able to** speak Spanish.	**(i)** He **is not supposed to** speak Spanish at school. **(l)** He **wasn't supposed to** speak Spanish at school.	**(j)** Where **was** he **allowed to** speak it? **(m) Is** he **allowed to** speak it at home? Yes, he probably **is.**
PHRASAL MODALS WITHOUT *BE* *have to* *used to*	**(n)** Victor **has to** speak English in class. **(q)** Victor **had to** speak English in class. **(t)** He **used to** speak Spanish all the time.	**(o)** He **does not have to** speak it at home. **(r)** He **didn't have to** speak it at home. **(u)** He **didn't use to** speak English at all.	**(p)** Where **did** he **have to** speak it? **(s) Does** he **have to** speak it at home? No, he **doesn't.** **(v) Did** he **use to** speak English? No, he **didn't.**

have got to *had better* *ought to*	(w) He **has got to** speak English at home. (x) He **had better not** speak Spanish in class. (y) He **ought to** try speaking English at home, too.	These modals do not usually appear in questions or negative sentences. One-word modals are used instead.

EXERCISE 1

The forms of the modals in these sentences are incorrect. Identify the problems and write the sentences correctly.

▶ **EXAMPLE:** Has Victor to speak English?

Does Victor have to speak English?

1. Sunyoon hasn't to do her homework.

   Sunyoon doesn't have to do her homework.

2. Does Victor able to speak Spanish at home?

   Is Victor able to speak Spanish at home?

3. Can Victor speak Spanish? Yes, he can speak.

   Yes he can speak spanish

4. Where he is allowed to speak Spanish?

5. Why he can't speak Spanish at school?

6. Ought Victor to speak Spanish at school?

   Should

7. Had Victor better speak English at school?

   Should

8. Used Victor to speak Spanish?

   Did victor used to speak spanish?

9. Does Victor allowed to speak Spanish in school? No, he doesn't allowed.

10. Why he should speak English in school? Why he shouldn't Spanish?

    not speak spanish

    he speak

Social Uses of One-Word and Phrasal Modals

Modals are commonly used for many basic social interactions.

USE	ONE-WORD MODALS	EXAMPLES	PHRASAL MODALS	EXAMPLES	SPECIAL NOTES
making requests	*would* *could* *will* *can*	(a) **Would** you open the window? (b) **Could** you turn down the radio? (c) **Will** you pass the salt? (d) **Can** you loan me a dollar?			The one-word modals are listed in order of most polite or formal to most informal.
asking for, giving, or denying permission	*may* *can*	(e) **May** I come in? (f) Of course you **can!** (g) You **can't** smoke here.	*be allowed to*	(h) You're **allowed to** bring a friend. (i) You're **not allowed to** smoke here.	*May* is considered more polite than *can.*
giving invitations	*will* *would* *can*	(j) **Will** you come for dinner? (k) **Would** you like to join us? (l) **Can** you come to my party?			
making offers	*will* *shall*	(m) I'll do the dishes. (n) **Shall** I help with the dishes?	*would . . . like*	(o) **Would** you **like** me to do the dishes?	Use *shall* to make offers of action by the speaker.

Continued

USE	ONE-WORD MODALS	EXAMPLES	PHRASAL MODALS	EXAMPLES	SPECIAL NOTES
making promises or expressing intention	*will*	(p) I'll do it (q) I promise I'll do it. (r) I'll do it, no matter what!	*be going to*	(s) **I'm going to** finish this, I promise. (t) **I'm going to** finish this whether you want me to or not.	*Be going to* expresses a stronger intention than *will*. See Unit 5, Focus 3, for more information on this difference.
making suggestions	*shall* *could* *can* *might*	(u) **Shall** we go out to dinner? (v) We **could** get Chinese food. (w) You **can** try that new restaurant. (x) Victor **might** try harder to speak English outside of class.			Use *shall* to suggest actions that involve both the speaker and the listener.
expressing advice	*could* *should*	(y) Victor **could** study harder. (z) Victor **should** study every day. (aa) He **shouldn't** speak Spanish at home.	*ought to* *had better* *had better not*	(bb) You **ought to** do your homework every night. (cc) You **had better** start working harder if you want to pass this class.	These forms are listed in increasing order of necessity. *Ought to* is rarely used in negative statements or questions.

FOCUS **2**

Continued

obligation, and necessity/ prohibition			
	be supposed to	**(dd)** You **had better not** skip class. **(ee)** You**'re supposed to** do your homework every night. **(ff)** You**'re not supposed to** ask your roommate to help you with the homework.	*Had better* is an emphatic form. It is often used as a threat. It is used in affirmative and negative sentences, but is not used with questions. Notice that the negative form is *had better not*, NOT *hadn't better*.
	must	**(gg)** We **must** leave before 5:00. **(hh)** You **mustn't** tell a lie	
	have to	**(ii)** You **have to** leave before 5:00. **(jj)** You **don't have to** work late if you don't want to.	*Have to* and *must* have different meanings in negative sentences: *must not* = prohibition *don't have to* = lack of necessity. *Have got to* is not used in questions or negatives.
	have got to	**(kk)** You**'ve got to** stop spending so much money	

EXERCISE 2

Look at the sentences below. Write the number of each sentence in the correct place in the chart to show how it is being used. Then, for each modal use, write one additional sentence of your own. Compare your completed chart to that of another student. The first three sentences have been done for you as examples.

FORM	USE
Sentences: ~~8, 14, 21~~ Your Own Example: ~~(4, 8, 14, 21)~~ ~~Can you give me change?~~	making requests
Sentences: #1 ~~# 8, 4, 10, 14, 21,~~ ~~(1, 10)~~	asking for, giving, or denying permission
Sentences: #3 ~~16, 5~~ ~~(3, 5)~~	giving invitations
Sentences: #2 ~~15, 22~~ ~~(2, 15, 22, 17)~~	making offers
Sentences: ~~18, 19,~~ ~~(18, 19)~~	making promises or expressing intention
Sentences: ~~7, 6, 17,~~ ~~(6, 7, 16)~~	making suggestions
Sentences: ~~9, 11, 12, 20, 23~~ ~~(9, 11, 12, 13, 20, 23)~~	expressing advice, obligation, necessity, or prohibition

1. May I have some cheese?
2. Shall I open a window?
3. Can you come to my party?
4. Would you help me?
5. Would you join us for dinner?
6. We could have Chinese food tonight.
7. We might try the Hong Kong Cafe.
8. Can you make me some coffee?
9. You mustn't forget John's birthday.
10. Aren't we allowed to watch television?
11. We don't have to study over the weekend.
12. You shouldn't stay up so late.
13. You ought to try harder in speech class.
14. Could you please turn down the radio?
15. Would you like me to help you with your homework?
16. Shall we go to Las Vegas for a vacation?
17. Shall I tell you the answer?
18. I'm going to pass the TOEFL, no matter what it takes!
19. I'll pay you back next Tuesday.
20. You'd better not leave.
21. Can you bring me a glass of water?
22. I can do that for you.
23. Victor can't speak Spanish in his English class.

FOCUS **3**

▲ Common One-Word and Phrasal Modal Meanings

Modals are also used to express important meanings.

MEANING	ONE-WORD MODALS	EXAMPLES	PHRASAL MODALS	EXAMPLES	SPECIAL NOTES
expressing general possibility	*can* *will*	**(a)** San Francisco **can** be foggy in the summer. **(b)** A good student **will** always do her homework before class starts.			See Unit 18 for more information.
expressing impossibility	*can't* *couldn't*	**(c)** You **can't** be telling the truth! **(d)** We **couldn't** be there already!			See Unit 18 for more information.
describing future activities	*will* *shall*	**(e)** Peter **will** be on vacation next week. **(f)** I **shall** pay you on Tuesday.	*be going to* *be about to*	**(g)** **I'm going to** spend a month in France before I start my new job. **(h)** **I'm about to** leave for the airport.	*Shall* is very formal in American English. *Will* is preferred. *Be going to* is discussed in Unit 15. *Be about to* is used to describe events in the immediate future.

Continued

MEANING	ONE-WORD MODALS	EXAMPLES	PHRASAL MODALS	EXAMPLES	SPECIAL NOTES
making predictions	*could* *might* *may* *should*	**(i)** I **could** be late. **(j)** I **might** be on time. **(k)** It **may** rain. **(l)** It **should** be sunny tomorrow.	*ought to*	**(n)** It **ought to** be sunny tomorrow.	Listed in order of increasing probability. *Ought to* is rarely used in negative statements or questions.
	will	**(m)** It **will** be sunny tomorrow.	*be going to*	**(o)** It **is going to** be sunny tomorrow.	
making logical inferences	*must*	**(p)** It **must** be raining, the streets are wet.	*have to*	**(r)** Denise **has to** be really sick because she didn't come in today.	These phrasal modals are not used in negative inferences or in questions.
		(q) Bob isn't studying for the test; he **must** not be worried about his grade.	*have got to*	**(s)** Bob **has got to** be the thief. No one else had a key to the cash box.	
describing abilities	*can* *could*	**(t)** I **can** speak English now, but I **couldn't** do it a year ago.	*be able to*	**(u)** Jack **was able to** get tickets, but he **wasn't able to** go himself.	Differences in meaning and use of these forms are discussed in more detail in Unit 24.
describing habitual actions in the past	*would*	**(v)** When Mary was young she **would** pretend to be a fairy princess.	*used to*	**(w)** I **used to** speak Farsi, but I've forgotten a lot of the vocabulary.	Using *would* and *used to* implies that the situation no longer happens.

EXERCISE 3

Look at the sentences on the bottom of this page and on the next page. Write the number of each sentence in the correct place in the chart to show how it is being used. Then, for each modal use, write one additional sentence of your own. Compare your completed chart to that of another student. The first three sentences have been done for you as examples.

FORM	MEANING
Sentences: #1 Your Own Example: _TOEFL questions can be very tricky._	general possibility
Sentences: #2 10	impossibility
Sentences: 6 5 13	future time
Sentences: 7 11 14	prediction
Sentences: 8 9 12	logical inference
Sentences: #3 9 9	ability
Sentences: 4 15	habitual actions in the past

1. It can be quite rainy this time of year.
2. You couldn't be hungry! You just ate.
3. I couldn't understand American TV programs a year ago.
4. I used to get frustrated when I watched TV.
5. Those naughty children will misbehave if you give them a chance.
6. I will be there at 5:00.
7. I may have to leave early.
8. Antonio got A's in all his classes. He has to be very smart.
9. I've been able to make friends in every country I've lived in.
10. It can't be midnight already! It seems like we just got here.

11. We should be there in twenty minutes unless there's a traffic jam.
12. Naomi must not have to worry about money. She buys really expensive clothes.
13. I'll graduate next June.
14. It might be too late to call John. He usually goes to bed early.
15. I would always have trouble going to sleep on the night before school started when I was a child.

EXERCISE 4

How are the modals being used in each of these sentences? Decide whether they express: request, permission, invitation, offers, promises, suggestions, advice, obligation, necessity, possibility or impossibility, future time, predictions, logical inferences, abilities, or past habitual actions.

▶ **EXAMPLES:** Can I ask you a question? ____request____

Can you speak Spanish? ____ability____

1. Will you open the door? ____request____
2. Will the office be open tomorrow? ____possibility____
3. I can't hear you. ____ability____
4. You can't smoke here; it's a church. ____obligation____ advice permision
5. You shouldn't smoke; it's bad for your health. ____advice____
6. You really ought to see a doctor. ____suggestion____ advice
7. The doctor has just finished with another patient, and ought to be ready to see you in just a minute. ____prediction____
8. You walked twenty miles today? You must be tired! ____logical inferences____
9. You must leave at once if you don't want to miss the train. ____necessity____
10. I may be late tonight, so plan on eating dinner without me. ____prediction____
11. Can I speak to Dr. Martinez? ____request____
12. You may not leave before the teacher tells you to. ____permition____
13. I'm interested in buying that car, but it could be too expensive. ____prediction____
14. Could you pass the butter? ____request____
15. Could you read when you were five years old? ____ability____

EXERCISE 5

Underline the one-word and phrasal modals in this paragraph. Then identify the meaning that each modal is used to express (permission, necessity, etc.). The first sentence has been done for you as an example.

▶ **EXAMPLE:** (1) *necessity*

(1) I'm not looking forward to this afternoon because I <u>have to</u> go to the dentist. (2) I have a broken tooth, and I can't eat anything tough. (3) I'm supposed to be there at three o'clock, and I mustn't be more than five minutes late, or they'll cancel my appointment. (4) So I guess I had better leave plenty of time to get there. (5) The bus is supposed to come every ten minutes, but it's often late. (6) I know that I ought to go to the dentist more often, but I really don't like to. (7) She's going to tell me that I have to take better care of my teeth. (8) I know I'm supposed to brush my teeth after every meal, but sometimes I just can't find the time. (9) After my appointment I won't be able to eat anything for six hours, and I'm not supposed to eat anything for three hours before my appointment, either. (10) I know I'm going to be hungry tonight!

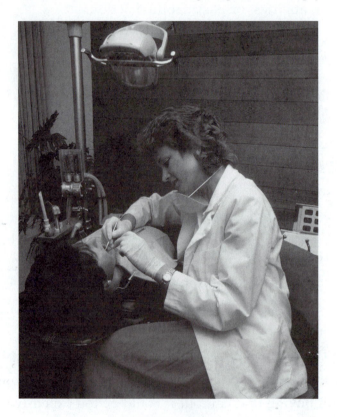

EXERCISE 6

Write a sentence with a one-word modal about the topics below:

▶ **EXAMPLE:** an activity to avoid if you want to be healthy

        You should avoid foods that are high in fat.

  1. a daily responsibility

  2. the best way to keep in touch with friends far away

3. advice for a lazy student

4. something you know how to do well

5. a possible event next year

6. something that is against school rules

7. something you don't know how to do

EXERCISE 7

Work with a partner. Use the phrasal modals below to ask your partner questions about daily life and activities. For each of the phrasal modals listed below ask:

a) one *yes/no* question.

b) one *Wh-* question.

Report your partner's answers in full sentences.

The first one has been done for you as an example.

▶ **EXAMPLE:** have to: Do you have to take the bus to get to school?

No I don't. I get a ride with a friend.

What time do you have to leave home?

About fifteen minutes before class.

My partner doesn't have to leave her house until just before class because she gets a ride in a friend's car.

1. have to

2. be allowed to

3. be supposed to

4. be able to

5. be going to

EXERCISE 8

Restate the ideas you wrote about in Exercise 6 by using phrasal instead of one-word modals. Are there any modal meanings that cannot be expressed with phrasal modals?

▶ **EXAMPLE:** You should avoid foods that are high in fat.

You ought to avoid foods that are high in fat.

Choosing One-Word Versus Phrasal Modals

Certain modal meanings and uses can only be expressed by one-word modals.

EXAMPLES	USE
(a) **Would** you help me? (b) **May** I have some cheese? (c) **Can** you turn down the radio?	Requests
(d) We **might** not have enough money. (e) We **could** fail the quiz if we don't study.	Some predictions
(f) **Can** you come to my party? (g) **Would** you join us for dinner?	Invitations
(h) We **could** have Chinese food tonight. (i) We **might** try the Hong Kong Cafe.	Suggestions
(j) A criminal **will** always return to the scene of the crime. (k) He **couldn't** have a TOEFL score of 600! He doesn't understand anything I say.	Expressions of general possibility or impossibility

In cases where both one-word and phrasal modals can be used, phrasal modals are preferred in the following situations:

To clarify modal meaning:

EXAMPLES	EXPLANATIONS
(l) Charlie **may not** bring a date	This one-word modal has two possible meanings: It's **possible** that he **won't** bring a date. He **doesn't have permission to** bring a date.
(m) Charlie **isn't allowed to** bring a date.	This phrasal modal has only one possible meaning: He **doesn't have permission to** bring a date.

To combine two modal meanings in the same verb phrase:

EXAMPLES	EXPLANATIONS
(n) A teacher **must be able to** explain things clearly. (o) NOT: She **must can** explain things clearly.	Two one-word modals cannot be combined.
(p) Poor people **shouldn't have to** pay the same taxes as rich people. (q) I **may be able to** get some extra tickets.	We can combine a one-word and phrasal modal.
(r) A firefighter **has to be able to** carry at least 250 pounds. (s) You **ought to be able to** speak French if you want a job in Paris. (t) I'm **going to have to** leave in a minute.	We can also combine two phrasal modals.

EXERCISE 9

What are the duties of citizenship? Decide whether people in society (a) **should have to do** or (b) **shouldn't have to do** these things. Add three more ideas of your own of what people should have to do and shouldn't have to do. Compare your sentences to those of a partner.

▶ **EXAMPLE:** People should have to send their children to school.

They shouldn't have to follow one particular religion.

1. send their children to school
2. follow one particular religion
3. go to work wherever the government sends them
4. work without pay on community projects
5. always obey their leaders
6. be required to vote in elections
7. report criminals to the police
8. get permission to leave the country
9. serve in the army
10. pay taxes

EXERCISE 10

What does it mean to "speak another language"? Read the skills listed below and decide whether each skill is in category A or category B.

Category A: A person **must** be able to do this in a new language in order to say that he or she "speaks the language."	*Category* B: A person only **should** be able to do this if he or she is a native speaker of the language.

Write the letter of the category in the space provided, and for each category think of one more skill of your own.

1. *should* read a newspaper
2. *should* understand native speakers perfectly when they speak to each other
3. *should* understand native speakers when they speak to foreigners
4. *should* have a perfect accent
5. *should* never make mistakes
6. *should* discuss abstract philosophy
7. *must* take care of day-to-day needs
8. *should* read and understand literature and poetry
9. *should* speak correctly enough that people can understand what you mean
10. A _____ *come to school every day to* ~~*must your classe*~~
11. B _____ *You should do exercies every day.*

Based on your definition, do you consider yourself to be fluent in English? Why or why not?

EXERCISE 11

What modal meanings are being expressed by the following sentences?

▶ **EXAMPLES:**   Don't leave the cheese anywhere that the dog is going to be able to reach. **(future activity, ability)**

1. You're going to have to leave soon.
2. If Alicia has another cup of coffee, she's not going to be able to fall asleep.
3. The management isn't going to allow anyone to go behind the counter.
4. Most people have to be able to get a full night's sleep in order to be alert.

5. Horses have got to be allowed to exercise enough if they are going to stay healthy.

6. Some people feel that anyone who wants to become an American citizen ought to be able to speak English.

7. Children under sixteen years old aren't supposed to be allowed to work without their parents' permission.

8. You don't have to be able to swim in order to enjoy the beach.

EXERCISE 12

Combine the modal meanings given below.

▶ **EXAMPLE:** You <u>might be allowed to</u> bring a guest. (possibility, permission)

1. Use a one-word and phrasal modal combination:

   (a) I _____ speak with the doctor. (necessity, permission)

   (b) Dogs _____ ride on buses. (advisability, permission)

   (c) Students _____ speak English in class. (advisability, necessity)

2. Use two phrasal modals:

   (a) A firefighter _____ carry at least 250 pounds. (necessity, ability)

   (b) I _____ not come to your party. (future, ability)

   (c) In order for plants to be healthy, they _____ grow freely. (necessity, ability)

   (d) You _____ speak French if you want a job in Paris. (advisability, ability)

EXERCISE 13

Make sentences that combine the following modal meanings. Compare your sentences with those of a partner and check your use of correct modals.

▶ **EXAMPLE:** future possibility and permission

   We may be allowed to speak to the president.

1. advisability and ability
2. necessity and ability
3. future possibility and ability
4. advisability and necessity
5. necessity and permission
6. advisability and permission

▶ **F**ormal and Informal Use of Modals

There are differences in the level of formality between some one-word and phrasal modals.

	MORE FORMAL	LESS FORMAL
ability *be able to/can*	**(a)** I'm **not able to** speak to you now.	**(b)** I **can't** speak to you now.
future activity *be going to/will*	**(c)** I **will** work a little longer.	**(d)** I'm **going to** work a little longer.
necessity *must/have to, have got to*	**(e)** We **must** go.	**(f)** We **have to** go. **(g)** We**('ve) got to** get out of here!
advisability *should/ought to*	**(h)** You **should** tell your parents.	**(i)** You **ought to** tell your parents.

EXERCISE 14

With a partner, discuss the following topics using informal language. Compare the modals you used with those in your partner's sentences.

1. a daily responsibility

2. the best way to keep in touch with friends far away

3. advice for a lazy student

4. a possible event or occurrence next year

Use Your English

ACTIVITY 1: SPEAKING

Below are descriptions of three people who have applied for citizenship in a new country. In a small group, pretend that you are a committee who has to decide who should be given a residence visa. Follow these steps:

STEP 1 Examine the applicants' reasons for wanting to immigrate. Decide whether they will be able to fulfill the basic duties of citizenship in the new country.

STEP 2 As a group, decide which applicant most deserves the residence visa and which one least deserves it.

STEP 3 Present your decision and your reasons to the rest of the class.

Applicant A

• belongs to a religion that is discriminated against in his or her country and will probably be imprisoned or executed because of those beliefs
• plans on maintaining the family's religion and language
• will not allow children of the family to go to public schools in the new country
• has few job skills and may need to be supported by public welfare

Applicant B

• wants to earn higher wages and send the money back to relatives in the home country
• has skills that are needed badly in the new country
• does not intend to vote or become involved in the politics of the new country
• believes in obeying the law, but will try to avoid national service

Applicant C

• was jailed for political activity in college and is now being threatend by the secret police
• doesn't agree with the politics or government of the new country and doesn't believe in paying taxes
• is engaged to someone from the new country
• has skills that are badly needed in the new country

ACTIVITY 2: READING/SPEAKING

Below there are three advertisements for jobs available in clerical administration, computer programming, and sales.

STEP 1 For each job, identify

1. the things that an applicant must be able to do

2. the things he or she should be able to do (although may not be absolutely required)

3. some things that are neither required nor recommended, but are still characteristics that the "perfect candidate" might have

4. what an interested candidate has to do in order to apply for the position.

STEP 2 Would any of these jobs interest you? Why or why not? Compare your ideas to those of other students in the class.

workaholic — work quickly Multitasking

PROGRAM ASSISTANT

Provide clerical and admin. support to five public program coord. involved in developing educational materials and providing training for hazardous waste workers.

QUALIFICATIONS: exper. operating word processing software and laser-printer hardware. Skill in establishing and maintaining master computer and paper files of program information. Interpersonal skills required to commun. with numerous instructors and staff on various university campuses. Organizational skills to estab. priorities. Related exper. working in a public service/public program atmosphere pref'd.

SALARY: $1799-2124/mo. with excel. benefits.

Send detailed resume to:
Personnel Office
Box 1012, 1066 Hastings St.
San Francisco, CA

LAW FIRM PROGRAMMER/ANALYST

Exciting opportunities exist in our office as we continue to develop, install, refine, and enhance automated solutions to law firm information processing. If you are a professional with 51 years of programming experience, have a background in 4 computer languages, and have business software development exp., we'd like to hear from you. We seek individuals who strive for excellence in their work product, who prefer a challenging, fast-paced environment, and who are service oriented. Excellent communication skills are a must!

Send resume and salary history to:
Human Resources
PO Box 7880
San Francisco, CA

SALES CAREER OPPORTUNITY

College Textbook Sales McGruder-Hall Western Region Office has immediate openings for 2 Assoc. Sales Reps. These positions involve both office sales support & selling textbooks to professors on college campuses.

Qualifications include:
* 4 yr. College Degree
* Exc. Communications Skills
* Strong Organization Skills w/ Ability to Prioritize Multiple Tasks
* Desire to Move into Outside Sales Position
* Strong Motivation to Succeed
* Willingness to Travel

We offer excellent salary & benefits package. Please send resume to:
Sales Manager
McGruder-Hall Inc.
55 Francisco St., Ste. 738
SF, CA 94133
No Phone Calls Please

ACTIVITY 3: WRITING

Write your own want ads advertising the qualifications and skills necessary for these occupations. First decide on necessary and desirable qualifications, and then tell interested people what they should do in order to apply.

English teacher

United Nations translator

firefighter

police officer

executive secretary/administrative assistant

computer programmer

ACTIVITY 4: READING/SPEAKING

Look in the want ads of your local newspaper and find two examples of jobs that you think you would like. Describe the positions to the rest of the class, and tell why you think you would be a good candidate for the jobs.

ACTIVITY 5: LISTENING

STEP 1 Listen to the following conversations. Write the topic of each conversation in the chart below. Notice any modals that the speakers used and the context for using them.

STEP 2 Listen to the conversations again and list at least two examples of modals that you heard in each conversation. What meanings did these modals communicate? Write your answers in the chart

	Topic	Modals	Meaning
Conversation #1		1. 2.	1. 2.
Conversation #2		1. 2.	1. 2.

STEP 3 Compare your findings to those of other students.

• What differences in level or formality could you hear?
• Based on what you heard, think of one question you want to ask your teacher about using modals in English.

ACTIVITY 6: LISTENING

Listen to a conversation between two people. This conversation could be on television or a real-life conversation that you were able to overhear. Follow the same procedure that you used in Activity 5.

INFINITIVES

UNIT GOALS:

- To review the form of infinitives and gerunds and the meaning of infinitives
- To understand and use sentences with verbs followed by infinitives
- To use infinitives as the subjects of sentences

▶ OPENING TASK
The "To Do" List

TO DO	Check with Mary	Check with Charlie
✗• buy Mary a present	✗• Does she really understand why I'm going?	• remind about helping move boxes to Mary's garage?
• say good-bye to Prof Montaigne		• check with landlord about cleaning deposit
• buy address book	✗• Is she still planning to visit? When?	• clean the kitchen
• buy suitcase		✗• change name on the bill for the electric company
• buy new jacket	• move boxes to her parents' garage	
• get small gifts for my host family	✗• drive me to airport?	• get address of his old girlfriend (ballet dancer)– don't tell Mary!
✗• have farewell dinner with Mom & Dad	• have farewell dinner? Where?	✗• get money he owes me
• get traveler's checks		
✗• reconfirm ticket and get seat assignment		

STEP 1 In two days John Tealhome is leaving to spend a year studying in France. On page 86 is his list of the things he needs to do before he goes, and the things that he would like his girlfriend, Mary, and his roommate, Charlie, to do for him. Look at John's "To Do" list and discuss these questions with a partner.

- What things does John still need to do?
- What things does he need Mary to do?
- What things does he want Charlie to do?
- What things does he want Charlie not to do?
- Has he forgotten to do anything?
- How ready do you think John really is?
- If he doesn't have time to get everything done, what things should he be sure to do, and what things could he decide not to do without creating problems?

STEP 2 Present your answer to the last question to the rest of the class.

▶ **O**verview of Infinitives and Gerunds

Infinitives and gerunds are formed from verb phrases.

EXAMPLES	EXPLANATIONS
(a) We need **to use** infinitives in certain situations.	Infinitives are formed by adding *to* before a verb (*to* + verb).
(b) Other situations require **using** gerunds.	Gerunds are formed by adding *-ing* to a verb (verb + *ing*).

Gerunds and infinitive phrases function like noun phrases.

EXAMPLES	EXPLANATIONS
(c) **Using gerunds and infinitives** can be tricky. **(d)** **To know which form is correct** requires some experience.	They can be used: • as subjects
(e) Some verbs require **using gerunds.** **(f)** With other verbs you'll need **to use infinitives.**	• as objects of verbs
(g) This unit and the following one will focus **on using** infinitives and gerunds. **(h)** By the end you should feel confident **about choosing** the correct form most of the time.	• as objects of prepositions
(i) But once you understand the principles, it's not **difficult to decide on the correct form.**	• with adjective phrases

EXERCISE 1

Underline the infinitive and gerund phrases in this passage. Tell how three of the forms you have identified are used in the sentence.

▶ **EXAMPLE:**   Norman likes <u>to collect stamps</u>.

   used as object of verb likes

(1) Norman likes to collect stamps. (2) He likes getting them from anywhere, but he is particularly interested in collecting stamps from Africa. (3) He has tried to get at least one stamp from every African country. (4) This hasn't always been easy to do. (5) He has tried writing to the post offices of various countries, but they haven't always responded to his request. (6) A friend suggested looking in commercial stamp-catalogs for hard-to-find stamps, and Norman has had pretty good luck finding rare or unusual stamps there. (7) He has also begun corresponding with stamp-collectors in other countries and has asked them to send him stamps when they first come out. (8) They are usually happy to do it and have urged him to do the same thing for them. (9) He enjoys learning about other countries and finds that collecting stamps is a good way to do this.

▶ **Infinitives**

EXAMPLES	EXPLANATION
(a) I want **to go to Tahiti next year.** **(b)** I am afraid **to open that door** because something bad might happen if I do.	Infinitives usually refer to the possiblity of an action occurring. The action has not yet happened.

Infinitives can contain the same information as any verb phrase.

EXAMPLES	EXPLANATIONS
(c) John decided **to go** to Paris. **(d)** Mary decided **not to go** with him. **(e)** We want **to find** another restaurant because they have asked us **not to smoke** in this one.	**Affirmative/Negative** Affirmative infinitive: *to* + verb Negative infinitive: *not to* + verb
(f) I need **to wash** my car. **(g)** My car needs **to be washed.** **(h)** Yoko intends **to become** active in student government, and hopes **to be elected** to the student council.	**Active/Passive** Active infinitive: *to* + verb Passive infinitive: *to* + *be* + past participle
(i) I would prefer **to have left** yesterday, but Lev would prefer to leave tomorrow. **(j)** We hope **to be living** in our new house by next summer.	**Perfect/Progressive Aspect** Perfect infinitive: *to* + *have* + past participle Progressive infinitive: *to* + *be* + present participle
(k) We want **to have washed** the car when he gets here. (We'll finish washing the car before he gets here.) **(l)** We want **to be washing** the car when he gets here. (We'll start washing the car before he gets here.) **(m)** We want **to wash** the car when he gets here. (We'll start washing the car after he gets here.)	Aspect tells us when the infinitive happens in relation to the main verb.

EXERCISE 2

Complete the sentences by expressing the idea in the infinitive as a verb phrase. Be sure to include all the information about time, aspect, and active or passive in your verb phrase.

▶ **EXAMPLE:** I hope **to be elected** to the student council.

I hope that I <u>will be elected to the student council.</u>

1. Morris claims **to have been born** in Russia.

   Morris claims that he _____ .

2. We expected you **to have done** the assignment already.

   We expected that you _____ .

3. The teacher reminded the students **not to forget** the homework.

   The teacher said, "_____ ."

4. We expected Hani **to be studying** when we got home.

   We expected that Hani would _____ .

5. My sister is never happy **to be left alone** on a Saturday night.

   If my sister _____ , she is never happy.

EXERCISE 3

Complete the sentences by expressing the underlined clause as an infinitive phrase. Be sure to include all the information about time, aspect, and active or passive in your infinitive phrase.

▶ **EXAMPLE:** I hope that I <u>will pass the TOEFL next month.</u>

I hope <u>to pass the TOEFL next month.</u>

1. Peter has the optimistic hope that <u>he will have finished the report by next week.</u>

   Peter hopes _____ by next week.

2. A strict teacher requires that <u>all students stop talking when class begins.</u>

   A strict teacher requires all students _____ .

3. The doctor told his patient: "<u>Don't take this medicine more than twice a day.</u>"

   The doctor reminded his patient _____ .

4. We thought that <u>the children would be sleeping</u> when we got home.

   We expected _____ when we got home.

5. When <u>my brother is bothered while he is doing his homework</u>, he doesn't like it.

My brother never likes _____.

EXERCISE 4

Interview a partner to get two or three answers for each of these questions.

▶ **EXAMPLES:**   What things do your teachers expect you **to do?**

They expect me to speak up in class.

What things do your teachers expect you **not to do?**

They expect me not to copy my homework from other students.

1. What things does your partner's family expect him or her **to do?**
   What things do they expect him or her **not to do?**

2. How does your partner like **to treat** people he or she has just met?
   How does your partner like **to be treated** by his or her teachers?

3. What things do your partner's teachers expect him or her **to do** at the beginning of class?
   What things do teachers expect your partner **to have done** before the beginning of class?

4. What does your partner plan **to do** when school ends?
   What does your partner plan **to be doing** when school ends?

▶ **N**oun or Pronoun Plus Infinitive

EXAMPLES	IMPLIED MEANING	EXPLANATIONS
(a) Norman wants **to collect foreign stamps.** **(b)** Norman wants **us to collect foreign stamps.**	**Norman** will collect the stamps. **We** will collect the stamps.	Sometimes it is necessary to identify who is performing the action described by the infinitive.
(c) This question is easy **to answer.**	It's easy for everyone.	*to* + verb: The performer of the infinitive is usually the same as the subject of the main verb or "everybody."
(d) This question is easy **for experts to understand.** **(e)** The problem was difficult **for him to solve.**	It's only easy for experts; it's not easy for other people. He had difficulty, but she didn't.	*(for)* + noun phrase + *to* + verb: The performer of the infinitive can be a noun or an object pronoun (*him, us, etc.*).

EXAMPLES	EXPLANATIONS
(f) Norman **reminded us to give** him the stamps. **(g)** NOT: Norman **reminded to give** him the stamps.	Certain main verbs require using noun or pronoun + infinitive. (See Focus 5.)
(h) Infinitives are difficult **for students to understand.** **(i)** NOT: Infinitives are difficult **students to understand.**	With certain verbs (see Focus 6) and adjectives, the noun/pronoun + infinitive **must** occur with *for*.

EXERCISE 5

In these sentences identify who performs the action described by the high-lighted infinitive.

▶ **EXAMPLES:**   We were expecting Ilana **to arrive** before now.

   Ilana.

   We were asked **to bring** presents to the party.

   We.

1. Malcolm claims **to be speaking** for the entire class.
2. This hotel requires people **to turn** in their room keys by 11.00.
3. Wendy requested her students **to bring** their books to class.
4. My sister promised **to stay** after the party.
5. Gladstone intends **to lose** thirty pounds by Christmas.
6. The child convinced his friend **to put** a frog in the teacher's desk.
7. Norman wasn't allowed **to stay up** late when he was a child.
8. My parents encouraged all their children **to start working** part-time while they were still in high school.

▶ **V**erbs Followed by Infinitives: Pattern I

Pattern 1: Verb + Infinitive

EXAMPLES	EXPLANATION
(a) I **decided to go** shopping but I **neglected to bring** my checkbook.	With certain verbs the infinitive immediately follows the main verb.
(b) Peter **tried to help** Denise, but she **refused to accept.**	
(c) She **seemed to have** too much work, but she **was** only **pretending to be** busy.	

EXERCISE 6

There are seventeen Pattern 1 verbs in the following paragraph. Identify them and write them in the blanks.

(1) The Acme Stamp Company agreed to send Norman some stamps, but when he got them they didn't appear to be in good condition. (2) The company claimed to be reputable, but Norman still felt the stamps were bad. (3) He didn't care to pay good money for bad stamps and he felt that he deserved to get a refund. (4) So he decided to phone the company directly. (5) He demanded to speak to the manager. (6) The manager pretended to be concerned, but he hesitated to make any firm promises about refunds. (7) The company offered to exchange the stamps, but Norman refused to accept the offer. (8) All the stamps from that company seemed to be of poor quality. (9) The company also tended to be very slow in filling orders. (10) Norman has learned to make sure a company is reputable before placing a large order with them. (11) He neglected to do this with the Acme Stamp Company. (12) Norman still hopes to get a refund. (13) He is waiting to see if the company will give him one before he files a formal complaint with the post office.

1. *agree*
2. *appear*
3. _____
4. _____
5. _____
6. _____
7. _____
8. _____
9. _____
10. _____
11. _____
12. _____
13. _____
14. _____
15. _____
16. _____
17. _____

EXERCISE 7

Complete these sentences with infinitive phrases. Express your real opinion. Compare your answers with other students'.

▶ **EXAMPLE:** An honest person should never pretend . . .

      to be something that he or she really isn't.

1. A good parent should never neglect . . .
2. Most children in elementary school learn . . .
3. Most poor people can't afford . . .
4. The world situation today seems . . .
5. Shy students sometimes hesitate . . .
6. Selfish people rarely offer . . .
7. A good friend should never refuse . . .
8. Criminals deserve . . .
9. Most children hope . . .
10. In general, good students tend . . .
11. Most American teenagers can't wait . . .
12. Most good teachers seem . . .
13. An honest person should never agree . . .
14. Excellent athletes often appear . . .

EXERCISE 8

Interview a partner and find out about five of the following topics. Report your information to the rest of the class in full sentences.

▶ **EXAMPLE:** *My partner often neglects to do her homework.*

1. a responsibility he or she often neglects to do
2. something he or she learned to do in English class
3. something he or she can't afford to do
4. a kind of assistance that she or he would never hesitate to accept
5. something he or she would refuse to do, no matter how much she or he were paid to do it
6. a reward she or he thinks he or she deserves to receive
7. how he or she tends to behave in a room full of strangers
8. something he or she would pretend to do as a child
9. how people in this class appeared to be on the first day of school
10. a famous person she or he would never care to meet

▶ # Verbs Followed by Infinitives: Pattern 2

Pattern 2: Verb + Noun/Object Pronoun + Infinitive

EXAMPLES	EXPLANATIONS
(a) Other stamp collectors have **advised Norman to order** stamps from catalogs.	Some verbs are followed by a noun/object pronoun plus infinitive. They describe situations where the subject causes or influences someone or something else to perform the action described by the infinitive.
(b) They **warned him not to spend** a lot of money unless he could **trust the stamp company to send** genuine stamps.	

Verbs that occur only with this pattern are:

advise	*convince*	*hire*	*persuade*	*tell*
allow	*encourage*	*invite*	*remind*	*trust*
cause	*forbid*	*order*	*require*	*urge*
command	*force*	*permit*	*teach*	*warn*

EXERCISE 9
Create sentences using the cues given.

▶ **EXAMPLES:** (advise/study) **My parents advised me to study English.**

(force/cancel) **The heavy fog forced the airport to cancel all flights.**

1. remind/pay
2. warn/not forget
3. convince/help
4. hire/work
5. require/pay
6. forbid/marry
7. invite/join
8. teach/speak
9. allow/leave
10. order/send
11. urge/vote
12. trust/spend
13. tell/eat
14. encourage/ask
15. force/leave

▶ Verbs Followed by Infinitives: Pattern 3

Pattern 3: Verb (+ Noun Phrase) + Infinitive

EXAMPLES	EXPLANATIONS
(a) We **expect to leave** in an hour, and we **expect you to come** with us. **(b)** Norman **wants to get** stamps from every country, and he **wants us to help** him.	Many verbs can be followed by either an infinitive or a noun phrase plus infinitive.
(c) Mary's father **arranged for John to get** a cheap ticket. **(d)** He never **intended for Mary to be** unhappy.	A few verbs of this kind must use *for* before the noun phrase. Verbs that follow this pattern are: *arrange, intend, consent, afford*.

EXERCISE 10

Interview other students in the class about one of the following topics. Report your answers in full sentences.

▶ **EXAMPLES:** My partner likes to do the dishes, but he prefers someone else to do the cooking.

My partner needs to write a statement of purpose for her university application, but she needs a native English speaker to check over her grammar.

1. things they **like to do** versus things they **like someone else to do**
2. things they **expect to do** versus things they **expect someone else to do**
3. things they have **asked to do** versus things they have **asked someone else to do**
4. things they **need to do** versus things they **need someone else to do**
5. things they have **arranged to do** versus things they have **arranged for other people to do**

EXERCISE 11

Combine these sentence pairs by replacing **"this"** with an infinitive phrase made from the information in the first sentence.

▶ **EXAMPLE:** John will spend a year in France. Mary doesn't want **this.**

Mary doesn't want John to spend a year in France.

1. John will write a long letter once a week. Mary has requested **this.**
2. John might postpone his trip until next year. Mary would prefer **this.**
3. She will try to visit him while he's there. She has decided **this.**
4. She was upset by the news of his plans. He didn't expect **this.**
5. John got a very cheap ticket. Mary's father arranged **this.**
6. John didn't apply for a passport. He neglected **this.**
7. John will report to the police when he arrives. French law requires **this.**
8. Mary will begin to study French herself. John has encouraged **this.**
9. Mary feels hurt that John is leaving. John never intended **this.**

Using Infinitives with Passive Verbs

EXAMPLES	EXPLANATION
(a) **People warned Norman not to pay** a lot of money for stamps from unfamiliar companies. (b) **Norman was warned not to pay** a lot of money.	Pattern 2 and Pattern 3 verbs (except those that require *for*) can be used in passive sentences.

EXERCISE 12

Complete these sentences with infinitives. Use real information that expresses your true opinion. Compare your ideas with those of other students in the class.

1. Most people can be trusted . . .
2. Children should be allowed . . .
3. All teachers should be encouraged . . .
4. Noisy people should be told . . .
5. Teenagers should be warned . . .
6. Students should be expected . . .
7. Guests should be invited . . .
8. Rich people should be required . . .

▶ Infinitives as Subjects of a Sentence

AWKWARD	BETTER	EXPLANATION
(a) To collect stamps is fun.	**(b) It's** fun **to collect stamps.**	Infinitive phrases can be used as subjects in a sentence. We usually begin such sentences with *it* and put the infinitive phrase at the end of the sentence.
(c) To have been introduced to you is an honor.	**(d) It's** an honor **to have been introduced to you.**	
(e) For John to study in France is a good idea.	**(f) It's** a good idea **for John to study in France.**	

EXERCISE 13

Complete these sentences with ideas that express your true opinion. Compare your answers with other students'.

1. It's always a good idea . . .
2. It's enjoyable . . .
3. It's never wise . . .
4. It's every parent's dream . . .
5. It's never a teacher's responsibility . . .
6. It's sometimes difficult . . .
7. It's usually necessary . . .
8. It's seldom easy . . .

Use Your English

ACTIVITY 1: WRITING

In the Opening Task on page 86 you examined the things on John Tealhome's mind a couple of days before his departure for a year overseas. Have you ever left for a long trip? How prepared and well-organized were you two days before your departure?

STEP 1 Make a list like John's that indicates the things you still needed to do, and some of the things that you needed other people to do for you. Compare your list and John's. Who was better organized?

STEP 2 Write a paragraph describing your experience. Did you have chance to do everything you needed or wanted to do? Was there anything you forgot to do? What advice would you give someone preparing for a similar trip?

ACTIVITY 2: SPEAKING

Do parents treat boys and girls differently?

STEP 1 Interview some classmates and find out what things children in their culture are taught to do when they are growing up.

	Boys are encouraged to . . .	Boys are encouraged not to . . .	Girls are encouraged to . . .	Girls are encouraged not to . . .
Examples	be brave defend their sisters	cry play with dolls	be neat and tidy play with dolls	play roughly get dirty
Student 1				
Student 2				
Student 3				

STEP 2 Compare the responses of the people you interviewed. What differences are there? What might be the reasons for some of these differences? What things are taught to all children regardless of their gender or culture?

ACTIVITY 3: READING/SPEAKING

STEP 1 Below is a list of some possible strategies for learning to speak English. Decide whether the listed strategy is something that language learners should **try to do** or something that they should **try not to do** in order to learn more effectively.

- Try to use new vocabulary in writing and conversation.
- Stop to look up every unfamiliar word in the dictionary.
- Be very very careful not to make any mistakes.
- Guess at the meaning of unfamiliar words by using other clues in the sentence.
- Become discouraged if you don't understand 100% of everything you hear.
- Always think of your ideas in your own language first, and then translate them word-by-word into English.
- Listen for the general idea in conversations.
- Look for opportunities to speak English as often as possible.
- Go over your mistakes on homework and try to understand why you made them.
- Go over your mistakes on homework and write the correct answer.
- Find ways to punish yourself if you make a mistake.
- Don't speak unless you are sure the answer is correct.

STEP 2 List three more strategies language learners should try to use, and three strategies they should try not to do.

STEP 3 Compare your list with several other students', and present any interesting similarities and differences to the rest of the class.

ACTIVITY 4: SPEAKING

A **superstition** is a folk belief about lucky or unlucky events. For example, in some cultures the number 13 is considered to be an unlucky number. Friday the thirteenth is supposed to be a particularly unlucky day. Some people don't want to attend a party or sit at a table where there are thirteen people. Many buildings, especially hotels, do not have a thirteenth floor. Other superstitions still affect basic manners in society. Because of an old superstition it is considered polite to say "God bless you" when someone near you sneezes, even to someone you do not know.

STEP 1 Work with other students to develop a presentation for the rest of the class about some modern superstitions and their results. Identify some things that people try to do and some things they try not to. You may wish to compare the superstitions of several different cultures. Are there any superstitions that are universal? Why do you think superstitions come into being?

STEP 2 Present your ideas to the rest of the class.

ACTIVITY 5: WRITING

Write about your favorite hobby or leisure time activity. What is it? Why do you like to do it? What skill does someone need to develop or what special equipment does a person need to buy if he or she wants to pursue this hobby?

ACTIVITY 6: LISTENING

STEP 1 Read the questions below and then listen to the following conversation for information to answer them in complete sentences.

STEP 2 Compare your answers with another student's. Listen to the conversation a second time to confirm or clarify any questions you're not sure of.

1. What information should the students expect to be tested on?

_____

2. What were they told not to study?

_____

3. What had the man been planning to do tonight?

_____

4. Why wasn't the man in class yesterday?

_____

5. What had he been told to do in order to improve his chance for graduate school?

_____

6. Why doesn't he want a paid position at the library?

_____

UNIT 7

GERUNDS

UNIT GOALS:

- To understand the form and meaning of gerunds
- To understand and use sentences with verbs followed by gerunds
- To learn some basic principles about when to use an infinitive and when to use a gerund

STEP 1 Read these two definitions of different kinds of people and how they spend their free time.

DO-ERS like **doing things** during their free time. They have hobbies and activities that keep them busy. They plan their free time. A good vacation is one that lets them do many different things and have many new experiences.

BE-ERS prefer **not doing things.** They like to spend an afternoon relaxing, reading a magazine, or just doing nothing at all—sleeping, daydreaming. They don't plan their free time; they just let it happen. A good vacation is one that makes them feel relaxed.

STEP 2 In this chart, list ways you spend your free time. Two examples for each category have been provided. Add three more that are true for you.

Activities I enjoy doing in my free time (I do them, and I enjoy them).	Activities I enjoy *not* doing in my free time (*I don't do* them, and I enjoy not doing them).	Activities I don't enjoy doing in my free time (I do them, but I don't enjoy them).
1) reading the paper	1) not getting up early	1) doing chores (cleaning and laundry)
2) talking with friends	2) not driving to work	2) taking work home from the office
3) _____ _____	3) _____ _____	3) _____ _____
4) _____ _____	4) _____ _____	4) _____ _____
5) _____ _____	5) _____ _____	5) _____ _____

STEP 3 Describe the activities in your chart to a partner. Your partner should decide whether you appear to be a do-er or a be-er. What category does your partner seem to be in? Present your findings about each other to the rest of the class.

Gerunds

EXAMPLES	EXPLANATIONS
(a) Norman enjoys **collecting stamps.** He doesn't mind **paying a lot of money** for rare ones.	Gerunds are formed by adding *-ing* to the simple form of the verb. They are used in many of the same ways that infinitives are used. In general they refer to an action that is already happening or has been completed.
(b) The librarian doesn't like **our talking.** Maybe we'd better stop.	
(c) I hate **listening** to boring lectures. I wish this class were over!	

Gerund phrases can contain the same information as any verb phrase.

EXAMPLES	EXPLANATIONS
(d) I enjoy **staying in bed** on Sunday mornings.	**Affirmative/Negative**
(e) I like **not getting up** early.	Affirmative gerund: verb + *-ing*
(f) Peter likes **having a responsible job,** but he hates **not having enough time** for his family.	Negative gerund: *not* + verb + *-ing*
(g) Matt and Jeff enjoy **inviting friends** for dinner.	**Active and Passive**
(h) Matt and Jeff enjoy **being invited** to their friends' homes for dinner.	Active gerund: verb + *-ing*
(i) Sofia likes **giving orders,** but she hates **being told** what to do.	Passive gerund: *being* + verb
(j) Ayo was nervous about **taking** tests.	**Simple/Perfect Aspect**
(k) Ayo was happy about **having gotten** a good grade on his exam.	Simple gerund: verb + *-ing*
	Perfect gerund: *having* + past participle
	We don't often use perfect gerunds, and there is no progressive gerund.

EXERCISE 1

Complete the sentences by expressing the idea in the gerund as a verb phrase.

▶ **EXAMPLE:** I enjoy **not doing** anything on Sunday mornings.

  <u>I don't do anything on Sunday</u> , and I enjoy that.

1. We hate **being asked for** money all the time.

When _____, we hate it.

2. I really appreciate **your having taken** such good care of my dog while I was on vacation.

I really appreciate that _____.

3. They suspect him of **taking** the money.

They suspect that _____.

4. We didn't plan for **their having** problems with the homework.

We didn't plan for the fact that _____.

5. I think John resents **not being invited** to the party.

I think John resents the fact that _____.

EXERCISE 2

Complete the sentences by expressing the underlined clause as a gerund phrase. Be sure to include all the information in the verb phrase in your gerund phrase.

▶ **EXAMPLE:** <u>I don't ever do any homework on Saturday nights,</u> and I enjoy that.

  I enjoy <u>not doing (never doing) any homework on Saturday nights.</u>

1. When <u>I am asked for my suggestions about ways to improve the company,</u> I like it.

I like _____.

2. I really appreciate <u>that you have been so careful with this homework.</u>

I really appreciate your _____.

3. Mary suspected <u>that John was planning to contact his old girlfriend.</u>

Mary suspected John of _____.

4. The teacher didn't plan <u>for the fact that the students had completely forgotten the grammar rules.</u>

The teacher didn't plan on _____.

5. I think John is disappointed <u>that he wasn't selected for the scholarship.</u>

I think that John is disappointed about _____.

EXERCISE 3

Interview a partner and find out two or three things for each of these topics.

▶ **EXAMPLE:**   Things your partner enjoys doing:

What things do you enjoy doing on Sunday mornings?
I enjoy reading the paper.

Things your partner enjoys not doing:

What things do you enjoy not doing on Sunday mornings?
I enjoy not getting up early.

1. Things your partner enjoys **doing** on the weekends.

   Things your partner enjoys **not doing** on the weekends.

2. Things your partner hates **doing.**

   Things your partner doesn't mind **other people doing.**

3. Things or services your partner likes **giving to other people.**

   Things or services your partner likes **other people giving to him or her.**

4. Things that attending a college typically requires **doing.**

   Things that attending a college typically requires **having done.**

▶ Noun or Pronoun Plus Gerund

EXAMPLES	IMPLIED MEANING	EXPLANATIONS
(a) Denise doesn't approve of **taking** time off. **(b)** Denise doesn't approve of **Peter's taking** time off.	She doesn't like anybody's doing it. She doesn't like Peter to do it.	As with infinitives, it is sometimes necessary to identify who is performing the action described by the gerund.
(c) Peter can't understand **being** so serious about work.	He can't understand why he or anybody should do this.	verb + *-ing:* The performer of the gerund is the same as the subject of the main verb or "everybody."
(d) Peter hates **her complaining** about his absences.	Maybe he doesn't mind when other people complain; he just doesn't like it when she does it.	possessive noun phrase + gerund: The performer of the gerund is stated as a possessive noun (e.g., *Peter's* in **(b)**) or pronoun.

EXERCISE 4

In these sentences, underline the gerund and draw a line to the person who performs the action it describes.

▶ **EXAMPLES:** Is there any way we can delay underline{taking} the test?

No politician will ever admit underline{not having} a solution to the budget problem.

1. Jeff enjoys living in San Francisco.
2. I really appreciate your helping us get ready for the party.
3. Peter has considered looking for a new job.
4. Matt could never imagine leaving San Francisco.
5. Mary resents John's spending a year overseas.
6. Miss Manners will never excuse her having behaved so rudely.
7. We wanted to postpone leaving for the trip, but we didn't anticipate not being able to change our tickets.
8. We'll really miss your singing and dancing in the school talent show.

► # Verbs Followed by Gerunds: Pattern I

Pattern 1: Verb + Gerund

EXAMPLES	EXPLANATION
(a) Charlie **can't help falling** in love with a new woman every few weeks. **(b)** Mary **gave up smoking** because she knows it's bad for her health.	Some verbs are followed immediately by a gerund.

EXERCISE 5

Underline the verbs in this passage that follow Pattern 1. The first two have been done for you.

LIVING THE LOW-FAT LIFE

(1) Nutritionists <u>recommend</u> reducing the amount of fat in one's diet. (2) They <u>suggest</u> eating foods that are high in fiber and avoiding foods that are high in fat. (3) Some people deny having a high-fat diet and would never consider changing their eating habits. (4) Other people admit consuming more fat than they would really like to. (5) But nutritionists feel that everyone could benefit from the low-fat life.

(6) Most people can't help consuming a certain amount of fat, no matter how careful they are. (7) But here are a few very simple, basic changes in eating and cooking habits that will greatly decrease the amount of fat in your diet.

• (8) You can give up using rich, creamy sauces and use natural cooking juices to give your food flavor.

• (9) You should avoid consuming large amounts of red meat and quit having such foods as bacon or sausage on a regular basis.

• (10) You can practice cooking your food in different ways. (11) Such changes include not frying food in oil, but steaming or boiling it whenever possible.

(12) Initially these changes may be difficult, and you may resist changing old habits. (13) But if you keep on following the basic principles listed above, it will get easier to keep doing it.

EXERCISE 6

Use five verbs that you found in Exercise 5 to talk about some of your own health habits. Tell about things that you regularly avoid doing and things that you do regularly and intend to keep on doing.

Verbs Followed by Gerunds: Pattern 2

Pattern 2: Verb + { Gerund
Noun Phrase + Infinitive

EXAMPLES		EXPLANATION
Gerund (a) Doctors **advise reducing** fats in one's diet. (c) They **urge giving up** fried foods.	**Infinitive** (b) My doctor **advised me to reduce** my fat intake. (d) He **urged Peter to give up** fried foods.	Some verbs are followed by a gerund when referring to "everybody," and by an infinitive when referring to a specific person.

EXERCISE 7

For each of these Pattern 2 verbs listed below write two sentences—one with a noun phrase and one without. If you wish, you can write a single sentence that uses both patterns.

▶ **EXAMPLE:** Advise:

Most people advise taking a nice hot bath if you don't want to catch a cold, but my doctor advised me to take vitamin C instead.

1. require
2. encourage
3. urge
4. advise
5. forbid

Verbs Followed by Gerunds: Pattern 3

Pattern 3: Verb (+ Noun Phrase) + Gerund

EXAMPLES	EXPLANATION
(a) I **don't mind borrowing** money, but I **dislike Peter's doing** it. (b) I **dislike swimming** in cold water, but I **don't mind your doing** it.	Many verb-gerund combinations can be used with or without noun phrases.

Common verbs that follow this pattern are:

anticipate	*delay*	*don't mind*	*imagine*	*resent*
appreciate	*deny*	*enjoy*	*miss*	*tolerate*
consider	*dislike*	*excuse*	*postpone*	*understand*

EXERCISE 8

Complete these sentences with true information. Use gerunds in your answers, and if the highlighted verb can be used with a noun phrase, try to use a noun phrase in your answer:

1. I usually **avoid** . . .
2. When I was a child I used to **imagine** . . .
3. My English teacher **recommends** . . .
4. I would like to **quit** . . .
5. I am **considering** . . .
6. Honest people shouldn't **tolerate** . . .
7. To be a good soccer player it's necessary to **practice** . . .
8. A teacher's responsibility **includes** . . .
9. Becoming a really good speaker of a foreign language **requires** . . .
10. I **appreciate** guests . . .

EXERCISE 9

Combine these sentence pairs by replacing "**this**" with a gerund phrase made from the first sentence.

▶ **EXAMPLE:** John will spend a year in France. Mary resents **this**.

Mary resents John's spending a year in France.

1. John sings a funny song whenever he sees her. Mary will miss **this**.

_____

2. He wants to become really fluent in French. Mary doesn't really understand **this**.

_____

3. He applied to the program without consulting Mary. She resents **this**.

_____

4. She will not have a chance to talk with him every day. She's not looking forward to **this**.

_____

5. John is leaving in two weeks. He is quite excited about **this**.

_____

6. John needs at least three weeks to get a passport. He didn't anticipate **this**.

_____

7. This will make his departure even later than expected. John wanted to avoid **this**.

_____

Gerunds in Other Positions in a Sentence

Gerunds can be used in other places in the sentence where noun phrases normally appear.

Subjects of a sentence

EXAMPLES	EXPLANATION
Gerund Subjects (a) **Collecting stamps** is fun. (b) AWKWARD: **It's** fun **collecting stamps.** **Infinitive Subjects** (c) **It's** fun **to collect** stamps. (d) AWKWARD: **To collect stamps** is fun.	Unlike infinitive subjects, gerund subjects usually begin a sentence and are not usually used with *it* constructions.

Objects of prepositions and two-word verbs

EXAMPLES	EXPLANATION
(e) I am happy **about meeting** you. (f) This steak is too tough **for frying** in butter. (g) He is exhausted **from staying up** all night. (h) I'm **giving up smoking.** (i) I'm **looking into changing** majors.	Objects of prepositions and phrasal verbs must be expressed by nouns, pronouns, or gerunds, but never infinitives.

EXERCISE 10

Complete these sentences with information that describes your true feelings about these topics. Compare your answers to those of other students in the class.

1. Talking to strangers . . .
2. Eating ice cream . . .
3. I'm nervous about . . .
4. I'm never afraid of . . .
5. My friends are concerned about . . .
6. I would like to give up . . .
7. Growing older . . .
8. I get tired of . . .

Choosing Infinitives Versus Gerunds

There is a basic difference in meaning between infinitives and gerunds that can help us choose the correct form in many cases.

EXAMPLES	EXPLANATIONS
(a) I plan **to study** all weekend, so I guess I can relax this afternoon.	Infinitives usually refer to the possibility of an action occurring. The action has not happened yet.
(b) I don't enjoy **studying** all weekend, but we have a big examination on Monday.	Gerunds usually refer to an action that has already started or has already been experienced.
(c) I **want to swim** in the ocean this summer. (d) I **intend to take** the TOEFL at the end of the semester.	Verbs of desire (*hope, wish, plan, want,* etc.) imply that the speaker hasn't experienced the action yet, but may in the future. They are typically followed by infinitives.
(e) I **enjoy swimming** in the ocean. (f) I can't stand **taking** tests because they make me so nervous. (g) I can't stand **to take** tests because they make me so nervous.	Certain verbs of emotion (*enjoy, appreciate,* etc.) imply that the speaker has already experienced the cause of that emotion. They are typically followed by gerunds. Other verbs of emotion (*like, love, hate, can't stand*) can be followed by gerunds or infinitives without much difference in meaning.

Some verbs have an important difference in meaning depending on whether they are followed by an infinitive or a gerund.

VERB	EXAMPLES	IMPLIED MEANING
forget	**(h) I forgot to meet** her.	I didn't meet her because I forgot about our appointment.
	(i) I forgot meeting her.	I met her, but I didn't remember that I did.
try	**(j) We tried to close** the window, but it was stuck	We couldn't close it.
	(k) We tried closing the window, but the room was still cold.	We closed it, but that didn't make the room warmer.
remember	**(l)** John **remembered to mail** the letter.	He remembered, and then went to the mailbox.
	(m) John **remembered mailing** the letter.	He mailed the letter, and remembered it later.
stop	**(n)** John **stopped smoking** last month.	He doesn't smoke anymore.
	(o) John **stopped to smoke** because he needed a break.	John took a break and smoked.

EXERCISE 11

Review the basic patterns and common verbs in each pattern. Work with a partner and try to write as many additional verbs for each pattern as you can remember without looking back in your book. A few have been done for you.

VERBS THAT TAKE INFINITIVES			VERBS THAT TAKE GERUNDS		
Pattern 1	**Pattern 2**	**Pattern 3**	**Pattern 1**	**Pattern 2**	**Pattern 3**
appear	advise	expect	can't help	encourage	appreciate
refuse	remind	arrange	keep on	urge	anticipate
seem					dislike

EXERCISE 12

Fill in the blank with the gerund or infinitive form of the word in parentheses. There may be more than one correct answer.

1. If you want to lose weight you should try _____ (avoid) all sweets. That might be better than going on a diet.

2. I know Dimitri was at the party, but I don't remember _____ (talk) to him.

3. On her way home my mother stopped _____ (pick up) a few things at the store.

4. Suddenly all the dogs in the neighborhood began _____ (bark) at the same time.

5. My sister has never been able to quit _____ (smoke).

6. Ruth couldn't watch TV because she forgot _____ (bring) her glasses with her.

7. Nowadays, children have stopped (a) _____ (play) traditional children's games and seem (b) _____ (prefer) (c) _____ (play) video games instead.

8. I'll try _____ (eat) any kind of food once.

EXERCISE 13

Fill in the blanks with the correct form of the verbs in parentheses. There may be more than one correct answer.

Before the invention of radio and television, people spent much of their leisure time (1) _____ (do) activities that required (2) _____ (do) or (3) _____ (make) something. They practiced (4) _____ (play) a musical instrument or studied (5) _____ (sing).

Most people learned (6) _____ (keep busy) by (7) _____ (try) (8) _____ (improve) their abilities in some way or by (9) _____ (practice) a skill. People who couldn't afford (10) _____ (spend) much money on hobbies often started (11) _____ (collect) simple objects, such as matchbook covers or stamps, or even things like buttons or bottle caps. Of course, most people spent a lot of time (12) _____ (read), and (13) _____ (write) letters to friends.

Children played games in which they pretended (14) _____ (be) pirates or cowboys or people they remembered (15) _____ (read about) in books. Many women were extremely clever at (16) _____ (make) and (17) _____ (decorate) articles of clothing. Men often kept busy by (18) _____ (make) toys for children or (19) _____ (carve) small sculptures out of wood.

EXERCISE 14

Fill in the blanks with the correct form of the verbs in parentheses. There may be more than one correct answer, so be prepared to explain why you chose the answer you did.

Since the invention of radio and television, leisure-time activities have changed. Nowadays people don't find it as easy (1) _____ (fill) their time with such productive activities. Television has encouraged many people (2) _____ (stop) (3) _____ (work on) their hobbies. Children are spending more and more time (4) _____ (watch) TV or (5) _____ (play) video games. As a result, traditional children's games which have been played for hundreds of years are beginning (6) _____ (forget). Traditional skills such as embroidery, sewing, and woodcarving are failing (7) _____ (be passed on) from parent to child. People seem (8) _____ (prefer) activities that allow them (9) _____ (be) passive observers rather than active participants. If these traditional forms of recreation keep (10) _____ (disappear) at the current rate, many of the things that people used to enjoy (11) _____ (do) will only be found on television documentaries about how people tried (12) _____ (spend) their leisure time in the days before television.

Use Your English

ACTIVITY 1 : SPEAKING

In the Opening Task you were asked to decide whether you are a **do-er** or a **be-er** in the way that you spend your free time.

STEP 1 Form a group with other people who are in the same category as you. Together come up with a list of the five or ten best ways to spend a rainy afternoon.

STEP 2 Compare your list of activities with that of a group from the other category What does this tell you about the differences between **do-ers** and **be-ers?**

ACTIVITY 2 : SPEAKING

Choose a partner that you know pretty well.

STEP 1 Describe two or three things you can't imagine him or her ever doing. Then identify two or three things you expect your partner to do on a routine basis. Explain your reasons. What is it about your partner that makes you think he or she would behave that way? Your partner should then do the same thing with you.

STEP 2 Were you or your partner surprised by any of the things you heard? For example, did your partner tell you that he couldn't imagine your doing something that you actually do quite frequently? Or perhaps your partner mentioned an expectation that you would never consider doing. Report any surprises to the rest of the class.

ACTIVITY 3 : WRITING

We all have bad habits that we would like to stop doing, and things that we know we should do, but don't. New Year's Eve is a popular time to make resolutions about ways to improve our behavior.

STEP 1 Make a list of "New Year's Resolutions."

• What are some things you would like to stop doing? (For example, *watching so much TV, eating ice cream before bed, gossiping.*)
• What are some things you would like to start doing? (For example, *getting more exercise, reading for an hour every night, writing letters to friends.*)

STEP 2 Compare your New Year's Resolutions to those of other people in the class. Are there any common categories or characteristics?

ACTIVITY 4: WRITING

Write a brief paragraph on things about other people that you can't stand but many other people don't seem to mind (For example: *I can't stand friends being too serious about their work, and having no other interests in life*), and things about other people that you don't mind, but many other people can't stand (For example: *I don't mind people being late*).

ACTIVITY 5: SPEAKING

Prepare a short talk for the rest of the class on one of these topics:
- your likes and dislikes: activities that you don't mind, can't stand, love, hate, resent, and enjoy.
- your future plans: activities that you anticipate, hope, or intend to do; and things that would make you postpone or delay those activities or consider not doing them.

ACTIVITY 6: LISTENING

STEP 1 Read the questions below. Then listen for the information to answer them from the following radio program about leisure time in the United States.

1. What amount of time per week are people expected to work in the United States, Germany, and Japan?
2. What is the average amount of annual vacation for workers in the United States, Germany, and Japan?
3. What do Americans typically do on the weekend?
4. What is the third reason mentioned for the decreasing amount of free time?
5. Give two examples of "working vacations."

STEP 2 Compare your answers with a partner's, and then listen to the program again to confirm any information you're not sure of.

UNIT 8

INTENSIFIERS (*very, too, enough, etc.*) AND DEGREE COMPLEMENTS (*so that, such that etc.*)

UNIT GOALS:

- To use intensifiers such as *very, too,* and *enough*
- To use the word *not* with intensifiers
- To correctly form *so that* and *such that* clauses
- To use *too* and *(not) enough* plus infinitive phrases

▶ OPENING TASK
How Much Is Too Much?

STEP 1 Read the article on the next page and in your own words describe the difference between an *enthusiast* and a *somethingaholic.*

124

The word *workaholic* is used to describe people who like their jobs so much that they are "addicted" to them. Workaholics usually have no other important interests outside of their jobs. They often neglect other responsibilities (to their families, to their own physical health, etc.) in order to concentrate on their jobs and do them well. Another word, *enthusiast*, also describes someone who likes something a great deal. However, there is an important difference in meaning between an enthusiast and an "-aholic." An enthusiast balances that interest with other things in life. The interest is **very** important, but not **too** important.

The word *workaholic* has an interesting history. It is based on the word *alcoholic*, which is used to describe a person who is addicted to alcohol. In recent years the suffix *-aholic* has been applied to other things. Although you will not find these words in a dictionary, you may hear them in conversations or on television, or read them in popular magazines. In addition to workaholics, people can sometimes be **sportaholics** (addicted to sports), **shopaholics** (addicted to shopping), **TVaholics** (addicted to watching television), or even **chocaholics** (addicted to chocolate).

STEP 2 What other kinds of **"-aholic"** people can you think of? You have read about workaholics, TVaholics, chocaholics. Work with a partner and invent at least one other term for people who carry their enthusiasm about something too far. Present your term and definition to the rest of the class.

▶ **D**escribing How Much or To What Degree

We can answer *how* questions about degree or intensity with *intensifiers* or *degree complements*.

	INTENSIFIERS very, too, quite, extremely, etc.	**DEGREE COMPLEMENTS** so/such . . . that . . . too/enough . . . to . . .
How devoted is Denise?	**(a)** Denise is **extremely devoted** to her job.	**(b)** Denise is **so devoted** to her job **that** she spends her weekends at the office.
How hard a worker is she?	**(c)** She's **quite a hard worker,** and even spends her weekends at the office.	**(d)** She is **such** a hard worker **that** she has no time for a personal life outside her job.
How interested is Peter in his job?	**(e)** Peter is **slightly bored** with his job.	**(f)** Peter is **too** interested in other things **to** make his job the focus of his life.
How quickly does he work?	**(g)** He works **rather slowly.**	**(h)** Peter works steadily **enough to** avoid being fired.

EXERCISE 1

Underline the intensifiers in the following passage. The first sentence has been done for you.

(1) Denise Driven is a <u>very</u> dedicated employee, but she's <u>a little too</u> serious. (2) Although she's extremely hard working and quite efficient, she's also rather competitive and not very friendly. (3) She comes in to work an hour earlier than anyone else and is always the last one to leave. (4) At the end of the day she's really too tired for other activities. (5) She has no hobbies and few friends. (6) She's actually a bit dull, since she's not really interested in anything but her job. (7) Peter Principle is a rather easy-going fellow. (8) Although he works fairly hard, and is

reasonably serious about his work, his job is not the most important thing in his life, and he likes to have time to pursue other interests. (9) He lives a fairly normal life. (10) He likes spending time with his children, and he is quite active in the Lions Club. (11) He is also a rather accomplished musician. (12) He plays the clarinet in a jazz band with some of the other people from the office. (13) Peter and Denise really don't get along. (14) She thinks he's a little lazy and "insufficiently motivated." (15) He thinks she's a rather humorless workaholic who is "not very nice." (16) It's somewhat difficult to decide who's right.

EXERCISE 2

Underline the degree complements in this paragraph. For each degree complement make a *how* question.

▶ **EXAMPLE:** Denise is <u>too serious to be able to appreciate Peter's laid-back point of view.</u>

How question: How serious is Denise?

Denise Driven and Peter Principle still aren't getting along. (1) Denise is so rushed at work these days that she doesn't have any free time. (2) She has too little energy at the end of the workday to have any hobbies. (3) She's feeling a little lonely, but she's too busy to make any close friends. (4) Peter has suggested that she take some time off, but she always says that there's too much going on at work for her to take a vacation. (5) Nothing moves fast enough for her to feel satisfied. (6) Even her secretary types too slowly to keep up with all the letters she writes. (7) Peter, on the other hand, still works hard enough to avoid being fired. (8) But, unlike Denise, he isn't so dedicated to his job that he is willing to give up everything else in order to get ahead. (9) He loves his family enough to make their needs his most important priority. (10) He's just not competitive enough about his job for Denise to consider him a threat to her authority.

▶ Intensifiers

MEANING	MORE FORMAL INTENSIFIERS	LESS FORMAL (CONVERSATIONAL) INTENSIFIERS
an excessive degree	**(a)** That's **too** expensive.	**(b)** She's **way too** serious.
a great degree	**(c)** Denise is **quite** busy. **(d)** She's **extremely** dedicated. **(e)** She works **very** hard.	**(f)** Denise is **really** busy. **(g)** She works **so** hard! **(h)** She's **awful(ly)** serious.
a moderate degree	**(i)** He's a **rather** accomplished musician. **(j)** It's **somewhat** difficult to decide who is right. **(k)** He's **fairly** hard-working. **(l)** He does his job **reasonably** well. **(m)** He works hard **enough.**	**(n)** Peter's **pretty** dedicated. **(o)** Denise is **kind of** depressed. **(p)** He's **sort of** easygoing.
a small degree	**(q)** He gets **slightly** annoyed. **(r)** She's **a bit** competitive. **(s)** Work can sometimes be **a little** monotonous.	**(t)** He's a **tad** lazy.
an insufficient degree	**(u)** He doesn't work hard **enough.**	**(v)** Peter doesn't get paid **near(ly) enough.**

The position of intensifiers in a sentence

EXAMPLES	EXPLANATIONS
(a) Denise works **extremely hard.** **(b)** Peter works **steadily enough.**	All intensifiers come before the adjective or adverb, except *enough*, which comes after.
(c) Denise is **a very dedicated** worker. **(d)** She is **quite a dedicated** worker.	In noun phrases, intensifiers come between the determiner (*a, the, some,* etc.) and the adjective, except for *quite*, which comes before the determiner.

EXERCISE 3

Use the intensifiers from Focus 2 to describe the skills and activities listed below. Make statements that are true for you.

1. **a skill you are proud of:** something you do well to a moderate degree

   ▶ **EXAMPLE:** I'm a pretty good tennis player.
   _____

2. **a favorite food:** a kind of food you like to a great degree

   ▶ **EXAMPLE:** I'm extremely fond of popcorn.
   _____

3. **something that is not enjoyable for you, but you don't hate:** an activity you dislike to a small degree

   ▶ **EXAMPLE:** Doing homework can be slightly boring.
   _____

4. **an ability you want to develop:** a skill you have in an insufficient degree

   ▶ **EXAMPLE:** I don't speak English fluently enough.
   _____

5. **a bad habit:** something you do to an excessive degree

   ▶ **EXAMPLE:** I eat too much ice cream.
   _____

6. **a special talent:** something you do well to a great degree

   ▶ **EXAMPLE:** I'm a really good musician.
   _____

EXERCISE 4

Are the following sentences written in formal or informal style? If they are in informal/conversational style, change the intensifier to make the sentence more formal. If they are in formal style, change the intensifier to make the sentence less formal. There are several possible answers, so be prepared to explain why you chose the answer you did.

▶ **EXAMPLES:** That sun is so hot! *(Informal)*

　　　　　　More formal: _That sun is very hot._

　　　　　　I'm rather tired, so I won't be able to attend your party. *(Formal)*

　　　　　　Less formal: _I'm pretty tired . . ._

1. I'm kind of sick today.
2. I'm somewhat confused by all your questions.
3. She's really unfriendly.
4. He's quite annoyed about the broken window.
5. I'm sort of busy right now.
6. It's rather hot here, don't you think?
7. Peter works pretty hard.
8. Denise is pretty serious.
9. That man is awfully hard to understand.

Too Versus *Very*

MEANING

VERY—a great degree	TOO—an excessive degree (so much of something that it is not good)
(a) This car is **very** expensive, but maybe I'll buy it anyway.	**(b)** This car is **too** expensive. I can't afford it.
(c) Denise is **very** serious about her work. She's a good worker.	**(d)** Denise is **too** serious about her work. She's a workaholic.

EXERCISE 5
Complete these sentences using *too* or *very*.

1. We got there _____ late. The plane had already taken off.

2. I'm _____ busy, but I think I can finish the report for you.

3. Denise works _____ hard for her own good. She's going to get sick if she's not careful.

4. Denise works _____ hard because she's ambitious and wants to get ahead.

5. Don't bother to invite Jose to the party. He's _____ serious to have any fun!

6. The accident happened _____ quickly, but I'm _____ sure that the driver of the sports car didn't use his turn signal.

7. Children are growing up _____ quickly these days. They try to act like adults while they're still kids!

8. We arrived at the party _____ late, but there was still a little food left.

9. We arrived at the party _____ late. All the guests had left.

10. I really like Mary. I think she's _____ intelligent and has a great personality!

11. It's _____ hot. Let's forget about the tennis game.

Using Intensifiers with *Too*

EXAMPLES	EXPLANATION
(a) It's **way too** difficult! (b) It's **really too** hot. (c) It's **a little too** expensive. (d) It's **a bit too** late.	We use a few intensifiers with *too* to indicate how excessive something is.

EXERCISE 6

Complete these sentences, using an intensifier with *too*.

▶ **EXAMPLES:** You just missed the plane. You   arrived a bit too late.

I can't reach the top shelf. It's   a little too high.

1. I don't have quite that much money. It's_____.

2. I wish she would smile more. She's _____.

3. There's no way I can help you finish that report. I'm _____ .

4. Only a couple of students passed the test. The test was _____ .

5. The coffee needs more sugar. It's _____ .

EXERCISE 7

Pick five things from the list below that you don't like. Add two other things that aren't on the list. Give reasons for your dislike, using *too* and an intensifier.

▶ **EXAMPLES:** I don't like workaholics. They're really **too** serious.

I don't like dogs. They're a little **too** friendly.

babies	workaholics	studying grammar
dogs	diamond necklaces	being away from my family
cats	summer weather	rap music
spinach	sports cars	police officers
liberals	conservatives	

▶ **U**sing Intensifiers with *Not*

These intensifiers (***too, very, so, really, quite***) can be used in negative sentences to "soften" a statement or make it more indirect or polite.

EXAMPLES	IMPLIED MEANING
(a) Tom's new dog is **not too bright**.	It's **rather stupid**.
(b) Sometimes Peter doesn't work **very hard**.	Sometimes he's **lazy**.
(c) Please **don't** drive **so fast**.	Please drive **more slowly**.
(d) She's **not really interested** in sports.	She's **somewhat bored** with sports.
(e) I'm **not quite sure** I like that dog.	I'm **afraid of** that dog.

EXERCISE 8

Make these sentences more polite by replacing or adding intensifiers that use *not*. There may be more than one way to "soften" your comment.

▶ **EXAMPLES:**   This movie's pretty boring. <u>It's not too interesting.</u>

He dances rather badly. <u>He doesn't dance too well.</u>

1. She's quite unfriendly. _____

2. Mary's somewhat unhappy with you. _____

3. I hate spinach. _____

4. Mark is a terrible cook. _____

5. Beth dislikes listening to other people's problems. _____

6. It's too crowded for me. _____

Degree Complements with *Too* and *Enough*

Too + infinitive phrase

	EXAMPLES
too + adjective	**(a)** Some teenagers are **too immature** to make really wise decisions.
too + adverb	**(b)** They grow **too quickly** for clothes to fit for very long.
too much/little + noncount noun	**(c)** They have **too much pride** to ask for advice from their elders. **(d)** They have **too little patience** to wait for complete freedom.
too many/few + count noun	**(e)** They have **too many controls** to be able to feel truly independent. **(f)** They have **too few chances** to exercise responsibility.
verb + *too much/little*	**(g)** Teenagers think they **know too much** to listen to their parents and **too little** to be responsible for their actions

Enough + infinitive phrase

	EXAMPLES
adjective + *enough*	**(h)** Most teenagers are **responsible enough** to do a good job.
adverb + *enough*	**(i)** They work **hard enough** to get the same pay as adults.
verb + *enough*	**(j)** They have **learned enough** to make wise decisions.
enough + noun	**(k)** Parents often give their teenagers **enough responsibility** to prepare them for adult life.

EXERCISE 9

Restate these pairs of sentences with statements of degree using *too* and *enough*.

▶ **EXAMPLES:** Denise is very serious about her career. She doesn't understand why Peter is so relaxed.

Denise is too serious about her career to understand why Peter is so relaxed.

Peter isn't terribly serious about his job. He doesn't want to spend every weekend at the office.

Peter isn't serious enough about his job to want to spend every weekend at the office.

1. Denise has lots of responsibilities. She can't take a vacation right now.
2. The pace of work is extremely hectic. Denise can't do her best work.
3. Denise's secretary types very slowly. Denise can't catch up on her correspondence.
4. Mr. Green hasn't assigned Denise much additional clerical support. Denise can't meet the contract deadline.
5. Denise is very proud. She doesn't want to ask her boss for more help.
6. Denise isn't nice to Peter. He won't offer to help her with the contract.
7. There is always a little free time. Peter spends it on his friends, his music, and his family.
8. Peter plays the clarinet quite well. He could be a professional musician.
9. He doesn't like Denise. He won't help her meet her contract deadline.
10. Work is not that important. Peter doesn't make it the focus of his life.

▶ Implied Meanings of *Too* and *Not Enough*

The implied meaning of the infinitive phrase depends on which degree word we have chosen and the situation we are using it in.

EXAMPLES	POSSIBLE IMPLIED MEANINGS
(a) Mr. Green is **too old to worry** about losing his hair.	He doesn't worry about losing his hair. OR He worries about it, but he shouldn't.
(b) Mr. Green **is not young enough to wear** the latest fashions.	He doesn't wear the latest fashions. OR He wears those fashions, but he shouldn't.
(c) He is **wise enough to listen** to both sides in the argument.	He listens to both sides.
(d) He is **wise enough not to take sides** in the argument.	He doesn't take sides.

EXERCISE 10

Choose the correct implied meaning for these degree complements:

1. Teenagers are too young to buy alcoholic beverages.
    (a) They can buy alcoholic beverages.
    (b) They can not buy alcoholic beverages.

2. Peter does not work hard enough to be promoted.
    (a) He will be promoted.
    (b) He won't be promoted.

3. Mr. Green is wise enough to avoid taking sides in the argument.
    (a) He avoids taking sides in the argument.
    (b) He never avoids taking sides in the argument.

4. Teenagers think they are smart enough not to make mistakes.
    (a) They think they might make mistakes.
    (b) They think they won't make mistakes.

EXERCISE 11

Decide whether you agree with the following statements about teenagers. Use *too* or *enough* and an infinitive to give your opinion about things that fifteen-year-olds are old enough or too young to do.

Fifteen-year-olds are old enough . . .

Fifteen-year-olds are too young . . .

▶ **EXAMPLES:** Fifteen-year-olds are old enough to drive.

Fifteen-year-olds are too young for their parents to let them live in their own apartments.

1. They should be able to drive.
2. They shouldn't live in their own apartments.
3. They can fall in love.
4. Schools should let them choose what classes they want to take.
5. Teachers should talk to them as adults.
6. They shouldn't be able to buy alcohol or cigarettes.
7. Their parents should give them some financial responsibility.
8. The law shouldn't treat them as adults.
9. They shouldn't be police officers or soldiers.
10. Society shouldn't give them total freedom.

EXERCISE 12

Working with a partner, ask and answer the following "foolish" questions. Answer the question with a *yes* or *no,* and give a reason for your answer using *too*. Then try to restate your answer using *enough*. Ask your partner five more "foolish" questions of your own.

▶ **EXAMPLES:** Can you swim to Hawaii?

No. It's too far for someone to swim.

No. Nobody is strong enough to swim to Hawaii.

1. Do you have any great-great-grandchildren?
2. Can you walk 150 miles in a single day?
3. Is $50 a fair price for a cup of coffee?
4. Can dogs read?
5. Do banana trees grow wild in Russia?
6. Can one person lift a grand piano?
7. Can you learn to speak English fluently in a week?
8. Can a hundred-year-old woman still have babies?
9. Do you remember what you did on your first birthday?
10. Can you eat fifty hamburgers in a single meal?

EXERCISE 13

Working with a partner ask and answer these questions. Give your real opinions. Use *enough* in your answer.

▶ **EXAMPLE:**   Why don't some people pass the TOEFL?

   Because they don't know enough English to get a high score.

1. How much money do you need for a happy life?
2. How well do you speak English?
3. When should children move out of their parents' home?
4. When should people get married?
5. How quickly or slowly should a person drive on a turnpike or freeway?
6. What's an ideal age to retire?
7. What kind of peson should be president?
8. What is an important characteristic for a basketball player?
9. Why can't monkeys learn languages?

EXERCISE 14

Do you have all the money or all the free time you wish you had? Are there some things you are **not** able to do because you don't have enough resources or time, or because you have too many responsibilities?

Write sentences that describe five activities you can't do, and what keeps you from doing them.

▶ **EXAMPLES:**   I don't have enough time to read novels.

   I'm too poor to take a vacation this summer.

► **Degree Complements with *So* and *Such***

So + *Such* + *that* clauses

	EXAMPLES
so + adjective	**(a)** Denise is **so serious** about her work that she rarely takes a vacation.
so + adverb	**(b)** Peter plays the clarinet **so well** that he once considered being a professional musician.
so + *many/few* + (count noun)	**(c)** Denise writes **so many letters** that her secretary can't type them fast enough.
	(d) She has **so few outside interests** that most people consider her rather boring.
so + *much/little* + (noncount noun)	**(e)** The project took **so much time** that Denise had to spend her weekend in the office.
	(f) Denise works **so much** that she never has time for friends or hobbies.
	(g) They have **so little time** to get the job done that they'll have to spend the weekend in the office.
such + (*a/an*) + (adjective) + noun	**(h)** The disagreement between Peter and Denise has become **such a serious problem** that they are not speaking to each other.
	(i) Denise gives her secretary **such large amounts** of work that she is thinking about quitting.

In spoken English and less formal written English the *that* in *so/such* constructions can be omitted.

(j) I'm so happy **that** I could fly	OR **(k)** I'm so happy, I could fly.
(l) Denise is such a serious person **that** she probably doesn't know how to have fun.	OR **(m)** Denise is such a serious person, she probably doesn't know how to have fun.

EXERCISE 15

Identify the degree complements in this passage by underlining the result clauses where *that* has been omitted. The first paragraph has been done for you as an example.

Tall Tales

(1) In American English we use the term *tall tale* to describe stories that are so exaggerated <u>they become funny.</u> (2) No one really believes that they're true. (3) That's part of the fun. (4) The point of a tall tale is to tell such incredible lies <u>everyone ends up laughing.</u> (5) American folklore is filled with examples of tall tales.

(6) One famous tall tale is the story of the winter when the weather was so cold everything froze. (7) Each day things got a little colder. (8) First the usual things froze: water, plants, pipes, machinery. (9) Then it got worse. (10) It was such a cold winter dogs and cats froze when they went outside, and birds fell out of the sky, frozen solid. (11) Then it got even worse. (12) It got so cold people's words froze whenever they tried to talk. (13) You couldn't hear a single sound. (14) Of course, people like to talk, no matter how cold it is. (15) So people kept talking and their words kept freezing just as soon as they came out of heir mouths.

(16) Then suddenly the cold weather came to an end. (17) One day it was so cold nobody could carry on a conversation because the words just froze right up, and the next day it was warm enough to wear shorts. (18) The change in weather was so great and so sudden everything became unfrozen all at the exact same minute. (19) All those frozen words thawed out at once, and the resulting noise was so loud everyone became deaf.

EXERCISE 16

Make statements of degree about the underlined items in these pairs of sentences by using *so* and *such*.

▶ **EXAMPLES:** There are <u>many plants</u> in the rain forest with possible medical uses. Scientists fear we may lose valuable medical resources if they are destroyed

There are <u>so many</u> plants in the rain forest with possible medical uses <u>that</u> scientists fear we may lose valuable medical resources if they are destroyed.

1. The world's forests are being destroyed at a <u>rapid rate.</u>

   We can't ignore the problem any longer.

2. The world population is growing <u>quickly.</u>

   We can't continue our old habits.

3. We have <u>few alternative materials.</u>

We haven't stopped using trees for fuel.

4. There has been <u>a rapid growth</u> in population.

There are no other places for people to live except the rain forests.

5. Some countries have <u>few other natural resources.</u>

They are forced to use the rain forests for economic development.

6. The problems appear <u>impossible</u> to solve.

Some countries haven't even begun to look for a solution.

7. The United Nations considers deforestation <u>a problem.</u>

They are trying to establish conservation programs throughout the developing world.

8. The loss of the rain forests is a <u>major global threat.</u>

The future of mankind may be at stake.

EXERCISE 17

Give true answers to these questions using *so/such*.

▶ **EXAMPLE:** What kind of student are you?

I'm such a good student that I always do my homework before class.

1. What kind of student are you?

2. How quickly or slowly do you walk or drive?

3. Have you ever wanted something a great deal? How badly did you want it?

4. Did you ever eat a huge amount of food? What happened?

5. How high are the Himalayan Mountains?

6. Did you have a good time on your first birthday?

7. How tall was the tallest person you've ever seen?

8. How hard is the TOEFL?

9. What happened in the most boring class you've ever been to?

10. How wonderful is your grammar teacher?

Use Your English

ACTIVITY 1: WRITING

In Exercise 15 you read an unbelievable story called a **tall tale.**

STEP 1 Work with a group to invent a tall tale or unbelievable story of your own to tell to the rest of the class. The more unbelievable the story is, the funnier it will be.

STEP 2 The class should decide which group told the "tallest tale."

ACTIVITY 2: SPEAKING/WRITING

Tell about a time when you or someone you know lost their temper, made a foolish mistake, or said or did something without realizing it. Here are some examples:

- The driver of the bus I was riding got so mad and shouted so loudly that his false teeth actually flew out of his mouth.

- My brother was so excited to get to Hawaii that he left his sweater and overcoat on the plane. He was pretty cold when he returned to Chicago.

- I was once in such a hurry to get to work that I left the house wearing one black shoe and one brown shoe.

Use one of the following situations, or think of some of your own:

- *I was once so happy that . . .*
- *My sister was so hungry that . . .*
- *When I was a child I was once so frightened that . . .*
- *A student I know once got so nervous in class that . . .*
- *I once experienced such frustration that . . .*
- *I was once so angry that . . .*

ACTIVITY 3: LISTENING/ SPEAKING/WRITING

When are adult children old enough to move away from home? Different cultures have different opinions about when (and if) this should happen. Interview people from three or four different countries. What is the average age at which people move away from home? What do other people think if someone leaves home at a much younger or much older age than the average? Are there different standards for men and women? Make a report on what you have discovered. It can be written report or an oral presentation to the rest of the class.

Intensifiers (very, too, enough, etc.) and Degree Complements (so, so that, such that, etc.)

ACTIVITY 4: LISTENING/ SPEAKING/WRITING

Using this chart, interview a partner about what things he or she thinks people are old enough to do at the age of fifteen, and what things he or she thinks people are still too young to do. Then ask your partner to think of one other thing that people are old enough to do at age fifteen, and one more thing they're still too young to do. For all the things that your partner feels people are still too young to do, find out what age he or she feels is old enough for those things. Some examples have been provided for you.

ACTIVITIES	OLD ENOUGH OR TOO YOUNG?	WHY?
marry and raise a family	too young	They are not mature enough to take that responsibility. They should be in their twenties.
decide on a future career	old enough	They already know the kinds of things they like to do and the kinds of things they are good at.
fall in love		
drive a car		
go on dates without a chaperone		
make wise decisions about life		
live independently outside their parents' home		
pay taxes		
serve in the army		
get a full-time job		
get a part-time job		
take care of young children		
write poetry		
be a professional athlete		
vote in national elections		
control their own money		
become parents		
	too young	
	old enough	

ACTIVITY 5: WRITING

Write a short (one page) essay that describes how you feel about the importance of work in your life. Here are some questions you may wish to answer:
- Is work more or less important than other things in your life?
- Could you ever become a workaholic? Why or not not?
- Who would you rather work with, Denise Driven or Peter Principle? Why?

ACTIVITY 6: WRITING

Write a short (one page) essay about the following topic:
There's a popular saying in America that it's not possible to be too rich, too good-looking, or too thin.
- Do you agree? Are there some qualities or characteristics that no one can have too much of? If so, what are they? Why do you feel that nobody can have too much of those qualities?
- Do you disagree? Is there a negative aspect to being extremely good-looking, wealthy, or fashionably slim?

ACTIVITY 7: LISTENING/ WRITING

STEP 1   Listen to the following lecture on the destruction of tropical rain forests. Use the outline below to organize the information from the lecture.

I. Economic impact of rapid population growth

   A.

   B.

II. Result of economic impact on rain forests

III. Problems with reforestation

IV. Primary reasons to maintain existing rainforest areas

   A.

   B.

STEP 2   Write a one or two sentence summary of the lecture.

_____

_____

_____

_____

MODIFYING NOUN PHRASES

Adjectives and Participles

UNIT GOALS:

- To put adjective modifiers in the correct order
- To form and to understand the meaning of present and past participle modifiers
- To use other noun modifiers in the proper order

▶ OPENING TASK
Going to a Flea Market

STEP 1 The objects above are all for sale at a flea market—a place where people sell things they don't want anymore. Match the objects with the descriptions.

- one slightly used, antique, blue Moroccan dish
- two interesting little wooden statues from China
- a really beautiful old Italian glass bowl
- a fascinating collection of rare, used English textbooks

STEP 2 Think of two things you own that you don't want anymore. Write a short description of each thing. Show your descriptions to your classmates. Try to find classmates who want to buy your things, and find two things you want to buy from classmates.

Word Order in Noun Phrases

A noun phrase consists of a determiner and noun plus all its modifiers.

TYPES OF NOUN PHRASES	PARTS OF NOUN PHRASES
determiner + noun **(a)** **the** books; **these** books **(b)** **my** books; **some** books	**Kinds of determiners** articles, demonstratives, possessives, quantifiers
determiner (+ modifiers) + noun **(c)** some **extremely interesting, really beautiful used** books **(d)** some interesting, really beautiful used **grammar** books	**Kinds of modifiers** adjectives and participles (with or without intensifiers) other nouns
determiner (+ modifiers) + noun + (modifying phrases and clauses) **(e)** some interesting, really beautiful used grammar books **with red covers** **(f)** some interesting, really beautiful used grammar books **printed in China** with red covers **(g)** some interesting, really beautiful used grammar books printed in China with red covers **that we studied last semester**	**Kinds of modifying phrases and clauses** prepositional phrases participle phrases relative clauses

Although it is rare to have more than three or four modifiers for a single noun phrase, this is the usual order for different categories of modifiers.

Determiner	Intensifiers	Adjectives and Participles	Noun Modifier	Noun	Modifying Phrases
the/a/an some/no my/your each/every these/those	really very slightly	old/new interesting well-known	stone university	wall campus	next to the river described in the brochure

EXERCISE 1

From the chart below, make five noun phrases that use more than one modifier. Then write a sentence for each noun phrase. Compare your sentences to the examples and those of several other students.

Determiners	Intensifiers	Adjectives and Participles	Noun Modifiers	Nouns
a	very	little	stone	teacher
some	rather	experienced	English	statue
your	extremely	cute	circus	animals
the	quite	famous	university	watch
this	wonderfully	relaxing	pocket	professor
those	really	expensive	three-week	vacation
	somewhat	good	grammar	
		pleasant		
		ugly		

▶ **EXAMPLES:** I like those really expensive pocket watches.

Only your very experienced English teachers will know the answer.

Many very famous university professors are not very good teachers.

FORM

Order of Descriptive Adjectives

Different categories of descriptive adjectives usually occur in the following order.

EVALUATION/ OPINION	APPEARANCE	AGE	COLOR	ORIGIN
good	*size/measure*	old	red	*geographical*
bad	big	young	green	French
ugly	small	new	blue	Mexican
interesting	low	antique	striped	Japanese
nice	high		bright green	*material*
intelligent	heavy		dark blue	wooden
	shape		deep purple	vegetable
	round			cotton
	square			brass
	triangular			
	condition			
	chipped			
	broken			
	rotten			

Within a category there is some possible variation.

EXAMPLES	EXPLANATIONS
(a) a **big, round, shiny** apple (b) a **big, shiny round** apple (c) a **shiny, big round** apple	Adjectives of **appearance** usually follow the order in (a): **size, shape, condition.** But other orders are also possible.
(d) a **Japanese silk** fan (e) a **silk Japanese** fan	Adjectives of **origin** usually follow the order in (d): **geographical, material.** But other orders are also possible.

EXERCISE 2

Put the descriptive adjectives in these noun phrases in the correct category in the chart below. Not every category is used in each noun phrase. The first one has been done for you as an example.

1. handsome, small, well-polished Italian leather shoes
2. a big shiny new red sports car
3. a cute little brown puppy
4. some beautiful old Thai silk pajamas
5. a round antique brass tea tray
6. a painted Japanese wooden screen
7. an interesting young French physics professor
8. a funky, broken-down old car

CATEGORY	1	2	3	4	5	6	7	8
EVALUATION/ OPINION	handsome							
APPEARANCE size shape condition	small — well-polished							
AGE	—							
COLOR	—							
ORIGIN geographical material	Italian leather							
NOUN	shoes							

EXERCISE 3

Add the modifiers in the correct order to the following passages. The first one has been done for you as an example.

My friend Wolfgang is a shopaholic. Whenever he goes out of the house he returns with some (1) __strange new__ (new, strange) "bargain." He rarely buys any (2) _____ (useful, really) items. Once he came home with some (3) _____ (bright, flannel, purple) blankets. "They match my (4) _____ (pretty, French, new) curtains," he said. But those curtains were still in their (5) _____ (plastic, original) wrappings. He was so busy shopping that he hadn't had time to hang them up.

Fortunately, Wolfgang refuses to buy anything second-hand. I can imagine all the (6) _____ (useless, incredibly ugly, antique) "art objects" he would bring home. He already has (7) _____ (brand-new, European, expensive, plenty of, brightly colored) shirts and sweaters. But that doesn't stop him from buying more. He just piles them into his (8) _____ (little, dark, bedroom, over-crowded) closet. He has some (9) _____ (Italian, nice, handmade) shoes that I have never even seen him wearing.

He's running out of space to put things. He has such a (10) _____ (new, nice) apartment with lots of storage space, but his closets look like some (11) _____ (old, poor) shopkeeper's (12) _____ (frightening, terrible) nightmare!

EXERCISE 4

Are these sentences correct or incorrect? If they are incorrect, identify the problem and correct it.

1. I bought a green, old, pretty vase at the flea market.
2. He's a university, brand-new dormitory resident.
3. It's an antique, genuine, black, old-fashioned umbrella.
4. Would you like some of these delicious, little, chocolate candies?
5. Would you like to hear about my summertime, exciting, vacation plans?

► **Participle Modifiers**

EXAMPLES	EXPLANATIONS
(a) **The interesting man** told wonderful stories about adventures in Sumatra.	Present and past participles can be used like descriptive adjectives to describe nouns.
(b) **The interested man** listened carefully to the wonderful stories about adventures in Sumatra.	

VERB	PRESENT PARTICIPLE	PAST PARTICIPLE	EXPLANATIONS
study	studying	studied	Present participles are formed by adding *-ing* to the verb.
forget	forgetting	forgotten	Past participles are formed by adding *-ed* to regular verbs or by using the third form (*-en* form) of irregular verbs. For a review of irregular past participle forms see Appendix 6.

EXERCISE 5

Underline all the participles in the following passage, and tell what noun they describe. The first paragraph has been done as an example.

▶ **EXAMPLES:** (1) revealing—present participle, describes "information"

(2) hidden—past participle, describes "emotions"

(3) widespread—past participle, describes "reactions"

(4) exciting—present participle, describes "situations" increased—past participle, describes "heart rates"

(5) no participle modifiers in this sentence

Body Language

(1) Unconscious facial expressions and "body language" often give <u>revealing</u> information to other people. (2) Many people's "<u>hidden</u>"emotions are actually quite visible to anyone who knows how to read people's faces. (3) Some reactions are so <u>widespread</u> in all cultures that there seems to be a physical basis for them. (4) All people react in the same way to certain <u>exciting</u> situations by breathing more rapidly and experiencing <u>increased</u> heart rates. (5) Facial expressions of basic emotions, such as anger, surprise, and amusement, appear to be universal.
(6) Other reactions are not so universal. (7) Many, but not all, individuals respond to an embarrassing situation by blushing (when the face and neck turn bright red). (8) Some people show that they are bored by growing less active and becoming sleepy or inattentive. (9) Others respond to boring situations by becoming more active and showing such physical signs as jiggling feet or wiggling fingers. (10) But for other people, such reactions may be unintended indications of nervousness or anxiety, not boredom. (11) When someone experiences a confusing situation, he or she may unconsciously try to hide that confusion by smiling, thus doing what is known as "the stupid grin." (12) But another person might respond by looking angry.
(13) There are not only variations in this "silent language" between different individuals, but there are also important differences between cultures. (14) Certain kinds of "silent language" give one particular message in one culture, but a conflicting message in another culture. (15) For example, eye contact (looking directly into the eyes of the person you are speaking to) has very different meanings in different cultures. (16) In American culture, if you do not look directly into someone's eyes while talking, the listener will think that you are dishonest. (17) If someone is described as "shifty-eyed" it means that he or she cannot be trusted. (18) But in many Asian cultures, avoiding eye contact is a sign of politeness and respect, and prolonged eye contact (which indicates sincerity in American culture) means aggression or hostility, and is seen as a threatening behavior. (19) Mistaken "body language" can often result in even more misunderstanding than using the wrong word or incorrect grammar.

Meanings of Present and Past Participles

EXAMPLES	EXPLANATIONS
(a) a **loving** mother (She loves her children.)	Present participles modify **agents.** The agents do the actions described by the participle.
(b) a **well-loved** mother (Her children love her.)	Past participles modify **receivers.** The receivers are affected by the action described by the participle.

EXERCISE 6

Paraphrase these sentences by choosing the correct participle for the cues given.

▶ **EXAMPLE:** Most of my friends enjoy reading novels.

Most of my friends are __interested__ (interest) in reading novels.

Novels are __interesting__ (interest) to most of my friends.

1. The audience didn't understand the lecture.
   (a) The audience was _____ (confuse).
   (b) The lecture was _____ (confuse).

2. The students didn't do well on the exam.
   (a) The exam results were _____ (disappoint).
   (b) The students were _____ (disappoint).

3. Children who watch scary movies may not be able to sleep afterwards.
   (a) (Frighten) _____ children may not be able to go to sleep.
   (b) (Frighten) _____ movies may keep children from sleeping.

4. That was quite a delicious snack.
   (a) The snack was quite _____ (satisfy).
   (b) We were quite _____ (satisfy).

5. Most students enjoy studying grammar.
   (a) Most students are _____ (interest) in grammar.
   (b) Grammar is _____ (interest) to most students.

EXERCISE 7

Use present or past participles to complete these definitions.

▶ **EXAMPLE:** Information that reveals thoughts can be described as
<u>revealing</u> information.

Emotions that people hide can be described as
<u>hidden</u> emotions.

1. Situations that excite people can be described as _____
   situations.

2. Interest rates that fluctuate can be described as _____
   interest rates.

3. A situation that embarrasses people can be described as an
   _____ situation.

4. Results that people prove in experiments can be described as
   _____ results.

5. News that depresses people seriously can be described as
   _____ news.

6. Individuals whom some bad news depresses seriously can be
   described as _____ individuals.

7. A question that puzzles people can be described as a
   _____ question.

8. People that a question puzzles can be described as
   _____ people.

FORM   MEANING

Adding Information to Participles

Noun + Participle

EXAMPLES	EXPLANATIONS
(a) a **man-eating** tiger (a tiger that eats people) (b) a **trend-setting** fashion (a fashion that sets a trend) (c) a **fire-breathing** dragon (a dragon that breathes fire)	Present participles usually describe the agent. You can also identify the receiver of the action by adding nouns.
(d) a **flea-bitten** dog (a dog that is bitten by fleas) (e) a **manmade** lake (a lake that was made by people) (f) a **male-dominated** society (a society that is dominated by males)	Past participles usually describe the receiver. You can add nouns to past participles when you want to identify the agent as well. Some noun-participle combinations appear without hyphens.

Adverb + Participle

EXAMPLES	EXPLANATIONS
(g) a **fast-moving** train (a train that moves fast) (h) some **homegrown** tomatoes (tomatoes that were grown at home) (i) a **much-visited** attraction (an attraction that is visited a lot)	You can add adverbs to both past and present participles to include important additional information to the participles. Some special cases appear without hyphens.

Special Cases

EXAMPLES	EXPLANATIONS
(j) a **blue-eyed** baby (a baby with blue eyes) (k) a **long-legged** ballet dancer (a dancer with long legs)	You can make "past participles" from some adjective-noun combinations to describe certain kinds of physical characteristics.
(l) a **barely concealed** dislike (m) a **deeply depressed** individual	Some adverb-participle combinations appear without hyphens

EXERCISE 8

Use the information in these sentences to make participles.

▶ **EXAMPLE:** The story is loved very much. It's a ___much-loved___ story.

1. In that incredible jump, Houdini defied death.

It was a _____ jump.

2. I had to go to the store to buy this cake.

It's a _____ cake.

3. Gladstone Gulp bought a machine to reduce his weight.

It's a _____ machine.

4. They trained the new employee well.

She was a _____ employee.

5. That poor kitten is starved for love.

It's a _____ kitten.

6. They filmed the movie with a camera that they held by hand.

It was filmed with a _____ camera.

7. Look at that man with the long hair!

Look at that _____ man!

8. Learning grammar can consume a lot of time.

It can be a _____ activity.

EXERCISE 9

Write original sentences that describe at least five of the following.

1. the most boring teacher you have ever had

2. the most self-satisfied politician you have ever heard or read about

3. the most surprised reaction you have ever seen

4. the most amazing thing you have ever seen

5. the most worried person in your family

6. the most modern-thinking political leader you know

7. the behavior of the most bored student you have ever known

8. the most irritating habit your best friend has

EXERCISE 10

Choose the correct participle form for these sentences from the cues given. The first paragraph has been done for you as an example.

Problems in communication can happen when some of the conscious and un-conscious actions of the (1) _nonspoken_ (non-speak) part of a language are misunderstood. There can sometimes be (2) _confusing_ (confuse) situations between teachers and students in the classroom.

Teachers in American classrooms, for example, may often become (3) _____ (annoy) when students don't volunteer answers to general questions in class. Silence in American classrooms often means that the students are (4) _____ (bore), (5) _____ (disinterest), or (6) _____ (uninvolve) in the class activity. Similarly, teachers interpret eye contact from students as a sign that the lesson is (7) _____ (interest) and (8) _____ (involve) for them, and that they are actively (9) _____ (engage) in the learning process.

Students are sometimes (10) _____ (confuse) about the best way to show that they are paying attention. In an American classroom, asking questions is one good way to do this, but students from other cultures may be (11) _____ (embarrass) by having to admit that they are (12) _____ (confuse). Sometimes they feel (13) _____ (worry) that asking questions may be interpreted as (14) _____ (teacher-challenge) behavior or as a somewhat (15) _____ (insult) suggestion that the teacher has not explained things clearly enough.

The best way to solve these misunderstandings is to talk about them in class. Both American teachers and international students alike are often very (16) _____ (surprise) to find out about their sometimes (17) _____ (mistake) assumptions about what classroom behavior means in different cultures.

Modifiers that Follow Noun Phrases

PARTICIPLE PHRASES	PREPOSITIONAL PHRASES	EXPLANATION
(a) The man **speaking to John** told him some shocking information.	(b) The man **with John** told him some shocking information.	Some modifiers occur after the noun.
(c) The woman **surrounded by reporters** is a world-renowned expert on AIDS.	(d) The woman **next to the window** is a world-renowned expert on AIDS.	

EXAMPLES	EXPLANATIONS
(e) The man **speaking to John** told him some shocking information.	Participle phrases usually come after the noun if they identify the noun (tell which particular noun we are talking about).
(f) **Speaking to the man,** John found out some shocking information.	They can come before the noun if that noun has already been identified and the participle describes more about the noun.

EXERCISE 11

Underline the modifying phrases in this article. Draw an arrow to indicate the noun each phrase modifies. The first paragraph has been done for you as an example.

(1) One aspect of nonverbal communication frequently mentioned by researchers discussing cross-cultural differences is the varying size of the "conversation bubble" in each culture. (2) This bubble is the amount of physical distance maintained between people engaged in different kinds of conversation. (3) Americans having polite social conversations usually stand about an arm's length apart. (4) Closer distances are permitted only between people having a more intimate relationship. (5) Unless you are a very close friend or family member, moving closer than an arm's length is usually interpreted as overly aggressive (either socially or sexually). (6) People growing up in Latin cultures tend to have a smaller conversation bubble than people coming from Northern European cultures. (7) As a result, North Americans or Northern Europeans sometimes come across as a little cold or unfriendly to people raised in Latin countries such as Italy, Spain, or Latin America. (8) In general, Middle Eastern cultures tend to have the smallest conversation bubble, while North Asian and Northern European cultures tend to have the largest.

Use Your English

ACTIVITY 1: WRITING

Go to a flea market, thrift shop, garage sale, or even a department store. Write brief descriptions of things you find there that fit these categories:

- something really cheap
- something that costs more than $25
- something you might like to own
- something funny
- something ugly

ACTIVITY 2: SPEAKING

Play **Adjective Tennis** with a partner. Here's how it's done:

STEP 1 One person thinks of a noun phrase (a noun plus a determiner) and a modifier.

STEP 2 The other person puts the modifier in its correct position and gives another modifier for the first person to add to the noun phrase. The modifier has to make sense. For example, if the noun is *radio, intelligent* is not an acceptable modifier.

STEP 3 The person who can't think of an appropriate modifier, or who puts it in the wrong place, loses. Keep going until one person puts an adjective in the wrong place or can't think of something new to add. You may want a third student to act as your referee.

EXAMPLE:

Student 1:	a ball . . . tennis
Student 2:	a **tennis** ball . . . old
Student 1:	an **old** tennis ball . . . rubber
Student 2:	an old **rubber** tennis ball . . . dirty
Student 1:	a **dirty** old rubber tennis ball . . . incredibly
Student 2:	an **incredibly** dirty old rubber tennis ball . . . huge
Student 1:	an incredibly dirty, **huge** old rubber tennis ball . . . etc.

ACTIVITY 3: SPEAKING/WRITING

Examine this list of common emotions and choose two or three.

boredom   embarrassment   depression   confusion

annoyance   worry   amusement   excitement

STEP 1 For each emotion identify two or three situations that cause you to feel that emotion. Next identify two or three typical physical or psychological reactions you have when you feel each of the emotions. The first one has been done as an example.

Boring Situations:	Bored Reactions:
1) long meetings	1) I yawn, get sleepy, fidget
2) gossip about people I don't know	2) I think about other things
3) talking about things that don't interest me	3) I draw pictures in my notebook

STEP 2 Compare your responses and the situations that cause those responses with those of other students in the class. Discuss these questions:
- Are there universal reactions to certain emotions?
- Which category showed more individual variation: the reactions or the situations?
- Do some cultures express emotions more readily than others?

STEP 3 Present your ideas to the rest of the class, or write answers to the discussion questions for your teacher to read and correct.

ACTIVITY 4: SPEAKING

Some cultures value people who express their emotions easily, while others value people who can keep their feelings to themselves. What are the advantages and disadvantages to each kind of behavior?

STEP 1 Think of at least two situations where hiding your feelings can be helpful (for example, playing cards). Next, think of two situations where it is a disadvantage (for example, when trying to communicate in a language that you don't speak very well).

STEP 2 Do the same for expressing your emotions clearly.

STEP 3 Compare your answers with other students' and report any interesting similarities or differences to the rest of the class.

ACTIVITY 5: SPEAKING/WRITING

Think of three characteristics that make someone fascinating and three characteristics that make someone boring. Compare your answers with those of several other people and make a list of characteristics that everyone agrees on. Present your list to the class.

ACTIVITY 6: SPEAKING

Are facial expressions universal? This is a chart used to teach a common "vocabulary" of facial expressions to deaf students. Examine these expressions in a small group made up of people from different cultures (if possible). Are there any feelings that are expressed in your culture by different facial expressions than the ones shown? How are facial expressions different in different cultures? Present your ideas to the class.

Determined Disappointed Disapproving Disbelieving Disgusted Bored Distrusting

Concentrating Enjoying Grieving Regretting Interested Satisfied Embarrassed

Shocked Eavesdropping Confused Undecided Withdrawn

ACTIVITY 7: SPEAKING

On the next page are some other facial expressions. The emotions they portray have been omitted. Choose four or five expressions.

STEP 1 Use adjectives or participles to describe these expressions. Be ready to explain why you have chosen the description that you did.

STEP 2 Compare your answers with those of several other students in the class. Did you interpret any of the expressions differently? Do those differences tell you anything about facial expressions in other cultures?

STEP 3 Report any significant differences or insights to the class.

ACTIVITY 8: WRITING/SPEAKING

What is the difference between an antique and junk? What makes a used item valuable? Make two lists. For each junk item write a description of a similar item you would consider an antique. Think of five examples of each. Compare your list to a partner's. Here's an example.

Junk	Antique
a dirty old cup	a fine, unbroken, hand-painted porcelain teacup

ACTIVITY 9: LISTENING

STEP 1 Listen to these brief conversations, and circle the sentences that best describe the situation.

STEP 2 Compare your answers with a partner's and then listen to the conversations and questions again to check any answers that you disagree on or are unsure about.

Conversation 1

1. (a) The water wasn't cold enough.
   (b) She wanted a glass of water.
2. (a) She wanted iced water.
   (b) She didn't want iced water.
3. (a) The tea was too warm.
   (b) The tea was too small.

Conversation 2

1. (a) The girl's grandmother is the one who teaches physics.
   (b) The girl's grandmother is the one who is retired.
2. (a) He's trying to organize a lecture program for senior citizens.
   (b) He's trying to organize a lecture program for physics.
3. (a) The girl's mother is the one who teaches physics.
   (b) The girl's mother is the one who teaches biology.

COMPARATIVES

UNIT GOALS:

- To correctly express various degrees of similarity and difference
- To correctly use different complex comparisons of amount
- To understand and use formal and informal statements of comparison

▶ OPENING TASK
Comparing Developing and Developed Countries

Here is some statistical information about four countries that were once British colonies. Use the information to discuss the following questions with a partner or in a small group.

- What are some things that Bangladesh and Pakistan have in common? What are some differences?

- What are some things that Canada and the United States have in common? What are some differences?

- What are some differences between developed and developing countries? Are there similarities? What are they?

People's Republic of Bangladesh

area:	55,600 square miles
population:	127 million
growth rate:	2.7%
density per square mile:	2230
languages:	(national) Bangla; (official) English
religion:	Muslim 83%, Hindu 16%
literacy rate:	38%
GNP:	$155 billion
per capita GNP:	$1,260 per year
politically independent since:	1947 from Britain/1971 from Pakistan

Islamic Republic of Pakistan

area:	307,000 square miles
population:	135 million
growth rate:	2.9%
density per square mile:	440
languages:	(national) Urdu, (official) English, (regional) Punjabi, Sindhi, Pashtu, Baluchi
religion:	Sunni Muslim 77%, Shi'a Muslim 20%, other 3%
literacy rate:	38%
GNP:	$297 billion
per capita GNP:	$2,300 per year
politically independent since:	1947 from Britain

Canada

area:	3.8 million square miles
population:	30 million
growth rate:	0.8%
density per square mile:	8
languages:	English, French
religion:	Protestant 41%, Catholic 47%, Jewish 1%, other 11%
literacy rate:	97%
GNP:	$721 billion
per capita GNP:	$25,000 per year
politically independent since:	1867 from Britain

United States of America

area:	3.6 million square miles
population:	270 million
growth rate:	0.7%
density per square mile:	74
language:	English
religion:	Protestant 56%, Catholic 38%, Jewish 4%, other 2%
literacy rate:	97%
GNP:	$7,662 billion
per capita GNP:	$28,600 per year
politically independent since:	1776 from Britain

Comparisons of Degree: Adjectives and Adverbs

EXAMPLES	MEANING	FORM
	MORE X > Y	X *is* (intensifier) $\left\{\begin{array}{l}\text{adjective} + er \\ more + \\ \qquad \text{adjective} \\ more + \\ \qquad \text{adverb}\end{array}\right\}$ *than Y.*
(a) Pakistan **is much larger than** Bangladesh is. **(b)** Bangladesh is growing **somewhat more quickly than** Pakistan is. **(c)** The people of Pakistan are **slightly more literate than** the people of Bangladesh.	large difference ↕ small difference	$\left.\begin{array}{l}\textit{much} \\ \textit{considerably} \\ \textit{substantially} \\ \textit{somewhat} \\ \textit{slightly/a bit}\end{array}\right\}$ intensifiers
(d) Pakistan's post-colonial history is **just as recent as** Bangladesh's is.	**THE SAME X = Y**	X *is* (intensifier) *as* $\left\{\begin{array}{l}\text{adjective} \\ \text{adverb}\end{array}\right\}$ *as Y.* $\left.\begin{array}{l}\textit{exactly} \\ \textit{just}\end{array}\right\}$ intensifiers
(e) Bangladesh's literacy rate is **nearly as high as** Pakistan's.	**LESS X < Y**	X *is* (intensifier) *as* $\left\{\begin{array}{l}\text{adjective} \\ \text{adverb}\end{array}\right\}$ *as Y.* small difference $\quad\left.\begin{array}{l}\textit{almost} \\ \textit{nearly}\end{array}\right\}$ intensifiers
(f) Pakistan is **not quite as crowded as** Bangladesh is. **(g)** Bangladesh is **not nearly as large as** Pakistan.	small difference large difference	X *is not* (intensifier) *as* $\left\{\begin{array}{l}\text{adjective} \\ \text{adverb}\end{array}\right\}$ *as Y.* $\left.\begin{array}{l}\textit{quite} \\ \textit{nearly}\end{array}\right\}$ intensifiers
(h) Bangladesh is growing **slightly less rapidly than** Pakistan. **(i)** Bangladesh is **substantially less prosperous than** Pakistan is.	small difference ↕ large difference	X *is* (intensifier) *less* $\left\{\begin{array}{l}\text{adjective} \\ \text{adverb}\end{array}\right\}$ *than Y.* $\left.\begin{array}{l}\textit{slightly/a bit} \\ \textit{somewhat} \\ \textit{substantially/} \\ \textit{considerably} \\ \textit{much}\end{array}\right\}$ intensifiers

EXERCISE 1

In the following chart, write statements of comparison about the United States and Canada. Use the information on page. 167 Use intensifiers to make accurate statements.

Meaning	Form	Comparative Statement
MORE	. . . er than more . . . than	The area of Canada is slightly larger than the area of the United States. _____
THE SAME	as . . . as	_____
LESS	nearly as . . . as not as . . . as less . . . than	_____ _____ _____

EXERCISE 2

Read the paragraph on the next page comparing Pakistan and Bangladesh and fill in the chart. For each feature listed, note whether it is greater in Pakistan or in Bangladesh, and whether the difference is large or small.

Feature	Greater in Pakistan or Bangladesh?	Small or large difference?
population	Bangladesh	small
area	Pakistan	large
population density		
standard of living		
population growth		
GNP		
educational development		
prosperity		

(1) Although the population of Bangladesh is slightly larger than that of Pakistan, its land area is considerably smaller. (2) This means that the population density of Pakistan is not nearly as great as that of Bangladesh, and as a result, the general standard of living is substantially higher. (3) Although the population of Bangladesh is not growing quite as quickly as Pakistan's, its GNP is quite a bit lower, and as a result, it will be a very long time before the standard of living for Bangladeshis becomes as high as for Pakistanis. (4) While educational development is almost as high in Bangladesh as in Pakistan, economic development is substantially lower, and people in Bangladesh are generally less prosperous.

EXERCISE 3

Make comparative statements about the countries below using the information provided. Use appropriate intensifiers to describe whether the difference is large or small. Compare your statements to those of a partner.

▶ **EXAMPLE:** The literacy rate in Brunei is substantially lower than in Bulgaria.

Brunei's per capita income is considerably higher than Bulgaria's.

	Brunei	**Bulgaria**
per capita GDP	$15,800	$4,630
population density	142 per square mile	192 per square mile
literacy rate	88%	98%

	Jamaica	**Japan**
per capita GDP	$3,260	$22,700
population density	621 per square mile	863 per square mile
literacy rate	85%	100%

	South Korea	**Turkey**
per capita GDP	$14,200	$6,100
population density	1,221 per square mile	214 per square mile
literacy rate	98%	82%

EXERCISE 4

Interview a partner to obtain the following information, and then make statements that compare you and your partner.

▶ **EXAMPLE:** My partner is substantially older than I am.

I am much younger than my partner.

QUESTIONS	YOUR PARTNER	YOU
how old	37	18
how long studying English		
when he/she usually goes to sleep		
how often he/she goes to the movies		
how quickly he/she thinks English skills are improving		
how big his/her family?		

Comparisons of Amount: Noun Phrases

EXAMPLES	MEANING	FORM
(a) Pakistan has **much more land area than** Bangladesh does.	**MORE X > Y**	X + VP + (intensifier) + *more* NP *than* Y (*does*)
(b) Bangladesh has **slightly more people than** Pakistan.	large difference ↕ small difference	*much /many considerably/ substantially slightly somewhat* } intensifiers
(c) One has **as much representation as** the other. **(d)** Pakistan sends **just as many representatives** to the U. N. **as** Bangladesh does.	**THE SAME** **X = Y**	X + VP + (intensifier) + *as much/many* NP *as* Y (*does*)* *exactly just* } intensifiers
(e) Pakistan has **almost as many people as** Bangladesh. **(f)** Pakistan does not have **quite as many people as** Bangladesh does.	**LESS X < Y** small difference	X + VP + (intensifier) *as much/many* NP *as* Y (*does*)* *almost nearly* } intensifiers
(g) Bangladesh does**n't** have **nearly as much land area as** Pakistan.	small difference large difference	X + *not* + VP + (intensifier) *as much/many* NP as Y (*does*)* *quite nearly* } intensifiers
(h) Pakistan has **slightly fewer people than** Bangladesh. **(i)** Bangladesh has **much less land than** Pakistan does.	small difference ↕ large difference	X + VP + (intensifier) *fewer/less* NP *than* Y (*does*)* *slightly somewhat substantially/ considerably much/many* } intensifiers

*NP = Noun Phrase   VP = Verb Phrase

EXERCISE 5

In the following chart, write statements of comparison about the United States and Canada. Use the information on pages 167. Use intensifiers to make accurate statements.

Meaning	Form	Comparative Statement
MORE	*more . . . than*	The United States had substantially more people than Canada.
THE SAME	*as much/many . . . as*	_____
LESS	*almost as much/many . . . as*	_____
	not + VERB + as much/ many . . . as	_____
	fewer/less . . . than	_____

EXERCISE 6

Read the paragraph comparing Pakistan and Bangladesh on pages 173 and 174. Underline the first comparison statement in each sentence and rewrite it. Then say whether the difference is big or small.

▶ **EXAMPLE:** **1.** Bangladesh has <u>somewhat more people than Pakistan.</u>
Bangladesh's population is greater than Pakistan's. It is a small difference.

2. _____
_____

3. _____
_____

4. _____
_____

5. _____
_____

6. _____
_____

(1) Although Bangladesh has somewhat more people than Pakistan, it has considerably less land area. (2) This means that Pakistan does not have nearly as many people per square mile as Bangladesh does, and as a result, there is much less pressure on basic resources such as roads and water supply. (3) As

a rule, people in Bangladesh have somewhat fewer opportunities for economic improvement than people in Pakistan. (4) Bangladesh has just about as many literate people as Pakistan, but it has fewer people living above the poverty line, and so there is somewhat less political and economic stability in Bangladesh than there is in Pakistan. (5) However, Pakistan has more regional ethnic groups than Bangladesh does, and there are more incidents of ethnic unrest in Pakistan than there are in Bangladesh. (6) Thus, Bangladesh has fewer extreme political conflicts than Pakistan.

EXERCISE 7

Make comparative statements about the countries below using the information provided. Use appropriate intensifiers to describe whether the difference is large or small. Compare your statements to those of a partner.

▶ **EXAMPLES:** Luxembourg has considerably less agricultural land than Libya.
Libyans don't make nearly as much money as people in Luxembourg.

	Luxembourg	Libya
per capita income	$13,988	$7,130
number of official languages	3	1
GNP	$4.9 billion	$27 billion
amount of land used for agriculture	210 square miles	40,772 square miles

	Switzerland	Swaziland
per capita income	$14,030	$740
number of official languages	4	2
GNP	$97.1 billion	$490 million
amount of land used for agriculture	4,144 square miles	540 square miles

	Taiwan	Thailand
per capita income	$8,750	$800
number of official languages	1	1
GNP	$72.8 billion	$44 billion
amount of land used for agriculture	3,335 square miles	75,413 square miles

EXERCISE 8

Interview a partner to obtain the following information, and then make statements that compare you and your partner.

▶ **EXAMPLE:**   My partner has taken the TOEFL several more times than I have.
I have taken the TOEFL fewer times than my partner.

QUESTIONS	YOUR PARTNER	YOU
times he or she has taken the TOEFL	5	1
rooms in your partner's house or apartment		
languages your partner understands		
number of children he or she would like to have		
countries he or she has visited		
family members		

▶ **Comparisons of Similarity and Difference: Noun Phrases**

Comparisons can also be made in terms of **similarity** and **difference,** in addition to amount and degree.

EXAMPLES	MEANING	FORM
(a) Pakistan uses **exactly the same official language as** Bangladesh. **(b)** Pakistan and Bangladesh use **the same official language.**	**IDENTICAL** **X = Y**	X + VP + (intensifier) + *the same* NP *as* Y (*does*).* *X and* Y + VP + (intensifier) + *the same NP* *exactly / precisely* } intensifiers
(c) Pakistan has **very much the same literacy rate as** Bangladesh (does). **(d)** Pakistan and Bangladesh have **almost the same growth rate.**	**SIMILAR** **X ~Y** great similarity ↕ small similarity	X + VP + (intensifier) *the same* NP* *as* Y (*does*). *X and* Y + VP + (intensifier) *the same NP.* *very much / basically / almost / somewhat* } intensifiers
(e) Bangladesh doesn't have **quite the same population as** Pakistan (does). **(f)** People in Pakistan and Bangladesh do **not** have **at all the same culture.**	**DIFFERENT** **X ≠ Y** small difference ↕ large difference	X + *not* + VP + (intensifier) + *the same* NP *as* Y (*does*).* *X and* Y + *not* VP + (intensifier) *the same NP.* *quite / nearly / at all* } intensifiers
(g) Bangladesh has a **slightly different growth rate from** Pakistan. **(h)** People in Pakistan and Bangladesh have **very different cultures.**	small difference ↕ large difference	X + VP + (intensifier) + *different* + NP *from/than* Y.* *X and* Y + VP + (intensifier) + *different* + NP* *slightly/a bit / somewhat / substantially/ considerably / much/very* } intensifiers

*NP = Noun Phrase   VP = Verb Phrase

EXERCISE 9

Underline the statements of similarity and difference in the following passage. For each comparative structure you find, (a) identify the things that are being compared, and (b) decide whether the comparison describes things that are identical, similar, or different. The first two sentences have been done for you as an example.

▶ **EXAMPLE:**   1) (a) different kinds of English; (b) similar
            2) (a) things like vocabulary and pronunciation; (b) different

REGIONAL VARIETIES OF ENGLISH

(1) Although English is spoken in many countries, <u>English speakers don't all speak quite the same kind of English.</u> (2) <u>Things like vocabulary and pronunciation are often substantially different.</u> (3) The differences between some varieties of English are easy to identify. (4) No one would mistake Indian English for Australian English. (5) The pronunciation features of these two "Englishes" are quite different. (6) British English is substantially different from American English, not only in terms of accent, but also spelling and vocabulary—especially slang.

(7) But the differences between some regional varieties are more subtle. (8) For example, many people think that Canadian and American varieties of English are exactly the same, but in fact, there are some differences, and not all words are pronounced alike. (9) In America the vowel sound in the word "out" is pronounced differently from that in *boot*. (10) But in Canada many people pronounce *shout* basically like *shoot*. (11) To most people Canadian English and American English seem very much alike. (12) But the careful listener will be able to find a number of examples of the ways Americans speak the language differently from their northern neighbors.

EXERCISE 10

Based on your own knowledge and the statistical information you read about in the Opening Task, make statements about general similarities and differences between developing countries and developed countries. Describe one characteristic of developing countries that is likely to be (a) identical, (b) similar, (c) somewhat different, and (d) very different from developed countries.

EXERCISE 11

Interview a partner about how she or he typically likes to spend a vacation. Identify two things about your partner's vacation likes and dislikes that are (a) identical, (b) similar, (c) somewhat different, and (d) very different from yours.

► **C**omparisons of Similarity
and Difference: Verb Phrases

EXAMPLES	MEANING	FORM
(a) Canadians pronounce most words **just the same as** Americans (do). **(b)** Canadians and Americans pronounce most words **very much the same.** **(c)** Canadian English sounds **almost like** American English (does). **(d)** American and Canadian English sound **very much alike.**	**IDENTICAL OR SIMILAR** identical ↕ similar ↕ less similar	X + VP* + (intensifier) + *the same as* Y (*does*). X *and* Y + VP + (intensifier) + *the same* X + VP (intensifier) *like* Y (*does*). X *and* Y + VP + (intensifier) *alike*. exactly/just almost very much } intensifiers quite/much somewhat
(e) Some Canadian words are**n't** pronounced **exactly like** American words (are). **(f)** Australian English and Indian English do **not sound at all alike.**	**DIFFERENT** small difference ↕ large difference	X + *not* + VP + (intensifier) *like* Y (*does*). X *and* Y + *not* + VP (intensifier) *alike*. exactly quite } intensifiers much at all
(g) Canadians do **not** pronounce "*out*" **quite the same as** Americans (do). **(h)** Americans and Canadians don**'t** pronounce "*out*" **at all the same.**	small difference ↕ large difference	X + *not* + VP + (intensifier) *the same as* Y (*does*) X *and* Y + *not* + VP + (intensifier) *the same*. quite a bit } intensifiers at all
(i) Canadians pronounce English **a bit differently from** Americans. **(j)** Australians and Americans pronounce English **quite differently.**	small difference ↕ large difference	X + VP + (intensifier) *differently from/than* Y. X *and* Y + VP + (intensifier) *differently*. a bit somewhat } intensifiers quite

*VP = Verb Phrase

EXERCISE 12

Use the information you read in Exercise 9 and your own experience to make statements of similarity and difference using these cues. Use intensifiers to indicate whether these differences are large or small.

▶ **EXAMPLES:** Indians/Australians/pronounce English/like

Indians don't pronounce English at all like Australians.

Canadians/Americans/pronounce English/alike

Canadians and Americans don't pronounce English quite alike.

1. British/American/use slang expressions/differently
2. No two countries/speak a common language/the same
3. Spanish in Spain/in Latin America/differently from
4. The word color/in Britain/in America/is spelled/not alike
5. Many Canadians pronounce "shout"/"shoot"/the same as
6. grammar/in regional varieties of English/alike

FOCUS **5**

▶ # Informal Usage of Comparisons

There are differences between formal (written) and informal (spoken) English when making comparative statements.

LESS FORMAL/ CONVERSATIONAL STYLE	MORE FORMAL/WRITTEN STYLE
(a) The culture of Pakistan is **different than** Bangladesh.	(b) The culture of Pakistan is **different from** that of Bangladesh.
(c) Canadians pronounce certain words **differently than** Americans.	(d) Canadians pronounce certain words **differently from** Americans.
(e) Pakistan had **much the same** colonial history **that** Bangladesh **did.**	(f) Pakistan had **much the same** colonial history **as Bangladesh.**

EXERCISE 13

Change these informal comparisons to their more formal variations.

1. Canadian English follows the same grammatical rules that American English does.
2. My partner usually spends his vacations differently than me.

3. My writing teacher doesn't put the same emphasis on accuracy that my mathematics teacher does.

4. The social values of Korea are quite different than Kuwait.

5. Many people in developing countries have a lower per capita income than many people in developed countries.

6. Cultural conflicts happen when people in one culture feel differently about certain social values than people in another culture.

7. My brother has almost the same hobbies that I do.

8. The English spoken in New Zealand is slightly different than in Australia.

Use Your English

ACTIVITY 1: SPEAKING

How can you tell if someone is from another country? What are some things people do differently when they come from another culture?

STEP 1 Working with a partner from another culture talk about how you know when someone is a foreigner. If you can, be sure to ask two or three Americans how they know when someone is from another country.

STEP 2 Identify some general or universal differences in behavior, dress, etc. that are true for all cultures. Some examples of generic differences are: speaking with an accent, clothing styles, and so on.

ACTIVITY 2: SPEAKING/WRITING

What are the similarities among people of a particular group?

STEP 1 Decide on a particular group of people. The group could be determined by nationality, culture, age, political beliefs, religion, or some other characteristic like Boy Scouts, people with blue eyes, teachers, tourists—the choices are unlimited!

STEP 2 As you think about things that define a particular group of people, make sure to avoid stereotypes in making your generalizations. **Generalizations** are statements of observation; for example: *Many people in culture X usually take a nap in the afternoon.* **Stereotypes** are statements of judgment; for example: *People of culture X are lazy.* A stereotype is an incorrect assumption that all members of a group share some characteristic.

STEP 3 Write a paragraph describing things that members of this group have in common.

ACTIVITY 3: WRITING

The Opening Task in Unit 12 on page 202 describes the true story of two identical twins who were separated at birth. Refer to the information on page 202 and write a paragraph that describes some similarities and differences between the twins.

ACTIVITY 4: WRITING/SPEAKING

Have you ever met someone who reminds you of someone else? What characteristics and actions were similar? In what ways were the two people different? In a brief essay or oral presentation, tell about two people who reminded you of each other.

ACTIVITY 5: LISTENING

Listen to the following conversation between Kim and Bob about a class in Anthropology. See if you can get enough information to answer the questions on the quiz that Professor Jordan gave them the next day. If necessary you can listen to the conversation more than once.

Anthropology 112: Cultural Geography
Quiz #3

1. Define "language family."

2. Define "culture family."

3. What two examples of culture families were mentioned in the lecture?

4. What is the relationship between culture and economic and political problems in developing countries?

ACTIVITY 6: READING/SPEAKING

In this unit you have examined some information on the economic differences between developing and developed countries. Based on the information in this unit as well as your own knowledge discuss the questions below in a small group.

- Which do you think is a more common source of conflict between nations: economic differences or cultural differences? Can you give examples to support your opinion?
- What do the differences and similarities between developed and developing countries mean for world peace and global development?

UNIT 11

CONNECTORS

UNIT GOALS:

- To correctly understand and use different coordinating conjunctions
- To correctly understand and use different sentence connectors
- To correctly understand and use different subordinating conjunctions.

▶ OPENING TASK
Improving Your Writing

My ⓔxperience with ⓒulture ⓢhock

Every person has experience with culture shock. (However) I am no exception. (And) I have experience with culture shock. Although I have lived in the United States for almost 1 year. I still often feel ~FRAG~ homesick and I miss my family. When I first came to the U.S., I was ~RUNON~ very comfortable <u>and because everything was new everything was ~RUNON~</u> <u>interesting for me</u>. I enjoyed my independence from my parents. I enjoyed (to experience) new food and making new friends. Everything was strange, nevertheless I enjoyed the new experiences. ~RUNON~

Soon I got used to many differences. Even though I was used to ~FRAG~ them. Still I wasn't comfortable. Little by little I grew tired of the differences. Because the things in America weren't new to me ~FRAG~ anymore. <u>The differences weren't interesting they were boring.</u> ~RUNON~ However I began to miss things in Indonesia. For example, food, my friends, the warm climate. I became (depress) and homesick. I stayed in my room, because I was tired of speaking English all the time. (Even though) I studied (however) my grades weren't so good.

So I visited my advisor. He told me about culture shock. I learned that every person has this kind of experience and it can't be (avoid) ~RUNON~ I learned that <u>this culture shock is temporary but universal</u>. My advisor told me I must (to keep) busy and talk about my culture shock with my friends. This was good advice, as a result, my culture shock became less and (in spite) I sometimes still miss my life in ~RUNON~ Indonesia. I don't feel depression (the same) as before.

(margin labels: AWKWARD, FRAG, AWKWARD, AWKWARD)

182

Bambang Soetomo asked his English teacher to point out grammatical problems in his essay about culture shock.

STEP 1 With a partner, go over the essay and the teacher's comments. What suggestions would you give to Bambang in order to improve his writing? Can you correct his essay?

STEP 2 Compare your corrected essay to one possible corrected version in Exercise 1 on page 187.

▶ **Overview of Connectors**

Connectors show logical relationships between clauses in a sentence, between sentences within a paragraph, or even between paragraphs.

EXAMPLES	EXPLANATIONS
(a) Matt grew up in Kansas, **but** he now lives in San Francisco. **(b)** Bambang **not only** misses his family, **but** he **also** wishes a few friends were in America with him.	There are three categories of connectors: **Coordinating conjunctions** connect two similar grammatical structures, such as noun phrases, prepositional phrases or independent clauses.
(c) Matt grew up in Kansas. **However,** he now lives in San Francisco. **(d)** Bambang misses his family. **In addition,** he wishes that a few friends were in America with him.	**Sentence connectors** show the logical connection between sentences.
(e) **Although** Matt grew up in Kansas, he now lives in San Francisco. **(f)** **In addition to missing** his family, Bambang wishes that a few friends were in America with him.	**Subordinating conjunctions** connect a dependent noun clause or a gerund phrase with the main clause.

The logical relationships that these connectors express can be divided into four general categories: **additive, contrastive, cause and effect,** and **sequence.** See the chart on pages 185–186.

MEANING	FORM		
	COORDINATING CONJUNCTIONS	SENTENCE CONNECTORS	SUBORDINATING CONJUNCTIONS
addition	(a) Bambang misses his family, **and** they miss him.	(b) Bambang misses his family. He **also** misses his friends. **In addition,** he is having culture shock. **Besides,** he's homesick.	(c) **In addition to** missing his family, Bambang misses his friends.
emphasis/intensifying	(d) **Not only** does Bambang miss his family, **but** he is **also** experiencing culture shock.	(e) **Furthermore,** he's not doing well in school. **In fact,** he failed two midterms. **Actually,** he's quite depressed. **Indeed,** he's thinking about going home.	(f) **Besides** being depressed, he's having trouble in school, **not to mention** feeling lonely all the time.
contrast	(g) Everyone experiences culture shock, **but** it eventually passes	(h) Some people have severe culture shock. Others, **however,** just feel a mild depression. Bambang's culture shock is almost over; yours, **on the other hand,** may just be beginning. Mild culture shock is a universal experience. Deep depression, **in contrast,** is not.	(i) Some people have severe culture shock, **while** others just feel a mild depression. **Whereas** some people have severe culture shock, others just feel a mild depression.
concession. . . (yes. . .but)	(j) The advisor told him culture shock can't be avoided, **yet** it is fortunately temporary.	(k) Bambang feels homesick. **Even so,** he will stay until he finishes his studies. Bambang studies hard. **Nevertheless,** he isn't getting good grades. **In spite of this,** he is still trying to improve.	(l) **Although** he feels homesick, Bambang will stay until he finishes his studies. He isn't getting good grades, **even though** he studies hard. **In spite of** experiencing culture shock/**In spite of the fact that** he still experiences culture shock, Bambang has decided not to go home.

Continued

Continued

MEANING	COORDINATING CONJUNCTIONS	SENTENCE CONNECTORS	SUBORDINATING CONJUNCTIONS
reason	(m) Bambang went to see his advisor, **for** he was worried about his grades.	(n) Bambang was worried about his grades. **With this in mind**, he went to see his advisor.	(o) He found it difficult to concentrate, **due to** being depressed. **Because/Since** Bambang was worried about his grades, he went to see his advisor.
result	(p) He was depressed, **so** he went to see his advisor.	(q) Bambang was worried about his grades. **Accordingly**, he went to see his advisor. His advisor told him that culture shock is universal. He **consequently** felt much better about his depression. **As a result**, he decided not to go home early. He **therefore** canceled his plane reservation.	(r) **As a result of** feeling depressed, he decided to talk with his advisor. He made an appointment **so that** he could find out about leaving school early. **In order to** find out more about culture shock, he decided to read some articles about it.
conditional	(s) The advisor told Bambang to keep busy, **or (else)** he would become more depressed.	(t) Bambang didn't want to go home early. **Then** he would feel that he had failed. **Under such circumstances**, he might even feel worse than he had in America.	(u) His advisor told him to get a lot of exercise, **providing/if** he could do that without neglecting his studies.
sequence	(v) He made an appointment, **and** he went directly to see his advisor.	(w) **First**, one must recognize culture shock. **Then** one must deal with it. **Eventually** everyone gets over it. **Soon** they start to feel more comfortable in the new culture.	(x) Bambang felt much better **after** he talked with his advisor. **When** he found out about culture shock, he was glad he hadn't decided to leave **before** talking with his advisor.

EXERCISE 1

Identify the form and meaning of the highlighted connectors. The first sentence has been done for you as an example.

▶ **EXAMPLE:** and: form: coordinating conjunction; meaning: additive

since: form: subordinating conjunction; meaning: reason

My Experience with Culture Shock

(1) Every person who has lived in a new culture has had some experience with culture shock, **and** I am no exception, **since** I, too, have had an experience with culture shock. (2) **Although** I have lived in the United States for almost one year, sometimes I still feel homesick, and still miss my family. (3) When I **first** came to the U.S., I was very excited. (4) **Because** everything was new, everything was interesting. (5) I enjoyed my independence from my parents; I **also** enjoyed experiencing new situations and making new friends. (6) **Although** everything was a little strange, I **nevertheless** enjoyed these new experiences. (7) **Eventually** I got used to many of the differences, **but even though** I was used to them, I still wasn't comfortable. (8) **In fact,** little by little I grew tired of the differences. (9) **Because** the things in America weren't new to me anymore, the differences weren't interesting. (10) **Indeed,** they had **actually** become boring. (11) **As a result,** I began to miss things about Indonesia, such as food, friends, and the warm tropical climate, more and more. (12) I **soon** became depressed and homesick. (13) I stayed in my room, **because** I was tired of speaking English all the time. (14) **Even though** I studied hard, my grades weren't good. I wanted to go home. (15) **Because of** these feelings, I decided to see my advisor, **so that** I could get some advice about returning home without finishing my studies. (16) He told me two important things about culture shock. (17) **First,** I learned that any person in a new culture has a similar kind of experience, **and** that culture shock can't be avoided. (18) **Furthermore,** I learned that culture shock is not only universal, but also temporary. (19) **As a result of** his advice, I realized that I should be patient, and that I shouldn't go home just yet. (20) My advisor **also** suggested that I try to keep busy and talk about my culture shock with my friends. (21) I followed this good advice, **and as a result,** my culture shock has become less troublesome. (22) **In spite of the fact that** I sometimes still miss my life in Indonesia, I don't feel as depressed as I did. (23) **Moreover,** I no longer want to return home before I finish my studies. I know that I can adjust to this new life.

EXERCISE 2

Circle the appropriate connector from the options in parentheses. There may be more than one correct choice.

Both Canada and the United States have large minorities that speak languages other than English. Canada has a large French-speaking minority. The United States, (1) (*on the other hand, furthermore, consequently, yet*) has a large Spanish-speaking minority. (2) (*But, However, So*) the way the two countries deal with this fact are rather different.

Canada has adopted a policy of bilingualism and has two official languages. All students study both languages in school. (3) (*Moreover, Nevertheless, Therefore*) all official government activities are conducted in both languages.

However, in the United States there is a movement to make English the only official language. (4) (*So, So that, As a result*), some people may be officially discouraged from using languages other than English at work. In some parts of the country, there are very few facilities available to people who can't speak English, (5) (*and, but, yet, so*) (6) (*under such circumstances, on the other hand, in addition to*) Spanish speakers may be required to provide their own translators in such places as hospitals or government offices. (7) (*In spite of, Even though, Consequently*) all students in the public schools are taught English, (8) (*but, and, for, no connector*) English-speaking students are not usually required to study Spanish.

These differences in bilingualism may result from geography. In Canada, the French speakers are actually a majority in certain parts of the country, primarily in the Province of Quebec. In the United States, (9) (*however, on the other hand, in spite of this, therefore*) Spanish-speaking communities are spread around the country. Large numbers of Spanish speakers are found in New York, Florida, New Mexico, and California. (10) (*As a result, Under such circumstances, In addition, Besides*) there are substantial numbers in many other large cities. (11) (*Although, However, In spite of*) they do not constitute a majority in any single region.

EXERCISE 3

Complete these sentences using information provided in Exercises 1 and 2.

1. In addition to missing his family, Bambang . . .

_____

2. In spite of sometimes still missing his family, ...

_____

3. Before he talked to his advisor about culture shock, ...

_____

4. Bambang now understands that his depression was the result of culture shock. Because of this, . . .

_____

5. Bambang sometimes does poorly on tests, even though . . .

_____

6. Bambang sometimes does poorly on tests, in spite of . . .

_____

7. Canada has an official policy of bilingualism. The United States, however, . . .

_____

8. Canada has an official policy of bilingualism. Consequently, . . .

_____

9. As a result of Canada's official policy of bilingualism, . . .

_____

10. Canada's French-speaking minority is concentrated in a particular part of the country. Consequently, . . .

_____

11. Canada's French-speaking minority is concentrated in a particular part of the country. Nevertheless, . . .

_____

12. Since all government business is conducted in both languages, . . .

_____

Using Coordinating Conjunctions to Connect Parallel Forms

Unlike other connectors, coordinating conjunctions (***and, but, or, nor,*** and ***yet***) can join any parallel grammatical structures.

EXAMPLES	STRUCTURES BEING JOINED
(a) **Jeff** and **Matt** are **roommates** and **best friends.**	nouns
(b) They **live** and **work** in San Francisco.	verbs
(c) They are **poor** but **hard-working** young men.	adjectives
(d) Every Saturday they clean their apartment **quickly** but **thoroughly.**	adverbs
(e) They hurry **down the street** and **around the corner** to do their shopping.	prepositional phrases
(f) They're always in a hurry **to go bike riding** or **to take their dog to the park.**	infinitives
(g) On Saturday nights they like **dancing at discos** and **going to nightclubs** to meet friends.	gerunds
(h) They enjoy living together because **they have many common interests** and **it's cheaper than living alone.**	clauses

EXAMPLES	EXPLANATIONS
(i) Jeff likes neither **dancing** nor **swimming.** **(j)** Matt **is** originally from Kansas but now **lives** in San Francisco.	**Parallel Structure (correct):** In formal written English, structures joined by coordinating conjunctions should have the same grammatical form.
(k) NOT: Jeff likes both **vacations** and **working.** **(l)** NOT: Matt **is** originally from Kansas, but now **living** in San Francisco.	**Nonparallel Structure (not correct)**

EXERCISE 4

Circle the coordinating conjunctions in this passage and underline the elements that each one connects. The first paragraph has been done for you as an example.

(1) Matt and Jeff first came to San Francisco in 1980, after they had graduated from college. (2) Both of them had grown up in small towns. (3) Jeff was from Wisconsin, and Matt grew up in Kansas, but neither one enjoyed living in a small town. (4) There wasn't enough freedom or excitement for their tastes. (5) Each one decided to move to San Francisco because he had heard that it was a beautiful city, and that it was filled with interesting people.

(6) When they first met, they were surprised and delighted to discover how many things they had in common and how similar their interests were. (7) Jeff liked weightlifting, and so did Matt. (8) Matt loved opera, and Jeff did too. (9) Jeff wasn't entirely comfortable with "big-city" life, nor was Matt, but neither one missed living in a small town at all. (10) They both liked dogs and wanted to have one for a pet, so they decided to look for an apartment and live together. (11) They both thought it would be cheaper and more fun to have a roommate.

(12) However, when they moved in together and began living with each other, they found that there were also a lot of differences between them. (13) Jeff was very neat, but Matt wasn't. (14) He preferred to let the dirty dishes pile up until there were "enough" to bother with, and he did not pick up his clothes or keep things neat. (15) Jeff, on the other hand, always wanted things to be washed immediately, even if there were only one or two dishes. (16) Matt liked staying out late every Friday night, but Jeff always wanted to get up early on Saturday mornings to clean the house and to finish chores so they could spend the afternoon relaxing or playing with their new puppy in the park. (17) They soon realized that they would either have to start making compromises or start looking for separate apartments, which neither Matt nor Jeff wanted to do. (18) Fortunately, their similarities outweighed their differences, and they settled into a pleasant life together.

► **P**roblems Using Coordinating Conjunctions

REDUNDANT	LESS REDUNDANT	EXPLANATION
(a) Jeff enjoys cleaning, **but he doesn't like to clean** on Saturday mornings.	**(b)** Jeff enjoys cleaning, **but not** on Saturday mornings.	When using coordinating conjunctions, repeated information should be omitted unless doing so makes the meaning unclear.
(c) Jeff didn't like life in a small town, and Matt **didn't like it either.**	**(d)** Jeff didn't like life in a small town, **nor did** Matt.	
(e) Matt and Jeff get phone calls **from** their parents **and from their friends** almost every week.	**(f)** Matt and Jeff get phone calls **from** their parents **and friends** almost every week.	

EXAMPLES	EXPLANATIONS
(g) Bambang Soetomo studies **hard, but** he sometimes has trouble understanding assignments. **(h)** NOT: Bambang Soetomo studies **hard but** he sometimes has trouble understanding assignments.	When coordinating conjunctions connect independent clauses, they must be preceded by a comma. Without a comma such sentences are called run-on or run-together sentences. They are considered incorrect in formal written English.
(i) Jeff doesn't plan to leave San Francisco, **nor does Matt want** him to. **(j)** **Not only do** the two **have** similar interests, but they also have similar personalities.	When clauses are joined with negative coordinating conjunctions (*nor, neither, not only*), the clause with the negative coordinating conjunction at the beginning must take question or inverted word order.
(k) AWKWARD: I began to miss my family, **and** I was getting more and more depressed, **so** I decided to talk with my advisor. **(l)** BETTER: **In addition to** missing my family, I was getting more and more depressed. **As a result,** I decided to talk with my advisor.	In formal written English, using coordinating conjunctions to connect independent clauses is often considered to be awkward or poor style. Other kinds of logical connectors—sentence connectors and subordinating conjunctions—are more frequently used.

EXERCISE 5

Combine these pairs of sentences to make them less redundant. There is more than one way to combine most of the sentences, so compare your answers with a partner's.

▶ **EXAMPLE:** Jeff lives in San Francisco. Matt lives in San Francisco.

   Jeff lives in San Francisco, and so does Matt.

   Both Jeff and Matt live in San Francisco.

1. Jeff likes cleaning. Matt doesn't like cleaning.
2. Jeff may go home for a visit on his vacation. Jeff may travel to France on his vacation.
3. Matt doesn't plan to return to his hometown to live. Jeff doesn't plan to return to his hometown to live.
4. Jeff likes getting up early. Matt doesn't like getting up early.
5. Jeff always wanted to have a dog. Matt always wanted to have a dog.
6. Matt might take the dog to the park this afternoon. Jeff might take the dog to the park this afternoon.
7. Matt likes dancing at nightclubs. Matt likes meeting friends at nightclubs.
8. Matt comes from a small town in Kansas. Jeff comes from a small town in Wisconsin.

EXERCISE 6

Connect the numbered pairs of sentences in one of these paragraphs with coordinating conjunctions. Make any necessary changes to remove redundancy or to correct word order.

Paragraph 1

(1) My mother doesn't smoke. My father doesn't smoke. (2) My father gave up smoking years ago. My mother only quit last year. (3) My mother had wanted to quit for a long time. She knew it was bad for her health. (4) She wasn't able to smoke only one or two cigarettes. She had to give it up entirely. (5) My mother sometimes still wants a cigarette. My mother won't smoke a cigarette no matter how much she wants to. (6) My father is proud of her for quitting. My father gives my mother a lot of praise for quitting.

Paragraph 2

(1) Canada has a large French-speaking minority. The United States has a large Spanish-speaking minority. (2) Many people in Canada speak French. All government publications are printed in both languages. (3) Canada has two official languages. The United States discourages the use of languages other than English for official purposes. (4) In Canada, the French-speaking minority is found primarily in the province of Quebec. In the United States, Spanish-speaking communities are found in New York, Florida, New Mexico, and California.

EXERCISE 7

Correct these run-on sentences from Bambang's essay. You can correct the punctuation or make two sentences using a sentence connector of similar meaning. Compare your solution to other students' solutions.

1. I still often feel homesick, and I miss my family.

_____

2. Everything was strange; nevertheless, I enjoyed the new experiences.

_____

3. The differences weren't interesting; they were boring.

_____

4. I learned that every person has this kind of experience, and it can't be avoided.

_____

5. This was good advice; as a result, my culture shock became less, but in spite of this, I still miss my life in Indonesia.

_____

_____

▶ **P**roblems Using Sentence Connectors

EXAMPLES	EXPLANATIONS
(a) I was getting more and more depressed. **As a result,** I decided to talk with my advisor. **(b)** I was getting more and more depressed; **as a result,** I decided to talk with my advisor. **(c)** NOT: I was getting more and more depressed, **as a result,** I decided to talk with my advisor.	Sentence connectors are used with sentences or independent clauses connected with a semicolon. Do not use them with commas to connect clauses. This produces run-on sentences.
(d) Jeff grew up in Wisconsin. **However,** Matt comes from Kansas. **(e)** Jeff grew up in Wisconsin. Matt, **however,** comes from Kansas. **(f)** Jeff grew up in Wisconsin. Matt comes from Kansas, **however.**	Sentence connectors normally occur at the beginning of a sentence, but some can also appear in the middle or at the end. See the chart in Appendix 4 (p. A-8) for more information.
(g) Living together has saved both boys a lot of money. **Besides,** Matt likes having a roommate. **(h)** NOT: Matt **besides** likes having a roommate. **(i)** NOT: Matt likes having a roommate **besides.**	Other sentence connectors cannot occur in the middle and/or end of a sentence. See the chart in Appendix 4 (p. A-8) for more information.
(j) Carmen had a lot of money in her bank account. **Therefore,** she was able to pay cash for her new car. **(k)** She was **therefore** able to pay cash for her new car. **(l)** NOT: She was able to pay cash for her new car **thus.**	

EXERCISE 8

These sentences have problems with sentence connectors. Identify the problems and correct them.

1. Every person has experience with culture shock. However, I am no exception.

2. Even though I studied however my grades weren't good.

3. In Canada all official government activities are conducted in both French and English. Under such circumstances, students also study both languages in school. Nevertheless, in the United States, there is no official bilingual policy in government operations. Besides, some local governments have policies that prohibit the use of any language other than English for official business.

▶ **P**roblems Using Subordinating Conjunctions

CORRECT SUBORDINATION	SENTENCE FRAGMENT	EXPLANATION
(a) **Because** things were no longer new to Bambang, **he** began to miss his friends and family back home.	**(b)** NOT: **Because** things were no longer new to Bambang. **He** began to miss his friends and family back home.	Subordinating conjunctions are used with dependent clauses, gerunds, or noun phrases. They cannot be used with sentences. This produces a **sentence fragment,** which is considered grammatically incorrect.
(c) **Even though** Bambang Soetomo studies **hard,** **he** sometimes has trouble understanding assignments.	**(d)** NOT: **Even though** Bambang Soetomo studies **hard. He** sometimes has trouble understanding assignments.	

EXAMPLES	EXPLANATION
(e) NOT: **Besides Bambang misses his family,** he also misses his friends. **(f)** **Besides missing his family,** Bambang also misses his friends.	Some subordinating conjunctions cannot be used with dependent clauses. They function as prepositions and are used with gerund or noun phrases instead. Common subordinating conjunctions of this type are: *besides, in spite of, despite, regardless of, due to, as a result of.* Adding *the fact that* to *in spite of* makes **(g)** grammatically correct.
(g) NOT: Bambang sometimes doesn't do well on tests, **in spite of he studies carefully.** **(h)** Bambang sometimes doesn't do well on tests, **in spite of studying carefully.** **(i)** Bambang sometimes doesn't do well on tests, **in spite of the fact that he studies carefully.**	

EXERCISE 9

Here are some problems with the form, meaning, or use of subordinating conjunctions that appeared in Bambang's essay. Identify the problems and correct them.

1. Although I have lived in the United States for almost one year. I often feel homesick and miss my family.

   _____

2. Even though I was used to them. Still I wasn't comfortable.

   _____

3. However I began to miss things in Indonesia. For example food, my friends, the warm climate.

   _____

4. In addition to he told me about culture shock, my advisor suggested that I should be patient.

   _____

5. Besides I was homesick, I was also having trouble getting used to the way classes are taught in the U.S.

   _____

6. In spite of the fact that being homesick, I didn't want to go home without completing my education.

   _____

7. As a result of my conversation with my advisor. My culture shock got a little better.

   _____

8. Despite I was having problems, I didn't stop doing my best.

   _____

Use Your English

ACTIVITY 1: WRITING

Give your teacher a piece of your writing. This may be something that you have written for this class or another class. Ask your teacher to indicate places where there are grammatical problems. Follow the same procedure that you used for the Opening Task to analyze your problems and correct your mistakes.

ACTIVITY 2: WRITING

Write a brief essay describing your own personal experience with culture shock. Be sure to connect your ideas with logical connectors and avoid run-on sentences or sentence fragments.

ACTIVITY 3: SPEAKING

What are some common connectors in your native language? How does "good style" affect their use? In this unit we learned that although it is grammatically possible to join sentences with coordinating conjunctions, it is not always considered to be "good writing." Think about the words you use to join ideas in your native language. Identify two situations where "good writing" may be different in your first language than it is in English. Present your ideas to the rest of the class.

ACTIVITY 4: SPEAKING

Examine the different meanings that are implied by choosing one connector instead of another.

STEP 1 With a partner or in a small group, discuss these three groups of sentences. What are the differences in implied meaning?

1. (a) Indian food is spicy, and I love it. (b) Indian food is, spicy, but I love it. (c) Indian food is spicy, so I love it.	2. (a) Although Indian food is spicy, I love it. (b) Although I love Indian food, it's spicy.	3. (a) Not only is Indian food spicy, but I also love it. (b) Because Indian food is spicy, I love it.

STEP 2 The following sentences are illogical. With a partner or in a small group, discuss how the incorrect use of a logical connector makes the meaning of these sentences strange or unclear.

(1) I love Indian food, and it is spicy.

(2) I love Indian food, so it is spicy.

(3) Since I love Indian food, it is spicy.

ACTIVITY 5: LISTENING

Listen to this story about **Silly Sally.** Silly Sally likes and dislikes various things. There is one single, simple reason for all the things she likes or doesn't like. The purpose of the game is to discover this simple reason.

STEP 1 As you listen to the description of her preferences, follow along on the chart on the next page, and put a check in the appropriate column.

STEP 2 Compare your answers with another student's and try to figure out the secret of her likes and dislikes.

STEP 3 With your partner come up with one additional example of something she likes and dislikes for each category. Your teacher will tell you if your examples are correct or not. If you think you know the secret of the game, don't tell other students. Just give more examples of the things that Silly Sally likes and doesn't like. Your teacher will tell you if you're correct.

Silly Sally's Likes and Dislikes

Category	Like	Dislike?	Category	Like?	Dislike?
styles of food			**movie stars**		
cooking	—	—	Johnny Depp	—	—
eating	—	—	Meryl Streep	—	—
Greek food	—	—	Marlon Brando	—	—
Chinese cuisine	—	—	Elizabeth Taylor	—	—
Brazilian	—	—	Denzel Washington	—	—
Japanese	—	—	Whoopi Goldberg	—	—
Moroccan	—	—	_____	X	—
_____	X	—	_____	—	X
_____	—	X			
			dating		
sports			restaurants for dinner	—	—
tennis	—	X	restaurants for lunch	—	—
baseball	—	—	art gallery	—	—
skiing	—	—	museum	—	—
horseback riding	—	—	kisses	—	—
hockey	—	—	hugs	—	—
jogging	—	—	marriage	—	—
walking	—	—	engagement	—	—
_____	X	—	_____	X	—
_____	—	X	_____	—	X
people			**vacations**		
queens	—	—	Greece	—	—
princesses	—	—	Italy	—	—
kings	—	—	inns	—	—
princes	—	—	hotels	—	—
Matt and Jeff	—	—	Philippines	—	—
Peter and Denise	—	—	Indonesia	—	—
John and Mary	—	—	travel in the summer	—	—
_____	X	—	travel in winter	—	—
_____	—	X	_____	X	—
			_____	—	X
fruits and vegetables			**animals**		
beets	—	—	sheep	—	—
carrots	—	—	goats	—	—
apples	—	—	cats	—	—
potatoes	—	—	dogs	—	—
oranges	—	—	puppies	—	—
cauliflower	—	—	kittens	—	—
_____	X	—	_____	X	—
_____	—	X	_____	—	X

RELATIVE CLAUSES

UNIT GOALS:

- To understand restrictive and non-restrictive modification
- To correctly form subject and object relative clauses in different parts of a sentence

- To correctly use or delete relative pronouns in different kinds of relative clauses
- To use **whose** in relative clause

▶ **O PENING TASK**

Which One is Which?

STEP 1 Read this article about twins who were separated at birth.

In 1943 two identical male twins were born in Ohio. Their mother was very young, so she gave the children up for adoption. They were separated the day after they were born, and grew up in different parts of the country. One grew up in Ohio and the other grew up in Oregon. Neither one knew he had a twin brother until the one twin moved back to Ohio, where the other twin was living. Then friends of the Ohio twin began to tell him that they had seen a man who looked exactly like him. The Oregon twin met several people who acted as if they knew him, even though he had never met them before. The two men each began doing research, and discovered their backgrounds and the fact that they were twins. They finally met each other in 1989, and the case was even reported on national television news programs.

Many researchers have been interested in this case because they want to see if the two men have any similarities even though they were raised in completely different environments. The researchers have found that there were, of course, many differences between the two men, but there are also some very interesting similarities: They had both married women with blonde hair and had three children. They had both painted their houses yellow. They both had dogs and shared similar interests and hobbies. They both had jobs that called for a lot of travel.

STEP 2   Look at this list of differences between the twins, and use the information to answer the questions that follow.

▶ **EXAMPLE:**   Which twin is married to Bernice?

The twin who <u>has an old-fashioned home is married to Bernice</u>

Here is some information about one twin:

His nickname is "Rosey."

He has a modern home.

He is married to a woman named Betty.

He has three children—all boys.

His children knew that he had been adopted.

He sells plumbing supplies.

He has a large dog named Prince.

His favorite sport is football.

He likes to listen to classical music.

Here is some information about the other twin:

His nickname is "Red."

He has an old-fashioned home.

He is married to a woman named Bernice.

He has three children—all girls.

His children didn't know that he been had been adopted.

He sells advertising space in magazines.

He has a small dog named King.

His favorite sport is basketball.

He likes to listen to jazz.

1. Which twin has children that are all girls?

   The twin who _____.

2. Which twin owns a dog named Prince?

   The twin who _____.

3. Which twin sells plumbing supplies?

   The twin whose _____.

4. Which twin likes classical music?

   The twin whose _____.

5. Which twin prefers basketball?

   The twin who _____.

6. Which twin lives in a modern home?

   The twin who _____.

7. Which twin is married to a woman named Betty?

   The twin whose _____.

8. Which twin's children didn't know that he had been adopted?

   The twin who _____.

► **R**estrictive and Nonrestrictive Relative Clauses

EXAMPLES	EXPLANATIONS
(a) Which book do you want? The one **that's under the dictionary.** **(b)** What kind of food do you like? I like food **that's not too spicy.**	Restrictive relative clauses answer the question "what kind" or "which one."
(c) Nitrogen, **which is the most common element on earth,** is necessary for all life.	Nonrestrictive relative clauses just provide additional information about noun phrases. They do not identify what kind or which one.

EXERCISE 1

Underline each relative clause in this passage and circle the noun phrase it modifies. The first two have been done for you as an example.

(1) My friend Charlie has fallen madly in love. (2) He told me he has finally met (the woman) that he has been looking for all his life. (3) He has always been attracted to (women) that are intelligent and independent and that have a good sense of humor and a love of adventure. (4) (The woman) that he has fallen in love with has all those things and more, according to Charlie. (5) Even though physical appearance isn't the most important (characteristic) that Charlie is looking for, he is quite happy his new friend is attractive and athletic. (6) She not only runs and skis, but also goes scuba-diving, and has (several other (interests) that Charlie also shares.

(7) Charlie was never completely happy with (the women) that he used to go out with. (8) There was always something that he wasn't satisfied with. (9) I used to tell him he was too choosy. (10) The "perfect woman" that he was looking for didn't exist. (11) No real person can equal the picture that someone has in his or her imagination. (12) But I'm glad he has found someone that he thinks is perfect. I've never seen him happier.

▶ Forming Restrictive Relative Clauses

EXAMPLES	EXPLANATIONS
(a) I read a book [Charlie really liked ~~the book.~~] last week. *(that)*	The relative pronoun [*that* in Example (a)] replaces the noun phrase in a relative clause in order to avoid repetition.
(b) I read a book [**that** Charlie really liked ↗] last week.	When the relative pronoun is in the object position, it is moved to the front of the relative clause.

Relative pronouns can replace any noun phrase within the relative clause.

RELATIVE CLAUSE	UNDERLYING SENTENCE	FUNCTION
(c) I read the book **that** was published last year.	**(d)** **The book** was published last year	subject
(e) I read the book **that** your professor wrote.	**(f)** Your professor wrote **the book.**	object
(g) I met the person **that** Charlie gave flowers to.	**(h)** Charlie gave **the person** flowers.	indirect object
(i) I met the person **that** Lin told me about.	**(j)** Lin told me about **the person.**	object of a preposition
(k) I read the book **that** was published last year. **(l)** NOT: I read the book that **it** was published year.	Remember that the replaced noun or pronoun of the underlying sentence does **not** appear in the relative clause.	

EXERCISE 2

In the following article underline the relative clauses. Then restate each relative clause as an independent sentence. The first three have been done for you as examples.

▶ **EXAMPLES:** (1) A new study may interest many people.

(2) They conducted a survey with several thousand American women all around the country.

(3) These women have common attitudes about men.

Scientists Identify Today's "Prince Charming"

(1) Sociologists at Mills College have released a new study <u>that may interest many people</u>, especially men. (2) They reported the results of a survey <u>that they conducted with several thousand American women all around the country</u>. (3) They wanted to examine common attitudes <u>that these women have about men</u>, so that they could identify important characteristics that women think are necessary in a good husband or boyfriend. (4) The study found a number of interesting results, which will probably not surprise most women, but may surprise some men.

(5) The women in the survey generally seem to prefer men <u>who can express their feelings</u>. (6) Most women prefer husbands <u>who they can talk to easily and that they can share their problems with</u>.

(7) There were also several other things <u>that women consider important in a partner</u>. (8) A man's character or personality is more important to many women than the job that he does for a living or the salary that he brings home. (9) Not surprisingly, most women want a husband that will take on an equal share of housekeeping and childraising duties.

(10) But the most important characteristic is this: Women want boyfriends who they can trust and husbands that they can depend on. (11) Unfortunately, more than 70% of the women who answered the questionnaires said they had husbands or boyfriends who lacked one or more of these important characteristics.

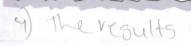

4) The results.

▶ Relative Pronouns

The relative pronouns are *who, whom, which,* and *that*.

EXAMPLES	EXPLANATIONS
(a) The man **who** told me about you last week is over there. **(b)** The man **whom** you mentioned last week is here today. **(c)** The man **whom** you told me about yesterday is here to see you.	Use *who* and *whom* to refer to humans. In formal written style, use *who* to refer to subjects in relative clauses and *whom* to refer to objects.
(d) I read the **book which** Kevin had recommended.	Use *which* to refer to nonhumans.
(e) The **man that** wrote this book is a teacher. **(f)** The **man that** you told me about is a teacher. **(g)** I read the **book that** Kevin had recommended.	Use *that* for humans or nonhumans, but only with restrictive relative clauses.
(h) Abraham Lincoln, **who** was the 16th president of the United States, died in 1865. **(i)** NOT: Abraham Lincoln, **that** was the 16th president of the United States, died in 1865. **(j)** San Francisco, **which** is on the Pacific Ocean, has a very cool climate. **(k)** NOT: San Francisco, **that** is on the Pacific Ocean, has a very cool climate.	Do not use *that* as a relative pronoun in nonrestrictive relative clauses. Use only *who, whom,* and *which*.

EXERCISE 3

Combine these pairs of sentences by using a relative clause with *that, who, whom,* or *which*.

▶ **EXAMPLE:** I finally met the woman. Charlie has fallen in love with the woman.

> I finally met the woman that Charlie has fallen in love with.

1. Last month Charlie fell in love with a young woman. He had been introduced to the woman by some friends.

2. She had a number of positive characteristics. Charlie found these characteristics quite attractive.

3. She has a responsible position in a company. The company produces computer programs.

4. That's a fast-growing field. Charlie is also interested in that field.

5. Hobbies involve athletics and being outdoors. Both of them like these hobbies.

6. Charlie introduced the woman to his parents. He had been dating the woman for several weeks.

7. She has a wonderful sense of humor. This makes their times together relaxing and enjoyable.

8. From the first time they met, Charlie felt there was a "special understanding" between them. He was unable to explain this understanding.

EXERCISE 4

Answer these questions using a relative clause ("I like people who . . ."; "People who I like . . ."). Compare your answers to those of a classmate.

1. What kind of people do you like?
2. What kind of people like you?
3. What kind of food do you like?
4. What kind of leisure activities interest you?
5. What kind of person do you want to marry?
6. What kind of person will want to marry you?
7. What kind of practice is useful in learning languages?
8. What kind of government is the best?

EXERCISE 5

The following sentences are incorrect. Identify the mistakes and correct them.

1. I read a book that it was published last year.
2. I saw an article which your professor wrote it.
3. Jeff and Matt have been living in the city of San Francisco, that is located in California, since 1985.
4. This is the person whom Charlie gave her flowers.
5. I met the person who Charlie told me about her.
6. The teacher that I studied with her has become quite famous.
7. The money which you loaned me some last week is there on the table.
8. The resort that we read about it in the newspaper is becoming more and more popular.
9. The people whom I visited them last year are coming here for a visit.
10. My father, that lives in San Diego, loves sailing.

▶ **Deleting Relative Pronouns**

You can delete relative pronouns that function as objects in restrictive relative clauses.

EXAMPLES	FUNCTION OF RELATIVE PRONOUNS
(a) I read the book **that** your professor wrote. (b) I read the book your professor wrote.	direct objects
(c) The lady **that** Charlie sent flowers to is on the phone. (d) The lady Charlie sent flowers to is on the phone.	indirect objects
(e) I read the book **that** Charlie was so excited about. (f) I read the book Charlie was so excited about.	objects of prepositions

You can only delete relative pronouns that function as subjects in restrictive relative clauses that contain *be* (either as a main verb or an auxiliary). In such cases both the relative pronoun and *be* are deleted.

EXAMPLES	EXPLANATIONS
(g) I want a book **that was written** by an expert. (h) I want a book **written** by an expert.	relative clauses with passive verbs
(i) I think I know that woman **who is carrying** the blue suitcase. (j) I think I know that woman **carrying** the blue suitcase.	relative clauses with progressive verbs
(k) I tried to get an autograph from the baseball player **who is beside** the fence. (l) I tried to get an autograph from the baseball player **beside** the fence.	relative clauses with prepositional phrases
(m) Anyone **who is foolish enough** to use drugs should be free to do so. (n) Anyone **foolish enough** to use drugs should be free to do so.	relative clauses with adjective phrases
(o) Have you read the book **that made** Darryl Brock famous? (p) NOT: Have you read the book **made** Darryl Brock famous?	You cannot delete relative pronouns if they are subjects of a relative clause without *be*.

EXERCISE 6

Underline all the relative clauses in this passage. Make sure that you also include the ones that have deleted relative pronouns. The first paragraph has been done for you as an example.

The War to End All Wars

(1) When World War I, <u>which was fought in Europe from 1914 to 1917</u>, was finally over, it was called "the war to end all wars." (2) It was the most destructive war <u>the world had ever fought until then</u>. (3) Over ten million young men <u>sent to battle from both sides</u> were killed or permanently disabled.

(4) The war introduced powerful new weapons <u>the world had never before seen</u>. (5) The use of the airplane enabled armies on both sides to drop bombs with an effectiveness and precision that had been previously impossible. (6) Heavy casualties were also caused by the wide-scale use of a poison gas, called mustard gas, which permanently damaged the lungs of soldiers caught without gas masks.

(7) There were more than 8.5 million deaths. (8) Many people fighting this terrible war were killed in battles. (9) But many others died from intestinal diseases caused by the unsanitary conditions on the battlefield, or by infections which developed in lungs damaged by mustard gas, which was used by both sides.

(10) The peace established by "the war to end all wars" lasted less than a generation. (11) The most destructive war the world had ever known, like most wars, didn't solve the political and economic problems facing European governments at that time. (12) Less than twenty-five years after the conflict everyone hoped would bring world peace, Europe was again at war.

EXERCISE 7

Wherever possible, delete the relative pronouns in these sentences and make any other necessary changes.

▶ **EXAMPLE:** The kind of people **that** I like are usually people **who** have a good sense of humor.

1. I like people **who** think about other people's feelings.
2. I like people **who** are working to make the world a place **that** we can all share.
3. I like people **who** don't take the work **that** they do too seriously.
4. I don't like people **who** have no sense of humor.
5. I like people **who** don't worry about things **that** other people say about them.
6. I dislike people **who** try to hurt other people's feelings.
7. I dislike people **who** are very concerned with power and position.
8. I like people **who** question the things **that** they have been taught and the teachers **who** have taught them.
9. I like people **who** are like me.
10. I like people **who** like me.

EXERCISE 8

Write five sentences that describe the kind of people you like and five sentences that describe the kind of people you don't like. Compare your sentences with those of a classmate. Describe any common likes and dislikes.

Whose in Relative Clauses

When a relative clause contains a possessive form, *whose + noun* can be used in the same way as relative pronouns.

EXAMPLES	UNDERLYING SENTENCE	EXPLANATIONS
(a) I met a man **whose house** was destroyed in the earthquake.	**(b)** I met a man. **His house** was destroyed in the earthquake.	*Whose* can be used with: • the subject of a relative clause
(c) I got a letter from the man **whose house** we visited last week.	**(d)** I got a letter from a man. We visited **his house** last week.	• the object of a relative clause
(e) I spoke to the man **whose party** we got an invitation **to**.	**(f)** I spoke to a man. We got an invitation **to his party**.	• the object of a preposition
(g) I got a letter from the man **whose house** we visited last week. **(h)** NOT: I got a letter from a man **house** we visited last week.		You can never delete *whose* from a relative clause. It must always be used with a noun.

EXERCISE 9

Combine these sentences using *whose*.

▶ **EXAMPLE:** I got a letter from a man. We visited his house last week.

I got a letter from the man whose house we visited last week.

1. Samira met a man. His twin brother is a well-known geneticist.
2. Jeff and Matt are roommates. Matt's nickname is "Akbar."
3. People may have similar personalities. Their genetic make-ups are similar.
4. Nicole took a class from a teacher. She knew his wife in college.
5. Mary Rae would like to go to the lecture by the mountain climber. She read about his latest climb in *Adventure Magazine*.
6. My friend has a dog. Its eyes are different colors.
7. I keep getting phone calls for some stranger. His last name is apparently the same as mine.
8. Hans finally succeeded in meeting the artist. He had been admiring her work for years.

EXERCISE 10

Combine these numbered pairs of sentences in this paragraph using relative pronouns or *whose*.

(1) Charlie wants to make some changes in his life. These changes involve both his lifestyle and his social activities. (2) Charlie wants to find a new place to live. The place has to have enough room for a dog. (3) He's looking at a new apartment. The apartment has a balcony, so he can grow some flowers. (4) Charlie also wants to get married to someone. Her political beliefs are similar to his own. (5) He hasn't found anyone yet. No one seems to share his interest in politics and sports. (6) He's thinking of putting a personals ad in a paper. A lot of people advertise in that paper in order to meet others with similar interests and backgrounds.

EXERCISE 11

Answer these questions, using relative clauses. Compare your answers with one of your classmate's.

▶ **EXAMPLE:**   What kind of food do you like?

I like food that is not too spicy.

1. What kind of person do you want to marry?
2. What kind of person should be the leader of a country?
3. What kind of person makes the best teacher?
4. What kind of television programs do you like to watch?
5. What kind of place is the best for a vacation?
6. What kind of house or apartment would you like to live in?
7. What kind of books do you enjoy reading?
8. What kind of students get the best grades?

Use Your English

ACTIVITY 1 : SPEAKING

STEP 1 In Exercise 2 you read about some of the things that American women consider important in a husband. Divide into same-gender groups of men and women. In your group discuss the characteristics of "the ideal life partner." Prepare a list of five to ten statements like these.

The ideal partner is someone who takes an equal responsibility for raising the children.

The ideal partner is a person who is able to maintain a good sense of humor.

What ideals do you all agree on? Are there ideals that are controversial?

STEP 2 Present your statements to the other groups. Compare the ideals presented by women's groups and the ideals presented by men's groups.

STEP 3 Discuss these questions as a whole class or in mixed gender groups.

- What are the important similarities and differences between the statements of the two kinds of groups?
- Are there some ideals that all men share, no matter what culture they come from?
- Are there some ideals that all women share, no matter what culture they come from?
- Are there some ideals that both genders share?

ACTIVITY 2 : WRITING

Write a brief essay describing personal characteristics in people that you like and dislike. You may wish to look at Exercise 7 for some ideas about the kinds of characteristics other students have identified. Here are some questions you should try to answer in your essay.

- What kind of people do you like most?
- What personal characteristics do you appreciate and respect in other people?
- What personal characteristics do you find distasteful?

ACTIVITY 3 : SPEAKING/WRITING

The word *daffy* means silly. A *daffynition* is a made-up definition for a word that doesn't really exist. In fact the word *daffynition* is, itself, a made-up word.

STEP 1   Try to invent daffynitions for these made-up words.

EXAMPLE: Who or what is a **murphler?**

A murphler is someone who makes a lot of noise when he eats.

- What do **parahawks** do?
- What does **chemicophysiologicalistic** mean?
- What do **flurps** and **mompsquats** have in common?
- What are **quatchels?**
- Define **hypervoraciosity.**

STEP 2   Share your daffynitions with the rest of the class. Which one is the most believable? Which one is the most amusing daffynition for each term?

STEP 3   Make up some of your own imaginary words and provide definitions for them.

ACTIVITY 4: LISTENING

Listen to the following lecture about "hawks" and "doves," and write definitions for the following terms based on the information you heard.

What is a pacifist? _____

_____

What is a "hawk" ?_____

_____

What is a "dove"?_____

_____

What is the difference between a war and a revolution?_____

_____

_____

ACTIVITY 5: SPEAKING

Organize a debate between "hawks" and "doves" to consider the following questions:

- Is there a difference between a **war** and a **revolution?**
- Give some examples of armed conflicts that you feel were or were not justifiable.

- Under what circumstances is it acceptable to take up arms against your own government, other countries, or other groups of people within your own country?

You may wish to discuss wars in general, or a specific conflict that you are familiar with.

ACTIVITY 6: WRITING/SPEAKING

In English we often make a "dramatic introduction" in certain formal situations. A dramatic introduction lists a person's characteristics and accomplishments and ends with the person's name.
Here's an example of a "dramatic introduction":

> "Ladies and gentlemen, it is my great pleasure to introduce an individual whose honesty and sincerity are well-known, whose commitment to education is serious and wide-reaching, whose work in the field of linguistics has helped many students understand English better, and whose wit and kindness make working together a pleasure. Ladies and gentlemen, I give you our English teacher, Rebecca Buckley."

Make a dramatic introduction for one of your classmates or for a real person whose life and accomplishments you are familiar with.

ACTIVITY 7: SPEAKING

"Nicknames" are additional names that are given to people to describe some physical characteristic or aspect of their personality.

STEP 1 Here is a list of some common American nicknames. Working with a partner, decide what characteristics would be likely for someone whose nickname is one of these:

Blondie	Doc	Sport	Cowboy	Tubby
Sugar	Gramps	Tiger	Honey	

STEP 2 Report your ideas by using sentences like these:

We think that someone whose nickname is **Red** is probably a person who has red hair.

We think that someone whose nickname is **Curly** is probably a person who has curly hair (or perhaps someone who is bald).

We think that someone whose nickname is **Sunny** is probably a person who has a cheerful, outgoing personality.

STEP 3 Discuss how nicknames are used in other countries. Do you have a nickname? Why do people call you that name?

PRESENT TIME FRAME

UNIT GOALS:

- To distinguish the use of progressive aspect from simple present
- To understand and use non-progressive stative verbs
- To understand common uses of the present time frame

▶ OPENING TASK
Outward Bound

WHAT IS OUTWARD BOUND? Outward Bound participants come from ordinary jobs and spend two weeks in the wilderness. The program is physically exhausting, but most people find it deeply satisfying. People go to Outward Bound programs in order to challenge themselves and test the limits of their physical and mental strength. Most people are surprised to learn that they are much braver, stronger, and more capable than they originally thought.

STEP 1 Mary Rae is in Florida, participating in a program called Outward Bound. Use the information in the two charts below to write a paragraph that describes at least five differences between Mary Rae's normal life and her life at Outward Bound. Here are some examples:

Mary Rae normally spends her day as an account executive in a busy advertising firm, but at Outward Bound, she is spending twelve to fourteen hours a day in vigorous physical activity. In New York she supervises twenty-five employees, but in Florida, she is only supervising herself. . . .

MARY RAE'S LIFE IN NEW YORK	MARY RAE'S LIFE AT OUTWARD BOUND
Occupation: advertising account executive; visits clients, supervises a 25-person office	Occupation: program participant; rows, hikes, climbs trees, builds fires
lives in a small apartment	sleeps in a tent, lives in a canoe
often eats take-out Chinese food	cooks all her own food, catches fish, and picks wild fruit
worries a lot about her career	doesn't think about her career at all
doesn't get much exercise	hikes or rows 12–14 hours each day
doesn't spend much time outdoors	doesn't spend any time indoors
often has trouble falling asleep	falls asleep almost instantly
doesn't feel challenged by her daily routine	feels very challenged by each day's activities
is somewhat bored with life	is excited about growing stronger and more capable
feels that she is not learning anything new	feels that she is learning something new every day
finds making new friends difficult	finds making new friends easy

STEP 2 Compare your paragraph with a classmate's. Did you use the same verb tenses to describe Mary Rae's life in New York and Florida?

STEP 3 Based on Mary Rae's experience, would you ever consider going to an Outward Bound Program? Why or why not?

Using Simple Present Versus Present Progressive

USE SIMPLE PRESENT TO DESCRIBE	USE PRESENT PROGRESSIVE TO DESCRIBE
• **General statements about recurring habits and skills** (a) My friend **speaks** Spanish. (b) I **study** every night after dinner. (c) The children **sleep** in the upstairs bedroom.	• **Actions in progress at the time of speaking** (d) He **is speaking** Spanish. He must be talking with Carlos. (e) Please turn down the TV. I'**m studying.** (f) Don't make too much noise. The children **are sleeping.**
• **Timeless facts** (g) Baking soda **works** well as a cleaner.	• **Situations in progress around the time of speaking** (h) The refrigerator **is working** well. I just had it repaired.
• **Permanent situations** (i) I **live** in Texas.	• **Temporary Situations** (j) I'**m living** with my uncle for the summer.
• **States and conditions** (k) I **think** you're right. (l) We **have** three dogs at home.	• **Actions** (m) Be quiet! I'm **thinking.** (n) We'**re having** fun!

EXERCISE 1

Choose the correct verb tense (simple present or present progressive) for these sentences. More than one answer may be correct.

1. Don't turn on the TV. I _____ (talk) to you!

2. My brother _____ (speak) a little Spanish. Let's ask him to help us read this letter from Mexico.

3. Tamar _____ (study) for a biology quiz, so I don't think she can come to the party.

4. I _____ (leave) for work about 7:30 every morning.

5. Peter _____ (make) a big mess in the kitchen. Please go help him.

6. Ed _____ (do) his best, but he still can't run as fast as the others.

7. I _____ (try) to understand you, but you will have to speak more slowly.

8. Scientists _____ (discover) that many forms of mental illness are caused by chemical imbalances in the brain.

9. The traffic situation _____ (get) worse every year.

10. Learning a language _____ (get) easier when you practice outside of class.

EXERCISE 2

Write the correct form of the verb in parentheses (simple present or present progressive).

Luis (1) _____ (not take) a vacation this summer, because he (2) _____ (not think) that he (3) _____ (have) enough money. He (4) _____ (teach) high school chemistry, so he (5) _____ (get) three months of vacation, but teachers (6) _____ (not make) much money. So he (7) _____ (look for) a temporary job, since he can't afford to go anywhere. He (8) _____ (try) to find work as a computer programmer. But most companies only (9) _____ (hire) workers on a permanent basis. Luis (10) _____ (find) that it is difficult to locate short-term employment. He (11) _____ (get) depressed about the prospects of three months of nothing to do and nowhere to go. No matter how hard he (12) _____ (search), he (13) _____ (begin) to realize that he may have to take a vacation, whether he (14) _____ (want) one or not.

EXERCISE 3

Describe your typical day starting from the time you wake up and ending with going to sleep at night. Write at least eight sentences about things you do on a regular basis. Now describe three things that you are currently do-ing differently from normal, and why you have changed your routine.

▶ **EXAMPLE:** *I'm living in a dormitory, because I have moved to a new city to go to school.*

► **N**onprogressive (Stative) Verbs

EXAMPLES	EXPLANATION
(a) I **know** that you are unhappy right now. **(b)** NOT: I **am knowing** that you are unhappy right now.	Nonprogressive verbs describe conditions or states. They do not usually take progressive forms.

Common Nonprogressive Verbs

SENSORY PERCEPTION	KNOWLEDGE & BELIEF	FEELING & ATTITUDE	LOGICAL RELATIONSHIP	
see *hear* *feel* *appear* *look* *seem* *smell* *sound* *taste* *resemble* *look like*	*agree/disagree with* *believe* *doubt* *feel (believe)* *imagine* *intend* *know* *recognize* *realize* *remember* *suppose* *think (believe)* *understand* *consider*	*love* *like* *hate* *dislike* *appreciate* *prefer* *want* *need* *mind*	**Cause and Effect** *results in* *requires* *depends on* *means* **Possession** *belong to* *possess* *have* *own* *owe*	**Measurement** *weigh* *cost* *measure* *equal* **Inclusion** *contain* *consist of* *include*

EXERCISE 4

Work with a partner and ask W*h*-questions for the cues given. Your partner should give true answers, and then ask the same questions of you.

▶ **EXAMPLE:**   which parent/resemble most

Which parent do you resemble most?

I resemble my mother more than my father.

1. what kind of fruit/taste best
2. what way/think/most effective to learn a foreign language
3. how/a sick person/appear
4. what/your notebook/contain
5. what/a handshake/mean
6. what activity/your family appreciates/your doing
7. what/learning another language/require
8. how many _____/you/own
9. who/that _____/belong to
10. what/not understand/American culture

EXERCISE 5

Report your partner's answers from Exercise 4 to the rest of the class.

▶ **EXAMPLES:**   **Yoshiko resembles her mother more than her father.**

FOCUS **3**

▶ Verbs with Both Nonprogressive and Action Meanings

Some nonprogressive verbs can also be used to describe actions.

VERB	NONPROGRESSIVE MEANING	ACTION MEANING
have	**(a)** I **have** three brothers. **(possess)**	**(b)** We**'re having** a great time. **(experiencing)**
mind	**(c)** I **don't mind** smoke. **(object to)**	**(d)** He**'s minding** the children now. **(taking care of)**
see	**(e)** I **see** your point. **(understand)**	**(f)** Yuji **is seeing** a specialist about his back. **(consulting)**
think	**(g)** I **think** you're right. **(opinion)**	**(h)** Be quiet! I**'m thinking**. **(mental activity)**
consider	**(i)** I **consider** money to be the cause of many problems. **(opinion)**	**(j)** I**'m considering** going to Hawaii for vacation. **(mental activity)**
depends on	**(k)** Athletic ability **depends on** strength and practice. **(requires)**	**(l)** I**'m depending on** Yuji to help me move next week. **(relying upon)**
be	**(m)** Mei **is** a teacher. **(identity)**	**(n)** Those children **are being** very noisy. **(behaving)**
feel	**(o)** I **feel** that you're the best choice. **(believe)**	**(p)** I**'m feeling** a little sick today. **(experiencing)**

Other nonprogressive verbs can indicate the **act** of perception or measurement, or the perceptions or measurements themselves.

VERB	PERCEPTION/MEASUREMENT (NONPROGRESSIVE MEANING)	ACT OF PERCEPTION/MEASUREMENT (ACTION MEANING)
smell	**(q)** The flowers **smell** wonderful.	**(r)** The dog **is smelling** the clothes of the missing boy.
taste	**(s)** That cake **tastes** delicious.	**(t)** Our host **is tasting** the soup to make sure it's not too salty.
feel	**(u)** My arm **feels** broken!	**(v)** The doctor **is feeling** my arm to see if it is broken.
weigh	**(w)** Joe **weighs** almost 100 kilos.	**(x)** The butcher **is weighing** that piece of meat.

EXERCISE 6

Decide whether the verbs indicated express an action meaning or a nonprogressive meaning and write the simple present or present progressive tense in the blanks. In some cases both answers may be correct.

1. This cloth _____ (feel) really nice.

2. I _____ (consider) applying to go to Outward Bound.

3. Why did you ask that question? You _____ (be) really rude!

4. I _____ (believe) that Mary Rae _____ (have) a good experience at the Outward Bound program.

5. I don't like this coffee. It _____ (taste) bitter to me.

6. I like people who _____ (mind) their own business and don't try to tell others what to do.

7. Bambang _____ (doubt) that he will be able to pass the TOEFL next week.

8. It _____ (look) as if we will get some rain later this week.

9. John _____ (feel) a little guilty about leaving Mary for so long. But I'm sure he'll get over it.

10. Learning a new language _____ (require) a lot of hard work.

11. These days the government _____ (require) people to take drug tests in order to get a government job.

12. Those children _____ (be) so naughty. I wish someone would make them stop teasing that poor kitten!

▶ Uses of the Present Time Frame

EXAMPLES	EXPLANATIONS
(a) Supply **affects** demand in several ways. If supply **exceeds** demand, the cost of the commodity generally **decreases.** When cost **increases,** demand often **drops.** Decreased demand eventually **results** in decreased supply.	Use present time frame • to state general truths and relationships in scientific and technical writing
(b) Here's how we **make** cookies. First we **mix** a cup of flour and two eggs together in a bowl. Next, we **mix** in some sugar. A cup-and-a half **is** probably enough, but if we **want** sweeter cookies, we **add** at least 3 cups of sugar.	• to describe actions as they are performed in live demonstrations
(c) Shimazu **throws** the ball. Martinez **hits** it. He **passes** first base. He**'s making** a run to second base. He**'s** out!	• for reporting in radio and television broadcasts such as sporting events
(d) One day I**'m walking** down the street. I **see** this guy talking on a pay phone. I **know** he**'s** mad about something because I **can hear** him screaming all the way down the block. So, anyway, when I **get** next to the pay phone, he **stops** shouting and **asks** me if I have an extra quarter. I **tell** him, "Sorry, man," and all of a sudden . . .	• to tell stories orally in informal situations

EXERCISE 7

Here are reports of two scientific experiments. Change them into present time so that they are statements of general scientific principles, rather than accounts of specific experiments.

▶ **EXAMPLE:** *when baking soda is added to vinegar, a chemical reaction occurs.*
       . . .

Experiment 1

(1) When baking soda was added to vinegar, a chemical reaction occurred. (2) The baking soda bubbled and CO_2 was produced by the combination of elements. (3) When a candle was put next to the container while the chemical reaction was taking place, the flame on the candle went out.

Experiment 2

(1) We wanted to determine whether gravity affected the rate of acceleration of objects falling through space. (2) Two objects of similar size and shape, but substantially different weights—a cannonball and a volleyball—were dropped from the same height. (3) We found that both objects hit the ground at the same time. (4) This indicated that the attraction of gravity was constant.

EXERCISE 8

Tell this story aloud, as if you were Mary Rae describing her own experience. Tell it in present time to make it more vivid and less formal. The first two sentences have been done as examples.

▶ **EXAMPLE:** There I am, standing in dirty swamp water as deep as my waist, but I'm having a wonderful time! The canoe we're rowing has gotten stuck on a log, so somebody has to get into the water and try to lift one end of it.

There I was, standing in dirty swamp water as deep as my waist, but I was having a wonderful time! The canoe we were rowing had gotten stuck on a log, so somebody had to get into the water and try to lift one end of it. I looked into the water. It looked really dark and dirty. I knew there were a lot of poisonous snakes in this area. I knew there were also alligators. All of a sudden, I realized that I wasn't afraid of any of these things. I had complete confidence in my ability to free the canoe and to avoid getting eaten or bitten. Without another thought, I jumped into the water and started to pull at the canoe. At that moment I knew that there was nothing that I was afraid to do, and nothing that I couldn't do if I put my mind to it.

Use Your English

ACTIVITY 1: SPEAKING

Give the class a demonstration of how to do something. This could be how to prepare a favorite food, how to perform some physical activity, or how to make some simple object. While you are demonstrating the activity, tell how it is done.

ACTIVITY 2: SPEAKING

"How much does that cost?" "How much money do you earn." "How much do you weigh?" "How old are you?" Most Americans think that these would be rude questions to ask anyone who is not a very close friend. In other cultures, people don't consider these to be rude questions but they might hesitate to ask other kinds of questions, such as "How many daughters do you have?" "What do you do—what kind of job do you have?" or even "What kind of house do you live in?" Form a group and talk about what are considered to be rude questions in other cultures that you are familiar with. Present your findings to the rest of the class.

ACTIVITY 3: WRITING/SPEAKING

Describe some of the things that are happening in the drawings on page 218.

ACTIVITY 4: WRITING/SPEAKING

We all learn our basic cultural values when we are very young. A first step in learning about different cultures is learning to identify some of these basic cultural values.

STEP 1 Write down at least five things your parents told you that were general truths when you were growing up. Make sure that these things are not orders or requests (My parents told me to clean my room), but rather, statements about things that are always true (Big boys don't cry. Good manners are important.)

STEP 2 Compare your list to the lists of several other students. Are any of the statements the same on all your lists? Are there any interesting similarities or differences based on different cultures? What does this tell you about the values your parents tried to teach you?

STEP 3 Report your ideas to the rest of the class.

A C T I V I T Y 5 : L I S T E N I N G

STEP 1 Listen to Professor Freemarket's lecture for his Introduction to Economics class, and take notes. You may want to listen to the lecture a second time to make sure you understand the information he describes.

STEP 2 Use your notes to answer the questions that he asked the class on his weekly quiz.

STEP 3 Compare your answers to another student's to check the accuracy of your information, and the grammatical correctness of what you wrote.

Economics 101—Dr. Freemarket
Weekly quiz #5
(Twenty-five points possible)

1. (ten points) Define the Law of Supply and Demand.

2. (ten points) How does transportation affect the Law of Supply and Demand?

3. (five points) What other forces affect the Law of Supply and Demand?

PRESENT PERFECT

Describing Past Events in Relation to the Present

UNIT GOALS:

- To use the present perfect to understand and express past actions that are related to the present moment by time
- To use the present perfect to understand and express past actions that are related to the present moment by logical relationship or present result
- To understand and express meaning differences with present perfect progressive instead of present perfect tense

▶ OPENING TASK
Identifying What Makes You Special

North American Institute of International Studies
Application for Admissions

Applying for: _____ SPRING _____ SUMMER _____ FALL _____ WINTER 20_____

Degree Objective: Undergraduate _____   Graduate _____

    Major _____   Minor _____

Personal Data: Name _____

Address _____

Telephone _____   Birthdate _____   Sex _____   Ethnic Background _____

Educational Background:
List all secondary and post-secondary schools attended, including language programs.

Name and location of school	dates of attendance	degree granted	GPA

_____

_____

_____

_____

Personal Essay / Writing Sample:
All applicants must provide a writing sample. On another sheet of paper, write at least 200 words on the following topic. It must be handwritten, and written *only* by the applicant.

What are some characteristics that make you different from other people you know?
How have your experiences in life shaped you as a person? What are some achievements
that you have accomplished that you feel particularly proud of?

Signature _____   Date _____

All applications must be accompanied by official transcripts in English, proof of finances,
and a nonrefundable $40 application fee.

When American students apply to colleges and universities, they often have to write a personal essay about their individual character and achievements. Below are the ideas that Aliona Fernandez used for her successful application to the North American Institute of International Studies. (Her personal essay has been reprinted in Exercise 1 on page 233.)

STEP 1 Think of some of your own special characteristics that might be of interest to a university admissions committee. Identify one special **characteristic,** one **experience** that helped you develop that characteristic, and one **achievement** that this characteristic has enabled you to do. Add your characteristics in the space below.

	Aliona Fernandez	You
Characteristic	flexibility	
Experience	living overseas—Peace Corps volunteer	
Achievement	speak other languages and understand different cultures	

STEP 2 Compare your special characteristic, experience, and achievement with those of another student in the class. Decide whose ideas would be the best to use in a personal essay for a university application. Tell your opinion and your reasons to the rest of the class.

▶ Choosing Past Time Frame or Present Time Frame

We can use both past time frame and present time frame to talk about things that happened in the past.

PAST TIME FRAME	PRESENT TIME FRAME
Use past time frame (in the form of the simple past tense) to show that **a past event has no direct, ongoing relationship to the present.** The event was fully completed in the past or happened at a specific time in the past.	Use a present time frame (in the form of present perfect tense) to show that **a past event is directly related to the present.** The event happened in the past, but **continues to influence the present in some way.**
(a) I **went** to Disneyworld three times while I was living in Florida. Now that I live in Ohio, it's too far away to visit.	(b) I **have gone** to Disneyworld three times, so I'm not really anxious to go again so soon after my last visit.
(c) I worked as a limousine driver during college. I **had** many opportunities to meet famous people.	(d) As a limousine driver, I **have had** many opportunities to meet famous people. It's one of the things I like about my job.
(e) I started that book, but I **didn't finish** it. It was too boring.	(f) I **haven't finished** that book yet. I've been reading it for several hours, and I hope to finish it soon.

EXERCISE 1

Read the following personal essay written by a successful applicant to the North American Institute of International Studies. Underline the verb phrases and identify the tenses that are used. Then discuss these questions with a partner.

- Why did the author use present time in the first paragraph?
- Why did the author use past time in the second paragraph?
- Why did the author use present time in the third paragraph?

Personal Essay

by Aliona Fernandez

(1) One of the characteristics that makes me different from many people is my adaptability. (2) I am flexible and comfortable in new or unusual situations. (3) I think this is because I have had a lot of experience living in foreign countries. (4) This has given me a lot of opportunities to face unfamiliar situations and to learn about unfamiliar customs and beliefs.

(5) My first experience in a foreign country was as a Peace Corps volunteer. (6) I taught English in a small town in a rural area. (7) Life in my town was very simple. (8) Because there was no electricity and rather little contact with the outside world, my life was a lot like living in an earlier century. (9) I have been to other countries since that first experience, and everywhere that I have traveled has been interesting and educational.

(10) As a result of my experiences in other countries, I speak other languages and understand other cultures. (11) I have learned that relationships between people are very much the same, whether they have modern, busy lives, or old-fashioned, more peaceful lives. (12) I have learned to understand different ways of doing things and different ways of looking at the world. (13) Most of all, I have learned that "new" doesn't necessarily mean "better." (14) My experiences have made me adaptable, and this adaptability has allowed me to understand other people and cultures.

Relationship to the Present: Still True (Present Perfect Tense) Versus No Longer True (Past Tense)

One common way that past events relate to the present is if they are **still true.**

EXAMPLES	EXPLANATIONS
(a) I **have worked** in a factory for three years. I **have learned** how to operate three different kinds of machines so far.	**Present Perfect Tense:** Use the present perfect tense to show that something is **still true now.**
(b) I **worked** in an automobile factory for three years. I **did good work** on the assembly line, but they closed the factory.	**Past Tense:** Use the past tense to talk about something that is **no longer true now.**

EXERCISE 2

Choose past tense or present perfect tense for the verbs in parentheses. More than one answer may be correct, so be prepared to explain why you chose the form you did.

Bambang Soetomo (1) __came__ (come) to the United States last January to get a degree in mechanical engineering. Since he (2) _____ (be) in the United States, he (3) _____ (have) many new experiences. At home in Jakarta, servants (4) _____ (cook) all his food. But here in the United States, Bambang (5) _____ (have) to prepare food for himself. In Indonesia, a lot of his university classes (6) _____ (require) the ability to memorize large amounts of information. But here, Bambang (7) _____ (find) that memorization is not considered to be a very important skill in many of his classes. Of course, he (8) _____ (be) ready for obvious differences in things like food and social customs, but he (9) _____ (not/adjust) to the subtle differences. He (10) _____ (learn) that knowing about differences and dealing with them are two different things. In fact, he (11) _____ (be) rather homesick. In Jakarta he (12) _____ (have) a large group of friends, but here in the States he (13) _____ (meet) only a few other Indonesian students, and none of them are in his department. When he (14) _____ (be) planning his trip to America, he (15) _____ (plan) to go home for a vacation after his sophomore year, but he (16) _____ (change) his mind since he (17) _____ (get) here. He (18) _____ (speak) with his father about the possibility of coming home during his first summer vacation. His father (19) _____ (not decide) whether that's a good idea or not.

Relationship to the Present: Until Now

USE

Present perfect is used to describe things that began in the past but continue up to the present moment.

EXAMPLES	EXPLANATIONS
(a) Matt and Jeff **have seen** *The Wizard of Oz* over **a dozen times.** **(b)** I've **ridden** a motorcycle **once,** but I'll never do it again!	Use present perfect to describe: • the number of times something has happened
(c) The doctor **has just left** the office. Maybe you can catch him if you hurry to the parking lot. **(d)** We've **just been talking about** your suggestions. Won't you join us?	• very recent events with *just*
(e) I've **known** Stephanie **since** we were in high school **(f)** I've **never eaten** snake meat. **Have you ever tried** it?	• sentences with *ever, never,* or *since*

EXERCISE 3

Work with a partner. Take turns asking each other these questions. Ask at least ten questions. You can use the suggested topics or make up questions of your own.

1. Have you ever . . . (ridden a horse, been in love, seen a flying saucer . . .)

2. How many times have you . . . (eaten Chinese food, taken the TOEFL, driven a motorcycle . . .)

3. Name three things you have never done, but would like to do.

4. Name three things you have done that you don't want to do again.

Then tell the rest of the class about your partner. The class should decide who has asked the most interesting or unusual questions.

EXERCISE 4

Choose past tense or present perfect tense for the verbs in parentheses. More than one answer may be possible. The first sentence has been done for you as an example.

My friend Bob is a very happy man. He just (1) ____*found out*____
(find out) that he (2) _____ (win) a free trip to Hawaii.
He (3) _____ (buy) raffle tickets for years, but he never
(4) _____ (win) anything until six months ago, when he
(5) _____ (win) an electric toaster. Since then, apparently, his
luck (6) _____ (change). He (7) _____ (get)
more than a dozen prizes from various contests. Most of the
prizes (8) _____ (be) small until last month, when he
(9) _____ (win) a video cassette recorder and a color TV. I
wonder if he (10) _____ (think about) sharing his good for-
tune with his friends.

FOCUS **4**

Relationship to the Present: Present Result (Present Perfect Tense)

USE

Another common way that past events relate to the present is if the past event **continues to affect the present situation in some way.** Use present perfect tense to describe past events that cause a result in the present.

The present result can be stated directly.

PAST ACTION	STATED PRESENT RESULT
(a) I **have** already **seen** that movie,	so I **suggest** we go see a different one.
(b) He **has been wasting** so much money	that I **don't think** we should give him any more.
(c) I **have** always **felt** that teachers were underpaid,	so I **think** we should suggest that our teacher ought to get a raise.

The present result can be implied.

PAST ACTION	IMPLIED PRESENT RESULT
(d) You **have spilled** juice all over my new tablecloth!	The tablecloth is dirty.
(e) John **has obviously forgotten** about our meeting.	He is not at the meeting.

The present result can also be the speaker's/writer's attitude.

NOT CONNECTED TO THE PRESENT (PAST TENSE)	CONNECTED TO THE PRESENT (PRESENT PERFECT TENSE)	EXPLANATIONS
(f) **Did you find** the article you were looking for?	(g) **Have you found** the article you were looking for? Because if not, I think **I know where you can find it.**	The event is connected to the present in the speaker's mind.
(h) The White House **released** new figures **yesterday** concerning the economy.	(i) The White House **has released** new figures on the economy in the last quarter. These figures **show** that imports continue to exceed exports by more than 20%.	Reporters often introduce news stories with the present perfect tense to emphasize the connection with the present.
(j) The historian Toynbee **often observed** that history repeats itself.	(k) The historian Toynbee **has observed** that history repeats itself, and **I believe that he is correct.**	A writer may mention a past event that has a connection to a point she or he is about to make.

EXERCISE 5
Choose the sentence that reflects the most logical continuation of the ideas expressed in the first sentence, based on the tense used in the first sentence. Both sentences are formed correctly.

1. I have told you that I don't like the color green.
   (a) My brother didn't like that color either.
   (b) So why did you buy me a sweater in that color?

2. Jeff met Matt at a party.
   (a) They soon became the best of friends.
   (b) They share an apartment in San Francisco.

3. Bambang Soetomo arrived in America about eight months ago.
   (a) He has been adjusting to American life ever since.
   (b) He is living by himself in an apartment.

4. I have been trying to get in touch with my math professor since last week.
   (a) I didn't do well on the last exam.
   (b) Whenever I go to her office, she isn't there.

5. I don't think that Denise likes Peter very much.
   (a) Have you ever noticed that she avoids looking at him when she speaks?
   (b) Did she say anything about her feelings to you at the meeting last week?

EXERCISE 6

Discuss these questions about the short passages below with a partner and compare your ideas with other students'.

- Why do you think the speaker chose to use the present perfect tense instead of simple past tense in these sentences?
- How is the past action related to the present: by time relationship, by present result, or by a combination of both?

1. Scientists have discovered a number of interesting similarities between the atmosphere on Earth and on Titan, one of the moons of Jupiter. They have found significant concentrations of water vapor and other chemicals common on Earth. As a result, they are hoping to send another space probe to the planet later this year.

2. If I have told you once, I've told you a hundred times: I hate broccoli!

3. Guess what? We've been invited to Liz's wedding. What should we get her for a gift?

4. Conservative politicians have often stated that welfare payments to poor families do not help reduce long-term poverty, but recent statistics show that this may not be true.

5. Shakespeare's reputation as a psychologist has grown in recent years. His plays have always reflected a deep understanding of human motivations.

6. Has Jill found a summer job? I was talking with my aunt, and she said her office might need a temporary computer programmer.

▶ **Present Perfect Progressive Tense**

EXAMPLES	EXPLANATIONS
(a) He **has been living** with his parents, but he hopes to move out now that he has found a job. **(temporary)** **(b)** He **has lived** with his parents since he dropped out of college. **(permanent)**	Use the present perfect progressive tense (*have/has been* + verb + *-ing*) instead of present perfect to describe something that is: • temporary rather than permanent
(c) I **have been talking** to everyone about the problem, but I don't have a solution. Do you have any ideas? **(repeated occurrence)** **(d)** I **have thought** about the problem, and I have a solution. **(single occurrence)**	• repeated rather than a single occurrence
(e) It **has been snowing constantly** for the last three hours. I hope it stops soon! **(continuous)** **(f)** It **has snowed several times** since we got here, but there's still not enough snow for skiing. **(repeated)**	• continuous rather than repeated or recurring
(g) I **have been writing** my term paper. I still have to proofread it and staple it together. **(uncompleted)** **(h)** I **have written** my term paper Let's go celebrate! **(completed)**	• uncompleted rather than completed
(i) Living in foreign countries **has required** a lot of flexibility. **(j)** NOT: Living in foreign countries **has been requiring** a lot of flexibility.	Remember that nonprogressive verbs do not occur with the progressive aspect even when they refer to continuous states.

EXERCISE 7

Choose the correct form, present perfect or present perfect progressive, for the verbs. More than one answer may be possible.

1. I (a) _____ (read) about the development of early forms of photography, and I (b) _____ (learn) some very interesting facts about it. I would like to continue my research next semester.

2. That baby _____ (cry) constantly since we got here. I wish its parents would do something to make it be quiet!

3. Bob's brother _____ (resent) his winning that free trip to Hawaii ever since he heard the news.

4. I _____ (try) to explain that for ten minutes. Aren't you listening?

5. I _____ (try) to explain that every way I know how. I give up!

6. I _____ (work) on this problem all afternoon. It's time for a break.

7. Rebecca _____ (expect) the police to call about the accident. That's why she wants to stay home this afternoon.

8. Bob _____ (tell) the office that he doesn't want to take a summer job until after he returns from Hawaii.

9. The newspaper (a) _____ (try) to contact Bob about some contest. They (b) _____ (call) at least five or six times.

10. Bob (a) _____ (dream) about visiting Hawaii ever since he read a book about volcanoes. He (b) _____ (become) an expert on them.

EXERCISE 8

Decide whether the verbs in parentheses should use simple present, present progressive, present perfect, present perfect progressive, or the past tense. More than one answer may be correct.

Bambang Soetomo (1) _____ (speak) English quite fluently. I wonder where he (2) _____ (learn) it. He (3) _____ (study) mechanical engineering. He (4) _____ (plan) to go to graduate school once he (5) _____ (get) his B.S. degree. Bambang (6) _____ (live) by himself for the last few months. But he (7) _____ (think) about getting a roommate. He (8) _____ (miss) his friends back home a great deal, and this (9) _____ (affect) his studies. He (10) _____ (hope) that his father will let him come home during the summer, but his father (11) _____ (not decide) yet.

Use Your English

ACTIVITY 1: WRITING

Use the ideas you developed in the Opening Task on page 230 to write a personal essay like the one required for the application to the North American Institute of International Studies.

ACTIVITY 2: READING/SPEAKING

Bring in the front page of a daily newspaper and examine the articles with a partner or in a group. Find examples of sentences written in present time and past time. In what tense are headlines usually written? In what tense are the introductory paragraphs usually written? In what tense is the main part of the article generally written? Can you find a pattern? Why do you think the author chose one time frame rather than another? Discuss your ideas with your partner or group, and present them to the rest of the class.

ACTIVITY 3: SPEAKING

Experts in cross-cultural communication have found that most North Americans tend to believe that most changes in life result in improvement. This is not necessarily true in other cultures.

STEP 1 Find out what important changes your classmates have made in their lives. Interview three other classmates. Ask them the following questions:

- Have you changed any habits or routines recently?
- Describe the changes.
- Why have you made the changes?
- How have the changes affected you?

STEP 2 Based on the changes your group has experienced, decide whether you agree that changes in life are generally for the better. Present your group's ideas and reasons to the rest of the class.

ACTIVITY 4: SPEAKING

Experts in cross-cultural communication have found that North American culture tends to value individualism. As a result, many young children are taught to look for ways that they are different from other people. Most Americans can easily identify several personal experiences and characteristics that make them unique. What about people from other cultures?

STEP 1 Interview three or four people from various cultures and ask them these questions:

- What experiences have you had that most other people haven't?
- What things make you different from most other people?

STEP 2 Of the people you interviewed, who was able to think of the greatest number of individual differences?

ACTIVITY 5: SPEAKING

How do North Americans, as a group, compare to the students you interviewed for Activity 3 and 4?

STEP 1 Work with three other students. Two of you should interview three or four North Americans, asking the questions that you used for Activity 3. The second pair should ask the questions you used for Activity 4.

STEP 2 Compare the responses of the North Americans to the responses of the students you interviewed in those activities.

STEP 3 Discuss these questions with your group and summarize your ideas for the rest of the class.

- Were there differences between the answers given by North Americans and those of your classmates?
- Were North Americans able to identify their individual differences more readily than people from other cultures?
- Did North Americans feel differently about change than people from other cultures?
- What do the similarities and differences between the answers of various cultural groups tell you about cultural differences?

ACTIVITY 6: LISTENING/ SPEAKING

Which of these two people is most qualified to be accepted for admission to the North American Institute of International Studies?

STEP 1 Listen to the interviews with each candidate. Using the chart below, identify what the candidates say about their most important accomplishment, their background and experience, and their special abilities.

INTERVIEW QUESTIONS	CANDIDATE 1 NAME: _____ PROGRAM:	CANDIDATE 2 NAME: _____ PROGRAM:
What makes you different from other candidates?		
What relevant experience do you have?		
What is an achievement that you're proud of?		

STEP 2 Compare your chart with another student's, and listen to the interviews a second time to make sure you have heard all the important information.

STEP 3 You and your partner should decide which student is a better candidate for admission. Tell your choice and your reasons to the rest of the class.

UNIT 15

FUTURE TIME

Using Present Tenses, Using *Will* Versus *Be Going To* Versus *Shall* ; Adverbial Clauses in Future

UNIT GOALS:

- To understand and use different verb tenses to express actions and states in future time
- To correctly use, *will, be going to* and *shall* and other modals to express future time
- To correctly express future time in adverbial clauses

▶ OPENING TASK
Thinking About the Future

244

STEP 1 Write a short paragraph about the following question: **Do you think that life one hundred years from now will be better or worse than it is today? Why?** You can mention some of the current trends and issues listed below.

POSITIVE TRENDS	NEGATIVE TRENDS
Technological improvements, new medical treatments, longer life spans, better food crops, political changes, better communication, more rapid transportation, equal status for women, more education	Environmental problems (pollution, acid rain, global warming), population increase, new diseases, increased traffic, increasing government debt, changing family structures, decreasing natural resources, increasing economic inequality

STEP 2 Exchange paragraphs with a partner, and decide which one of you is more of an optimist (someone who generally expects good things to happen) and which one is more of a pessimist (someone who generally expects bad things to happen) about the future of the world.

STEP 3 Report your decision and some of the reasons to the rest of the class.

► # **R**ecognizing Future Time

We use simple present, present progressive, and modals to talk about future time.

EXAMPLES	EXPLANATIONS
(a) Luis **leaves** for work at 7:00 every day.	Simple present can describe present time.
(b) John **leaves** for Europe in three weeks.	It can also describe future time.
(c) Luis is **having** problems with his car, so he's taking the bus to work this week.	Present progressive can describe present time.
(d) We're **having** a test next Tuesday.	It can also describe future time.
(e) There's someone at the door. It **should** be Mehmet.	Modals can describe present time.
(f) When I am fifty years old, I **will have** a big party.	They can also describe future time.

EXERCISE 1

Do the verbs in these passages refer to future time or present time? Underline the verb phrases. Mark verb phrases that refer to future time with (F). Mark verb phrases that refer to present time with (P). The first sentence of each passage has been done for you as examples.

(P)

1. (a) School always <u>begins</u> in September in the United States. (b) This coming year, school begins on September 12. (c) Janet's going to start her third year of high school. (d) She's taking chemistry, history, English, and advanced algebra. (e) She might take a theater class, if she can fit it into her schedule.

(F)

2. (a) We<u>'re having</u> a class picnic in just a couple of weeks. (b) As you know, school ends on June 15, and the picnic will be on the next day, so we're already making plans. (c) Most people are being really cooperative. (d) For example, Lucia makes great potato salad, so she's bringing some to the picnic. (e) There should be enough for everyone to have some. (f) But George is being difficult. (g) He says he will come, but he won't bring anything. (h) Will you explain something to me? (i) Will you tell me why George is so stubborn? (j) He really should be more cooperative. (k) Everyone else is bringing something. (l) Why won't he?

USE

Present Tenses for Future Planned Events

EXAMPLES	EXPLANATIONS
(a) My birthday **comes** on a Sunday next year. (b) John**'s leaving** for France in a week (c) Next year **is** my parent's fiftieth anniversary.	Use simple present and present progressive tenses to describe future activities that are **already scheduled or planned** to take place in the future.
(d) We **will** go shopping if they have a big Spring Sale. (e) There **might** be a surprise quiz on Friday.	For future events that are **not already scheduled,** use *will* or other modals of prediction (*may, could, might*).

EXERCISE 2

Make at least five questions about things that will happen in this class at a future time and have already been scheduled. Ask your questions to another student.

▶ **EXAMPLE:** *When are we having our next grammar test?*

EXERCISE 3

Choose the best tense (present, present progressive, or a modal of prediction) for the verbs in the following sentences. Both forms may be grammatically correct, so be prepared to explain your choice.

▶ **EXAMPLE:** John *'s leaving*_____ (leave) for France in a week.

1. The boat _____ (sail) at dawn. Don't be late.
2. Filipe _____ (have) a party on Friday. Have you been invited?
3. John doesn't know when he _____ (return) from France.
4. Peter is hoping that Denise _____ (stop) demanding that everyone work so hard.
5. Marta's birthday _____ (be) Friday, so we'd better buy her a gift.
6. Perhaps there _____ (be) a test next Friday.
7. There definitely _____ (be) a test next Friday.
8. I _____ (graduate) next June.

▶ *Will* Versus *Be Going To*

Will

EXAMPLES	EXPLANATIONS
(a) I'm having trouble with my homework. **Will** you help me?	Use *will:* • for requests
(b) I need some milk from the store. Oh, **I'll** get it for you. **(c)** Denise **won't go** with us, no matter how much we ask her.	• to express willingness or unwillingness
(d) I'm sorry I forgot the book. **I'll bring** it tomorrow, I promise.	• to make a promise
(e) Plants **will die** if they don't get enough water.	• to express general truths

Be Going To

EXAMPLES	EXPLANATIONS
(f) **I'm going to go** to the party, whether you're there or not.	Use *be going to:* • to talk about intentions
(g) We shouldn't go hiking this afternoon. It**'s going to** rain any minute!	• to talk about the immediate future
(h) Are you going to Marta's party? I can't. I **am going to be** out of town that weekend.	• to talk about plans that have been made earlier

Will and *Be Going To*

EXAMPLES	EXPLANATIONS
(i) The weather **will be** fine for Reiko's wedding, and everyone**'s going to have** a wonderful time!	Use *will* and *be going to* to make predictions. When *be going to* is pronounced *"gonna"*, it is usually more informal than *will*.
(j) **I'm going to paint** my apartment. First, **I'll get** the paint and some brushes. Then **I'll get** to work. I **might** paint the walls green, but I haven't decided yet.	*Be going to* usually introduces a topic. Following sentences often use *will* and other one-word modals.

EXERCISE 4

Decide which form, *will* or *be going to,* should be used in the following sentences. In some cases both answers may be correct.

1. I've got an extra ticket to the opera. (a) _____ (you go) with me? It (b) _____ (be) a great performance. Pavarotti (c) _____ (sing) the part of Falstaff. I'm sure he (d) _____ (be) wonderful.

2. I don't know what to do for my vacation. Maybe I (a) _____ (go) to Mexico. I know the plane ticket (b) _____ (be) expensive. Perhaps I (c) _____ (take) the bus to save some money. Your brother's taken the bus before, hasn't he? (d) _____ (you ask) him how the trip was?

3. Lin (a) _____ (finish) her assignment tonight, even if she has to stay up until dawn. It (b) _____ (not be) easy. She has to finish reading *War and Peace,* and then write a ten-page paper. She (c) _____ (probably be) up all night. Maybe her roommate (d) _____ (make) some coffee for her and do the dishes, so that Lin (e) _____ (not have) to worry about anything else.

4. Different plants need different amounts of water. Too much water (a) _____ (kill) certain kinds of plants. Other kinds require daily watering, and they (b) _____ (die) if they don't get it. Setting out a garden (c) _____ (require) some advanced planning to make sure that plants with similar water requirements (d) _____ (be) planted in the same areas.

▶ **U**sing *Shall*

EXAMPLES	EXPLANATIONS
(a) I'll go to the store. (b) (?) I **shall** go to the store. (c) I **won't** do it. (d) (?) I **shan't** go.	*Shall* is not usually used in American English. Using *shall* to talk about future actions sounds quite formal and old fashioned to Americans. The negative contracted form (*shan't*) is almost never used.
(e) **Shall** I peel you a grape? (f) **Should** I answer the phone? (g) **May** I help you?	Use *shall*: • To make offers *Should* or *may* are often used in this context.
(h) **Shall** we dance? (i) **Shall** we begin with the first exercise? (j) **Let's go out** for dinner.	• To suggest activities that both speaker and listener will participate in. *Let's* is less formal and more common.

EXERCISE 5

Decide whether *will, be going to,* or *shall* is a better form to use in these sentences.

1. _____ we go to a movie tonight?

2. When _____ you graduate?

3. _____ I tell you the answer to the question?

4. He _____ not do it, even though his mother wants him to.

5. Water _____ not flow uphill.

Other Modals in Future Time

Modals (*will, should, may, might, could*) that describe future events also tell about the **probability** of the event. See Unit 16 for more information and practice with predictions about future events.

EXAMPLES	MEANING	FORM
(a) We **will** arrive in an hour.	**certain** 100% probability	*will*
(b) Aunt Emily **should** like this movie.	**probable** 65%–80% probability	*should*
(c) I **may** be a little late to the meeting, because I **may not** be able to find a taxi at that hour.	**quite possible** 35%–65% probability	*may* *may not*
(d) Peter **might** know the answer, but he **might not** be in his office right now. **(e)** It **could** rain before we get there.	**somewhat possible** 5%–35% probability	*might* *might not* *could*
(f) I **won't** be at the concert next week.	**certain** 0% probability	*will not*

EXERCISE 6

Use a modal to give your opinion about the following questions. Give a reason.

▶ **EXAMPLE:** What will life be like one hundred years from now?

> *Life should be more complex one hundred years from now, because of so many technological developments.*

1. Will there be enough coal and oil?
2. Will there be a decrease in air pollution?
3. Will the overall climate grow warmer?
4. Will the rate of population growth be greater?
5. Will there be increased use of automobiles?
6. Will there be political stability?
7. Will there still be large differences between developing and developed countries?
8. Will there be cures for cancer, AIDS, and other diseases?

9. What will be the problems that people face in the twenty-first century?

10. Will there still be wars between countries?

Make up three questions of your own and ask them to a partner. Compare your ideas about the future to those of your partner. Who is more optimistic about the future?

▶ Future-Time Adverbial Clauses

In future time, adverbial clauses always use present tenses, and not modal auxiliaries.

(a) I'll do it tomorrow, **when I finish school.**	**(b)** NOT: I'll do it tomorrow, **when I will finish school.**
(c) I'm going to watch TV **as soon as I have finished my homework.**	**(d)** NOT: I'm going to watch TV **as soon as I will have finished** my homework.
(e) Hani is planning to have party **while his parents are visiting relatives in Canada.**	**(f)** NOT: Hani's planning to have a party while his parents **will be visiting relatives in Canada.**

EXERCISE 7

Join the second sentence in each of these pairs to the first sentence using the linking word in parentheses. Make sure to change nouns to pronouns where necessary.

▶ **EXAMPLE:** I'll go to the movies. I will finish my homework. (after)

> I'll *go the movies after I finish my homework.*

1. All my friends will be relieved. The semester will end in a couple of weeks. (when)

2. I'm going to go to the movies every day. I will have finished all the household chores that have been postponed all semester. (after)

3. It will be almost three weeks after the last day of class. Lin will finally get her research paper completed. (by the time)

4. I'm going to read that novel. I'll have some time after the exams. (when)

5. Bob's going to spend every day at the beach. The weather will be sunny. (while)

6. Matt and Jeff will be really tired. They are going to finish their ten-mile hike from the beach. (by the time)

7. Mark and Ann are leaving for Europe. They'll finish their last exam. (as soon as)

8. Doug and Elena are going to get married. They will be on vacation in Mexico. (while)

9. Even our teacher's going to take some time off. She will have finished grading the final papers and correcting the exams. (when)

Use Your English

ACTIVITY 1: SPEAKING/WRITING

What day and time is it at this moment? Imagine what you will be doing **at this exact moment** ten years from now twenty years from now, fifty years from now. Describe these activities to a partner of write a brief essay about them.

ACTIVITY 2: SPEAKING

STEP 1 Tell several other students about your vacation plans. Listen to their plans.

STEP 2 Then answer these questions as a group.

- Whose plans sound like the most fun? Why?
- Whose plans sound like the most boring? Why?
- Whose plans sound like the easiest to arrange? Why?
- Whose plans sound like the best opportunity to practice English?

Decide on one additional category of your own.

STEP 3 Report your answers to the rest of the class.

ACTIVITY 3: WRITING

Choose one of these three questions and write a paragraph or make a presentation expressing your ideas.

- What major **political and economic changes** are going to take place in your lifetime? Describe them and explain why you think they are going to happen.
- What major **social changes** are going to take place in your lifetime? Describe them and explain why you think they are going to happen.
- What major **scientific advances** are going to take place in your lifetime? Describe them and explain why you think they are going to happen.

ACTIVITY 4: LISTENING/SPEAKING

STEP 1 Listen to these two speakers talk about the future. As you listen, note the speaker's predictions and the reasons for those predictions in the chart below. Based on those predictions and reasons, decide whether the speaker is optimistic or pessimistic about the future.

Speaker 1

Optimistic or Pessimistic?	Speaker's Prediction	Speaker's Reasons
public health and population		
life expectancy and nutrition		
energy and pollution		
political and economic stability		

Speaker 2

Optimistic or Pessimistic?	Speaker's Prediction	Speaker's Reasons
public health and population		
life expectancy and nutrition		
energy and pollution		
political and economic stability		

STEP 2 Imagine that you are one of the speakers. Using the notes you took above, try to give a speech in your own words to a partner explaining why you are optimistic or pessimistic about the future. Your partner should do the same with the other speech. If you wish, add some ideas and reasons of your own.

ACTIVITY 5: SPEAKING

Organize a debate between optimists and pessimists.

STEP 1 Using the Opening Task on page 245, decide whether you are an optimist or a pessimist. Form groups of four or more. Try to have an equal number of optimists and pessimists in each group.

STEP 2 As a group, choose one category of world affairs (see Opening Task for examples). Discuss the current trends related to that category. Add one or two significant additional trends of your own. Optimists will then give reasons why they think the world will be better one hundred years from now. Pessimists will give reasons why they think the world will be worse one hundred years from now.

STEP 3 Present both sets of predictions to the other groups. As a whole class, decide who has presented the most persuasive reasons, the optimists or the pessimists.

MODALS OF PREDICTION AND INFERENCE

UNIT GOALS:

- To understand and use different modals to express predictions in future time
- To understand and use different modals to express logical inferences in present time
- To correctly express predictions and logical inferences in past time

▶ **O P E N I N G   T A S K**

Solving a Mystery

MYSTERY #1

A man lives on the fortieth floor of a very tall building. Every day he rides the elevator down to the ground floor. When he comes home he rides the elevator to the twentieth floor, but he has to walk the rest of the way.

Why does he do this?

MYSTERY #2

In a room, a dead woman is hanging by a rope, more than three feet above the floor. There are no windows, and the door has been locked from the inside. The room is empty: no furniture, no ladder. The only thing in the room is a single piece of paper.

What happened to the woman?

MYSTERY #3

A police officer receives an emergency phone call about a terrible automobile accident. A boy and his father have both been very badly injured. The officer has to fill out the report and figure out what happened. The police officer takes one look at the boy and his father, and says "You'll have to find someone else to deal with this. I'm too upset. This boy is my son!"

How can the boy have two fathers?

STEP 1 Work with a partner. Choose one of the mini-mysteries above to try to solve.

STEP 2 Think of five possible explanations. Decide which ones are likely and which ones are not very likely.

STEP 3 Turn to page A-12 and read the additional clues. Then try to solve the mysteries.

▶ **Modals of Prediction**

Modals of prediction refer to future time. Use them to indicate how likely or possible it is that some future event will happen. (See Focus 3 for information about making predictions in the past time frame.)

EXAMPLES	FORM	MEANING/USE
(a) We **will** leave in an hour.	*will*	It will **certainly** happen. We can also use simple present or present progressive to describe these events.
(b) We **should** be able to get a good price for Andy's car.	*should*	It is **likely** to happen. Using *should* for predictions sometimes sounds like advisability. If you aren't sure, use *will probably* to make your meaning clear.
(c) They **will probably** be here in a couple of hours.	*probably will*	
(d) I **may** be late tonight.	*may*	It will **possibly** happen.
(e) You'd better take an umbrella. It **could/might** rain tonight.	*might* *could*	
(f) We **may not** have to wait.	*may not*	It will **possibly not** happen.
(g) We **might not** get there in time.	*might not*	
(h) This **shouldn't** hurt.	*shouldn't*	It is **not likely** that this will happen. Using *shouldn't* for predictions sometimes sounds like advisability. If you aren't sure, use *probably won't* to make your meaning clear.
(i) This **probably won't** take too long.	*probably won't*	
(j) We **won't** leave before Tuesday.	*won't*	It will **certainly not** happen.

EXAMPLES	EXPLANATION
(k) **Will** they be here by 5:00? Mary **should be** on time, but John **might** be a little late.	To ask for predictions about future events, use only *will*, not other modal forms.

EXERCISE 1

Make sentences from these cues using modals.

▶ **EXAMPLE:**   certain: Andy/drive to New York for a vacation.

Andy will drive to New York for a vacation

1. likely: Andy/decide what to do about his car next week.
2. certainly not: The car/work well enough for his trip to New York.
3. possible: Andy/get it repaired, if it can be done cheaply.
4. not likely: He/have trouble selling it.
5. likely: He/be able to get a good price.
6. possible: Andy's friend Paul/want to buy it.
7. possibly not: Andy/sell the car to Paul.
8. possibly not: The car/be in very good condition.
9. possible: Paul/expect a refund if he has troubles with the car.
10. certain: Andy/need the money to buy a plane ticket if he doesn't drive.

EXERCISE 2

How likely is it that you will be doing the following activities next Saturday night at 8:00 P.M.?

doing English homework	taking a bath
watching TV	speaking another language
thinking about personal problems	sleeping
sitting in a movie theater	writing letters to my family
reading a magazine	having a good time with friends

Work with a partner. Ask questions with *will*. Answer questions with the appropriate modal of prediction.

▶ **EXAMPLES:**   At 8:00 P.M. next Saturday do you think you will be doing English homework?

I won't be doing homework on a Saturday night. I might be at a party.

EXERCISE 3

Write twelve true sentences about your plans for your next vacation using modals of prediction.

two things that you will certainly do

_____

two things that you will likely do

_____

two things that you will possibly do

_____

two things that you possibly won't do

_____

two things that you won't likely do

_____

two things that you certainly won't do

_____

EXERCISE 4

Write twelve sentences about how you think life will be at the end of the next century using modals of prediction.

two things that will certainly be true

_____

two things that will likely be true

_____

two things that will possibly be true

_____

two things that possibly won't be true

_____

two things that won't likely be true

_____

two things that certainly won't be true

_____

▶ Modals of Inference

Modals of inference refer to the present time frame. Use them to express a logical conclusion, based on evidence. (See Focus 3 for information about making inferences in the past time frame.)

EXAMPLES	FORM	MEANING
(a) That **must** be John. I've been expecting him.	*must*	There is no other possible conclusion from the evidence.
(b) John **should** be here somewhere. He said he was coming.	*should*	This is a logical conclusion, based on the evidence we have, but it is possible that there is another conclusion.
(c) She **may** be unhappy.	*may*	This is one of several possibilities.
(d) They **might** have some problems.	*might*	
(e) John **could** be here.	*could*	
(f) She **may not** be here. I don't see her anywhere.	*may not*	This is one of several possibilities.
(g) We'd better turn down the music. The neighbors **might not** like rap.	*might not*	
(h) They **shouldn't** arrive for several more hours. There's a delay at the airport.	*shouldn't*	This is not a logical conclusion, based on the evidence we have, but it could be possible.
(i) I've looked everywhere for Mary. She **must not** be here.	*must not*	This is not a possible conclusion, based on the evidence we have.
(j) That **couldn't** be John. I know he's still out of town.	*couldn't*	This is impossible.
(k) He **can't** be in two places at the same time.	*can't*	

EXERCISE 5

Make logical conclusions by filling in the blanks with an appropriate modal of inference. Decide whether the logical conclusion you express is:

- the only one possible (*must*) or impossible (*must not/can't/couldn't*),
- more likely than other possible conclusions (*should*) or less likely (*shouldn't*),
- or one of several possibilities (*could/may/might/may not/might not*).

There may be more than one correct answer, so be prepared to explain why you chose the form you did.

1. There's someone at the door. That (a) _____ be my brother; I've been expecting him. But it (b) _____ be the postal carrier, or it (c) _____ even be a salesperson.

2. Someone is ringing the doorbell. It (a) _____ be my brother; he has a key. It (b) _____ be the postal carrier; he doesn't usually ring the bell. It (c) _____ be a friend; all my friends think I'm still in New York. It (d) _____ be a salesperson. Let's not answer it!

3. I hope I can go to the movies with you tonight, but I (a) _____ (not) have enough money. I (b) _____ have enough, because I cashed a check yesterday. But I won't be 100% sure until I buy groceries and see how much money I have left. I really hope I can go. Everyone who has seen that movie says it's really good. It (c) _____ be very funny.

4. Martha looks pretty unhappy. She and George (a) _____ be having another one of their fights. I don't know what the problem is this time. It (b) _____ be because George is always working on his car. It (c) _____ be because Martha wants them to spend every weekend at her mother's house. It (d) _____ (not) be about money, though. That's the fight they had last week. They (e) _____ (not) have a very happy marriage.

5. Where have I put my wallet? It (a) _____ be somewhere! It (b) _____ just disappear by itself. It (c) _____ be on my desk, since that's where I usually put it. But it (d) _____ be in my briefcase, too. I sometimes forget to

take it out when I get home.

6. Naomi (a) _____ (not) need money. She's always eager to pay when we go out for a night on the town. She never seems to have a job. It (b) _____ be nice to have enough money without having to work.

7. Frank (a) _____ have no trouble finding a job when he moves to California. It (b) _____ take a while, but I know he'll find a good position. He seems unhappy in New York. He (c) _____ (not) like living there very much.

EXERCISE 6

Decide whether the following sentences are predictions or inferences and choose an appropriate modal. Compare your choices with a partner's.

▶ **EXAMPLES:** It _shouldn't_ (not) be very difficult to find a parking place today, because it's Sunday, and usually there aren't many people downtown.

Jack _must not_ (not) have much money, because he drives a fifteen-year-old car.

1. Traffic is getting heavy; rush hour _____ be starting.

2. Commuters _____ be getting really tired of driving to work in such awful traffic.

3. Experts tell us that traffic _____ get worse every year unless we do something about the problem.

4. Some people think that traffic _____ flow more smoothly if we increase the number of highways.

5. But most experts feel that the problem _____ (not) be solved by building more highways.

6. That _____ just increase the number of cars on the roads.

7. The traffic problem _____ begin to improve, once we have increased public transportation.

8. This city _____ (not) have a very efficient public transportation system, because people seem to drive everywhere.

Modals of Prediction and Inference in Past Time

You can make predictions and inferences about things that happened in the past time frame by using **perfect modals.**

MODAL + *HAVE* + PAST PARTICIPLE

| Alice | might | have | | seen | | that movie. |

MODAL	EXAMPLES WITH PRESENT/FUTURE TIME	EXAMPLES WITH PAST TIME
must	**(a)** That **must be** John. I've been expecting him.	**(b)** Who left this note? It **must have been** Stephanie.
should	**(c)** Peter **should be** here somewhere. He said he was coming.	**(d)** Let's ask Peter what happened at the meeting. He **should have been** there.
may *might* *could*	Why is Martha crying **(e)** She **may be** sad. **(g)** She **might be** having problems. **(i)** George **could be** the reason.	Why was Martha crying? **(f)** She **may have been** sad. **(h)** She **might have been** having problems. **(j)** George **could have been** the reason.
may not *might not*	**(k)** She **may not be** here. I haven't seen her yet. **(m)** She **might not get** invited to the party.	**(l)** She **may not have been** there. I didn't see her. **(n)** She **might not have gotten** an invitation to this party.
shouldn't	**(o)** They **shouldn't be** here until tomorrow morning.	**(p)** That **shouldn't have been** the reason why Ali didn't come.
must not	**(q)** I've looked everywhere for Mariko. She **must not be** here.	**(r)** They don't know what happened at the meeting. They **must not have been** there.
couldn't *can't*	**(s)** That **couldn't be** John. I know he's still out of town. **(u)** We **can't take** a test on Friday! I'm not ready.	**(t)** You **couldn't have forgotten** my name. **(v)** I **can't have lost** it!

EXERCISE 7

Change this passage to the past time frame.

▶ **EXAMPLE:** Denise might not have enough time to finish the project today. That must be the reason why she isn't at the boss's birthday party.

> **Denise might not have had enough time to finish the project yesterday. That must have been the reason why she wasn't at the boss's birthday party.**

(1) Frank might change jobs. (2) He should have no trouble finding a new job. (3) It might take a while, but he has excellent qualifications and lots of experience. (4) He must be really unhappy to want to move to a brand new company. (5) He must not like working in such a big company very much.

EXERCISE 8

Write the appropriate modal form in the blank. There may be more than one correct answer.

1. Someone called me up in the middle of the night. They hung up before I could answer the phone. It (a) _____ (not be) my brother; he doesn't have a telephone. It (b) _____ (be) someone I know, but why would they call in the middle of the night? It (c) _____ (be) a wrong number.

2. Where were you last night? I thought you were going to join us at the movies. You (a) _____ (have) enough money to go with us, because the tickets weren't that expensive. It's too bad you didn't come. I (b) _____ (be) able to lend you the money. Or perhaps Peter (c) _____ (pay) for your ticket. He's so generous. The movie was really funny. You (d) _____ (be) disappointed to miss all the fun.

3. Janet looked really unhappy as she was leaving Professor Brown's office. She (a) _____ (failed) another exam. I know she's already failed one midterm, and she had two more last week. It (b) _____ (be) her chemistry test. I know she was really nervous about it. But it (c) _____ (be) her calculus exam. She's really good at mathematics, and I know she studied a lot for it.

4. Luis looked everywhere for the missing documents. They

(a) _____ (disappear) by themselves. He thought they

(b) _____ (be) on the desk, where he usually put things

he was working on, or they (c) _____ (be) in his brief-

case, too. But when he looked, they weren't in either place. Then he

remembered working on them at the office. He (d) _____

(leave) them there.

5. Who killed Judge Clarence? It (a) _____ (be) his wife.

She was in Switzerland learning how to ski. It (b) _____

(be) his accountant. Apparently there was some trouble with money.

But nobody thought his accountant would do such a thing. There

were a few clues. His wallet was missing. His brother's fingerprints

were found on the candlestick that was used to kill the judge. The

murderer (c) _____ (be) his brother. But Detective Nancy

Mann was not convinced. It all seemed too simple. The brother was

rich and didn't need the money. The murderer (d) _____

(be) someone else, someone who was actually trying to get the

brother in trouble with the law.

EXERCISE 9

Use modals of prediction and inference to give possible or probable reasons
for these situations.

▶ **EXAMPLES:**   The window was open. The TV was gone.

A thief must have broken into the apartment.

The students are quiet. They're listening carefully.

They might be taking a test.

The teacher could be telling them about their final examination.

1. The parents are laughing. They're looking at a picture.

2. Mary's waiting at the corner. She's looking at her watch.

3. Ahmad was smiling. A doctor was congratulating him.

4. The men were digging holes. They were looking at an old map.

5. A woman was crying. She had just received an envelope in the mail.

6. Denise stays late at the office every night. She tells her boss about it.

7. That man wears old clothes. He doesn't have enought to eat.

8. The police ran to their car. They drove quickly to the house.

Use Your English

ACTIVITY 1: WRITING

STEP 1 Watch a television program (comedy or drama) for a few minutes without turning on the sound. You should be able to see, but not to hear, what's going on.

STEP 2 Describe at least five interactions between characters. Describe exactly what happened, your interpretation of what happened, and your reasons for thinking so.

Description of What Happened— Who did what?	Interpretation of Action—What was the character's reason or purpose?	Reason for Your Interpretation— Why do you think so?
Example: One man kept poking the other man in the chest with his finger.	He was trying to start a fight.	The other man's expression became more and more angry.
Interaction 1		
Interaction 2		
Interaction 3		
Interaction 4		
Interaction 5		

STEP 3 Write a paragraph that describes what you saw and what you think was happening. Be sure to distinguish between things that **might** have been going on versus things that **must** have been going on. Give reasons for all of your interpretations.

ACTIVITY 2: SPEAKING/WRITING

Do you have friends or family living in another country? What time is it at this moment in that country? Talk or write about what you think they are doing at this moment.

ACTIVITY 3: SPEAKING

Look at these pictures of six household items that are no longer used today.

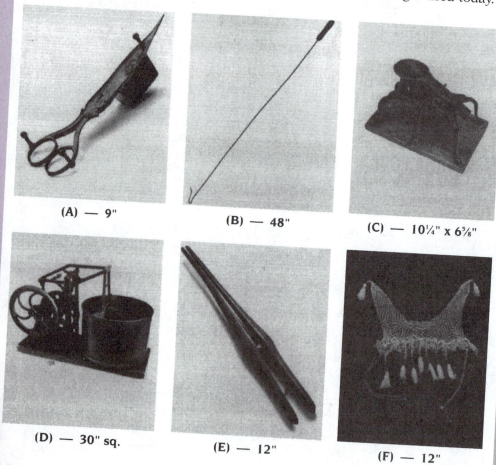

(A) — 9"

(B) — 48"

(C) — 10¼" x 6⅝"

(D) — 30" sq.

(E) — 12"

(F) — 12"

STEP 1 Work with a partner and discuss what you think each object might have been used for. Give reasons.

STEP 2 Compare your ideas with those of other students in the class. See page A-12 for answers.

ACTIVITY 4: SPEAKING

Do you know how to predict people's future by looking at their palms? Here is a diagram of some of the important "lines" of the palm. If the line is deep and strong, the person should have favorable developments in those areas. If the line is weak or broken, this indicates that the person may have trouble in that area. Using this reference guide, choose a partner examine his or her palm and make predictions about his or her future. Try to make at least two predictions about what will happen to your partner in the future and two inferences about his or her character or personality.

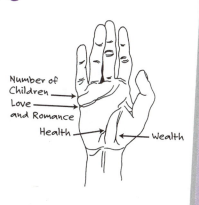

Number of Children
Love and Romance
Health
Wealth

ACTIVITY 5: LISTENING/SPEAKING

STEP 1 Listen to this conversation about a mystery. Decide whether each person listed below is a possible suspect, a probable suspect, or not a possible suspect.

Suspect	Likelihood of Guilt	Evidence
Mom	could not be guilty	she discovered the cookies were missing
Dad		
Nancy		
Eric		
Diane		

STEP 2 Work with a partner to decide who the criminal is. Give reasons to support your decision.

THE THIEF MUST HAVE BEEN _____.

HYPOTHETICAL STATEMENTS

UNIT GOALS:

- To correctly identify and understand sentences describing hypothetical or contrary-to-fact situations
- To correctly form hypothetical and contrary-to-fact statements in present, future, and past time frames
- To recognize and use various hypothetical constructions

▶ OPENING TASK
Differences in Educational Values

STEP 1 What are some important differences between educational values in the United States and in other countries? Here is a list of possible ways that teachers and students might behave. Think about the result of these behaviors in the United States and in your own country. Use the chart below to organize your ideas.

Situation	Result in USA	Result in the country you come from
Teacher Behavior: sitting on a desk wearing jeans to school saying "I don't know" making a lot of jokes in class hitting a student making a mistake		
not giving students homework		
Student Behavior: coming late to class		
asking a question		
making jokes in class		
not doing homework		
copying another student's answers		
making a mistake		

STEP 2 Explain your ideas to a group of three or four other students. (For example: In the United States if a student came late to class, the teacher would probably be annoyed. In Indonesia if a teacher said "I don't know," the students might think she was a bad teacher.) Compare the differences between what is expected of teachers and students in the United States and in other countries. Decide on the one or two important differences between the United States' educational system and the systems of other countries you are familiar with.

▶ **O**verview of Hypothetical Meaning

There is an important difference between **hypothetical** and **actual** meaning.

HYPOTHETICAL STATEMENTS	IMPLIED ACTUAL MEANING	EXPLANATIONS.
(a) If I had a million dollars, I would buy a nice house.	I don't have amillion dollars, so I probably won't be able to buy a nice house.	Hypothetical statements describe conditions that aren't true or are impossible.
(b) If we were in Hawaii right now, we wouldn't have to study grammar. We could by lying on the beach.	We're not in Hawaii—we're in English class. We can't lie on the beach because we're studying grammar.	
(c) You should be happy with your life. If I were you, I wouldn't feel so sorry for myself!	You aren't happy with your life. I am not you, but I think you feel too sorry for yourself.	We use hypothetical statements to imply that the opposite situation is actually true.
(d) You could have done a better job on your homework. You should have avoided a lot of these careless mistakes.	You didn't do a very good job on your homework. You made a lot of careless mistakes.	

EXERCISE 1

Here are some more hypothetical statements. Choose the sentence that expresses their implied meaning:

1. If you had done your homework, you would have gotten an A.

   (a) You didn't get an A because you didn't do your homework.

   (b) You did your homework, so you got an A.

2. You could have brought a friend to the party.

   (a) You had permission, but you came alone.

   (b) You brought a friend.

3. You could have been more careful with your homework.
   (a) You did your homework carefully.
   (b) You were careless with your homework.
4. You should have seen the doctor before you got so sick.
   (a) You followed my advice.
   (b) You didn't follow my advice.
5. I would have been here early, but the traffic was terrible!
   (a) I arrived early.
   (b) I arrived late.
6. I wish you had come to the lake last weekend.
   (a) You didn't come.
   (b) You were there.
7. Let's pretend that we had a new president.
   (a) We don't have a new president.
   (b) We have a new president.

▶ **A**ctual Versus Hypothetical Conditionals

ACTUAL VERSUS HYPOTHETICAL CONDITIONALS	IMPLIED MEANING
Actual Conditional: **(a)** If I **have** time, I always **clean** the kitchen before I go to work.	I always clean the kitchen when I have time.
Hypothetical Conditional: **(b)** If I **had** time, I **would** always **clean** the kitchen before leaving for work.	I don't usually clean the kitchen because I usually don't have time.
Actual Conditional: **(c)** If I **don't have to work**, I **will come** to your party.	I don't know if I can come, because there's a chance that I may have to work.
Hypothetical Conditional: **(d)** If I **didn't have to work**, I **would come** to your party.	I can't come because I have to work.
Actual Conditional: **(e)** If Miko **was** at the lecture yesterday, I'm sure she **took** very complete notes.	Maybe she was at the lecture and took notes.
Hypothetical Conditional: **(f)** If Miko **had been** at the lecture, I'm sure she **would have taken** very complete notes.	She wasn't at the lecture, so she didn't take notes.

EXERCISE 2

Match the statements in column 1 with their correct implied meaning in column 2.

STATEMENT

1. If John has the money, he always stops for a cup of coffee on his way to class.

2. If John had the money, he would always stop for a cup of coffee on his way to class.

3. If I had to work, I wouldn't be helping you with your homework.

4. If I have to work, I won't be able to help you with your homework.

5. If Bambang took the TOEFL yesterday, I'm sure he did very well.

6. If Bambang had taken the TOEFL, I'm sure he would have done very well.

IMPLIED MEANING

(a) He doesn't usually do this, because he usually doesn't have the money.

(b) He always does this whenever he has the money.

(c) I may have to work.

(d) I don't have to work.

(e) Bambang didn't take the TOEFL.

(f) Maybe Bambang took the TOEFL.

EXERCISE 3

Are these sentences hypothetical statements or statements about actual events? If they are hypothetical statements, state the implied meaning.

▶ **EXAMPLES:** Those two are always together, so if she attended the meeting, he did, too. **statement about an actual event**

If the weather hadn't been so cold yesterday, the picnic would have been a lot more fun. **hypothetical statement. Implied meaning: The weather was cold yesterday, so the picnic wasn't much fun.**

1. I would come to your party if I didn't have to work.

2. If Juan went to Hawaii on vacation, he must have spent a lot of money.

3. If Nancy could afford to retire, I'm sure she would have done so by now.

4. I wouldn't tease that dog if I were you.

5. Suppose you had your own private jet. You could take me to Las Vegas for lunch.

6. If they left when they had planned, they should be here any minute.

7. If my brother needed money, he always asked to borrow it from me.

8. If I cook a big casserole for the party, do you think there'll be enough food?

Hypothetical Conditionals in Present and Future Time Frames

EXAMPLES		EXPLANATIONS
Conditions	Results	
(a) If I **had** time,	I **would** always **clean** the kitchen before leaving for work.	Use past-tense verb forms to describe present and future hypothetical conditions. Use *would/could/might* + verb to describe present and future results.
(b) If I **didn't have to work,**	I **would come** to your party.	
(c) If I **won** the lottery,	I **would give** you a million dollars.	
(d) If I already **spoke** English perfectly,	I **wouldn't need** to read this chapter.	
(e) If we **didn't have to go** to school tomorrow,	we **could stay up** all night tonight.	
(f) If John **didn't plan to spend** next year in France,	Mary **might not be** so annoyed with him now.	

Using *were* in hypothetical statements

EXAMPLES		EXPLANATIONS
(g) If my mother **were** here, she would want us all to wash our hands.	**(h)** If Mary **were** coming to the party, she could bring the potato salad.	*If* clauses in hypothetical conditionals use *were* (rather than *was*) for singular subjects in formal English. *Was* is often used in informal situations.

Inverted Hypotheticals

EXAMPLES		EXPLANATIONS
Inverted Form	**Regular Form**	
(i) **Were** I in charge of this business, I would make big changes.	**(j)** **If I were** in charge of this business, I would make big changes.	In formal English, in clauses with a *were* auxiliary, we can indicate hypothetical conditions by omitting *if* and using question word or inverted order.

EXERCISE 4

Change these statements of actual condition and result into hypothetical conditionals.

▶ **EXAMPLE:**   Actual: (Condition:) I'm not the teacher. (Result:) We have too much homework.

Hypothetical: **If I were the teacher, we wouldn't have so much homework.**

1. I don't have a million dollars. I can't afford to buy you a new car.

2. I don't yet speak English perfectly. I still have to study grammar.

3. Doctors have to spend so many years in medical school. Medical care is quite expensive.

4. My mother doesn't know how I am living now. She's not worried about me.

5. I am not president of my country. I don't have influence on world events.

6. I have many good friends. My life is busy and rewarding.

7. The TOEFL is a difficult examination. Many people can't pass it on the first try.

8. There aren't enough places in universities in other countries. Many students come to North America for university study.

EXERCISE 5

Here are some hypothetical conditions. Add hypothetical results that are true for you.

▶ **EXAMPLE:**   If I could be anywhere in the world at this moment, . . .

I would be home in bed.

1. If I were going to attend any American university tomorrow, . . .

2. If I were president of the United States, . . .

3. If my teacher knew how I was studying now, . . .

4. If I were the teacher of this class, . . .

5. If I didn't have to worry about the TOEFL, . . .

6. If I went home next week, . . .

7. If I had all the money I needed, . . .

8. If I were the same age as my parents, . . .

EXERCISE 6

Here are some hypothetical conditions. Add hypothetical results that are true for you.

▶ **EXAMPLE:** I would take a vacation . . .

if I didn't have to pass the TOEFL.

1. I wouldn't need to work . . .

2. I would bring my family here for a visit . . .

3. We wouldn't come to school . . .

4. We wouldn't need umbrellas . . .

5. I wouldn't be studying English . . .

6. I wouldn't have to take the TOEFL . . .

7. The world would be a much better place . . .

8. I would give my English teacher a thousand dollars . . .

EXERCISE 7

Work with a partner. Choose five sentences that your partner wrote for Exercises 5 and 6 and rewrite them in nonhypothetical language.

▶ **EXAMPLES:** If I had a million dollars, I would give you a new car.

My partner doesn't have enough money to give me a car.

I would take a vacation if I din't have to finish this project.

My partner has to finish this project, so she can't take a vacation.

My partner can't tke a vacation because she has to finish this project.

EXERCISE 8

Look over the sentences that you and your partner wrote in Exercises 5 and 6. Which sentences can be rewritten as inverted hypotheticals?

Hypothetical Conditionals in Past Time Frame

EXAMPLES		EXPLANATIONS
Conditions	Results	
(a) If Miko **had been** at the lecture,	I'm sure she **would have taken** very complete notes. She **wouldn't have minded** sharing them. She **would have let** you borrow them.	Use past-perfect verb forms to refer to past hypothetical conditions. Use *would have/could have/might have* + verb to refer to past hypothetical results.
(b) If William the Conqueror **hadn't invaded** England in 1066,	the English language **would probably have** many fewer words of French origin.	Use *would/could/ might* + verb to refer to present or future hypothetical results.
(c) If I **had been born** in 1890,	I surely **wouldn't be** alive today.	
(d) If we **hadn't saved** enough money last year,	we **wouldn't be able to take** a vacation next summer.	

Inverted Hypotheticals

EXAMPLES		EXPLANATION
INVERTED FORM	REGULAR FORM	
(e) **Had I known** that you were coming so late, I woun't have waited.	**(f)** **If I had known** that you were coming so late, I wouldn't have waited.	In formal English, in clauses with a *had* auxiliary, we can indicate hypothetical conditions by omitting *if* and using question word or inverted order.

EXERCISE 9

Do these sentences indicate statements of past possibility, or hypothetical events that did not actually happen?

▶ **EXAMPLES:** I didn't see him, but he could have been there. *past possibility*

If John had been at the concert, he would have been able to explain how the composer was able to get those effects. *hypothetical event.*

1. My brother could have loaned me the money, but he's too cheap.

2. Assuming that the plane was on time, it should have landed a little while ago.

3. I don't know what the problem is. They should have been here by now.

4. You should have asked for a receipt when you bought those clothes.

5. Tiffany might have worked a little harder on this report. It's pretty careless.

6. The thief might have gotten in through the window. It's unlocked.

EXERCISE 10

Change these nonhypothetical statements of condition and result to hypothetical conditionals.

▶ **EXAMPLE:** I wasn't alive one hundred years ago. I have been able to fly all over the world.

If I had been alive one hundred years ago, I wouldn't have been able to fly all over the world.

1. My parents didn't speak English when I was a baby. I have to learn it in school.

2. English became a language of international business after World War II. Most developing countries require students to study it in high school.

3. Modern English developed from several different languages: French, German, Latin, Dutch, and even Norwegian. As a result, the grammar and spelling rules are very irregular.

4. England was invaded by France in 1066. Many French words replaced the traditional Anglo-Saxon ones.

5. English society changed a great deal after the French invasion. Modern English grammar is more similar to French grammar than to German grammar.

EXERCISE 11

Complete these sentences with past-time hypothetical results that are true for you.

▶ **EXAMPLE:**   If I had been born one hundred years ago, . . .

   I wouldn't have had a chance to travel.

1. If my family had used English at home when I was growing up, . . .
2. If World War II had ended differently, . . .
3. If the grammar of English hadn't developed from so many different languages, . . .
4. If advanced computer technology hadn't been developed, . . .
5. If I had never studied English, . . .

EXERCISE 12

Add present or future time results to the following sentences.

▶ **EXAMPLES:**   If I had been born one hundred years ago, . . .

   I probably wouldn't be alive today.

   my great-grandchildren might be entering the univerity in the next few years.

1. If I had been born in this country, . . .
2. If World War II hadn't ended over fifty years ago, . . .
3. If my parents hadn't wanted me to learn English, . . .
4. If computers hadn't become so inexpensive and widely available, . . .
5. If I had already gotten a score of 650 on the TOEFL, . . .

EXERCISE 13

Here are hypothetical results. Add appropriate past-time conditions.

▶ **EXAMPLE:**   I wouldn't have had a chance to travel . . .

   if I had been born one hundred years ago.

1. I wouldn't have asked you to join us . . .
2. I would not be studying English now . . .
3. English grammar would be much more regular . . .
4. Fax machines wouldn't be so popular . . .

5. America wouldn't be spending so much money on the military . . .

6. Transoceanic telephone calls wouldn't be possible . . .

7. There wouldn't have been such major political changes in Eastern European countries . . .

8. Modern antibiotics might not have been discovered . . .

9. Life today would be much more difficult . . .

10. I wouldn't have to answer this question . . .

EXERCISE 14

Look over the sentences that you and your partner wrote in Exercises 11, 12, and 13. Choose five sentences to rewrite as inverted hypotheticals.

EXERCISE 15

Work with a partner. Choose five sentences that your partner wrote for Exercises 11, 12, and 13 and rewrite them in nonhypothetical language.

▶ **EXAMPLES:** I wouldn't have asked you to join us, if I had known you were going to be so rude.

I asked you to come because I thought you would be more polite.

If I had been born one hundred years ago, I wouldn't have had a chance to travel widely.

A hundred years ago people like me didn't have a chance to travel widely.

Mixing Hypothetical and Actual Statements

We sometimes mix actual conditions and hypothetical results.

ACTUAL CONDITION	HYPOTHETICAL RESULT
(a) I had to work last night.	**Otherwise** I would have come to your party.
(b) Peter brought a doctor's excuse to explain his absence.	**Otherwise** Denise would have accused him of being irresponsible.
(c) It's going to rain tomorrow.	**Otherwise** we could have the luncheon outside.

HYPOTHETICAL RESULT	ACTUAL CONDITION
(d) I would have come to your party last night,	**but** I had to work.
(e) Denise would have accused Peter of being irresponsible,	**but** he brought a doctor's excuse to explain his absence.
(f) We could have the luncheon outside,	**but** it's going to rain tomorrow.

EXERCISE 16

Here are some actual conditions. State a hypothetical result by using *otherwise* or *but*.

▶ **EXAMPLE:** I'm not rich.

I'm not rich. Otherwise I would loan you the money you asked for.

I would loan you the money you asked for, but I'm not rich.

1. I don't have a million dollars.
2. I don't yet speak English perfectly.
3. Doctors have to spend many years in medical school.
4. My mother doesn't know how I am living now.
5. My father is not the leader of my country.
6. I have many good friends.
7. Many students come to the United States for university study.
8. The weather forecaster has predicted heavy rain for tomorrow afternoon.

▶ # **U**sing Hypotheticals for Unlikely Possibility and for Sensitive Topics

Use hypothetical statements to indicate unlikely possibilities.

STATEMENT	IMPLIED MEANING
Likely Possibility (Nonhypothetical) (a) If we **get** some free time, we **can go** to the movies.	There is a strong possibility that we may get free time.
Unlikely Possibility (Hypothetical) (b) If we **got** some free time, this weekend, we **could go** to the movies. (c) If I **had** free time, I **would go** to the movies.	The possibility of free time is not strong, but we are discussing it anyway. There is no possibility of free time, but this is what would happen if there were a possibility.

Use hypothetical statements to discuss potentially "sensitive" topics more easily and diplomatically.

STATEMENT	IMPLIED MEANING	EXPLANATION
Nonhypothetical (d) **Will** you ever leave your husband?	I think you might do this.	
Hypothetical (e) **Would** you ever leave your husband?	This is not a real situation, just an example. I don't really think that you would do this.	Using hypothetical indicates that the speaker does not believe the listener would actually consider doing the thing being discussed.

EXERCISE 17

Decide whether these statements are likely or unlikely possibilities for you, then make a hypothetical or nonhypothetical sentence that reflects that.

▶ **EXAMPLE:**   marry someone from another country

(likely possibility)—something that might actually be possible for me

If I marry someone from another country, I will probably become a citizen of that country.

(unlikely possibility)—something that I don't think will ever be possible for me

If I married someone from another country, my parents would be very disappointed.

1. go to Las Vegas for the next vacation
2. pass the TOEFL the next time I take it
3. become president of your country
4. have eight children
5. buy a new car within the next three months
6. join the army
7. get sick later today
8. look for a new place to live
9. have free time before class tomorrow
10. win the lottery
11. be on television sometime in my life

Using Hypotheticals to Imply that the Opposite Is True

Use hypothetical statements to talk about things that didn't actually happen.

STATEMENT	IMPLIED MEANINGS
(a) You could have brought a friend.	You had permission, but you came alone.
(b) You could have been more careful with your homework.	You had the ability to be careful, but you didn't do it.
(c) You should have seen the doctor.	You didn't see the doctor.
(d) You might have cleaned the house before my mother got here.	The house was still dirty when she arrived.

EXERCISE 18

Restate these sentences in nonhypothetical language. Compare your answers with those of a partner.

▶ **EXAMPLE:** You should have been there.

You weren't there.

1. You shouldn't have gone to so much trouble!
2. We could have been seriously injured in that bus accident.
3. You might at least have invited her to the party.
4. You should be happy that I was able to come at all.
5. She wouldn't have gone even if she had been invited.

Using Hypotheticals with *Wish* and Verbs of Imagination

We use hypothetical statements with *wish* to talk about situations that are not true or not likely to become true.

STATEMENT	IMPLIED MEANING
(a) I **wish** you **had come** to the lake last weekend.	You didn't come.
(b) I **wish** you **liked** Chinese food.	You don't like it.
(c) I **wish** you **would come** to my party.	You refuse to come.

We use hypothetical statements with verbs that indicate imagination.

STATEMENT	IMPLIED MEANING
(d) **Let's imagine** that we **had** a new president.	We know this is not a real possibility.
(e) **Pretend** that you **could** fly. Do you think you **would** still own a car?	This is an impossible situation.
(f) **Suppose** we **went** to Europe next summer. How much do you think it **would** cost?	We are only talking about it now; we're not making an actual plan.

EXERCISE 19

Read the following paragraph. Underline the hypothetical statements. Rewrite the sentences using nonhypothetical language. The first hypothetical statement has been done for you as an example.

▶ **EXAMPLE:** (3) For example, Sir Isaac Newton decided to take a nap under an apple tree, and as a result he was hit on the head by a falling apple.

(1) Many important scientific developments have happened by accident. (2) Discoveries have often been made because someone was in the right place at the right time, or because someone made a mistake and got an unexpected result. (3) For example, <u>if Sir Isaac Newton hadn't decided to take a nap under an apple tree, he wouldn't have been hit on the head by a falling apple.</u> (4) It was this event that gave him the idea about the Law of Gravity. (5) If Sir Alexander Fleming hadn't left a sandwich on a windowsill of his laboratory and forgotten about it, he wouldn't have discovered the fungus or mold that contains penicillin. (6) Had Christopher Columbus correctly calculated the actual size of the earth, he would never have tried to reach Asia by sailing west. (7) If that hadn't happened, the European discovery of the New World might have occurred in 1592, instead of 1492.

Use Your English

ACTIVITY 1: SPEAKING

Should drugs be legalized?

STEP 1 Form a group with three other students in the class to discuss your opinions on these issues:

- What three things might happen if the government legalized the use of drugs?
- What three things might happen if drugs remained illegal?
- Should drugs be legalized? Why or why not?

STEP 2 Based on your discussion, your group should answer these two questions:

- What is the strongest reason in favor of legalization?
- What is the strongest reason against legalization?

Present these reasons to the rest of the class.

ACTIVITY 2: WRITING

Think about some things that you would have done differently if you had known then the things that you know now. Identify:

- Things you wish you had done that you didn't do. For example: *I wish I had studied harder when I was in high school.*
- Things you wish you hadn't done that you did do. For example: *I wish I hadn't spent all my time watching television instead of exercising.*

Write a short essay about this topic or make a presentation to the rest of the class.

ACTIVITY 3: WRITING/SPEAKING

If you could have three wishes, what would they be, and why would you wish for them?

STEP 1 Write down your three wishes.

STEP 2 Compare your answers to those of someone else in class. What do someone else's wishes tell you about his or her life? What do your wishes tell someone else about you?

STEP 3 Make one statement about why you think your partner made the wishes that he or she did. Tell that statement to your partner, but not to the rest of the class.

ACTIVITY 4: SPEAKING/WRITING

Suppose that you had just been made President of the Entire World. What actions would you take to:

- end world hunger
- develop renewable energy sources
- control population growth
- protect the environment
- abolish war
- ensure political stability
- maintain economic growth

Choose one of these areas and make a plan for things you would do if you had the power and resources to accomplish them. Report your plan to the rest of the class. The class will decide who they would like to choose as President of the Entire World.

ACTIVITY 5: WRITING/SPEAKING

Identify some things you would and wouldn't do for ten million dollars, and compare them to those of other people in class. Ideas to consider: Would you tell a lie? Would you betray a friend? Would you give a child up for adoption? Would you become a citizen of another country? Would you leave your family? What would you refuse to do, even if you were offered ten million dollars?

ACTIVITY 6: SPEAKING

STEP 1 Think about what you would do if you were faced with the following problems.

- Your parents don't approve of the person you want to marry.
- Your friend and you both work at the same company. You feel very loyal to the company, but you discover your friend has stolen some of the company's money.
- You have fallen in love with the husband or wife of your best friend.
- Your best friend needs to borrow some money "for a serious emergency"—but he won't say what that emergency is. You had been planning to use that money to buy a birthday present for your boyfriend or girlfriend. Your friend needs the money right away, and the birthday celebration is also today. You can't get any more money: only what you have now.

STEP 2 Discuss your solutions in a small group. Together decide on one or two suggestions for what people can do if they are faced with any kind of difficult problem.

ACTIVITY 7: LISTENING

Listen to the following conversation between Peter and Denise. Then choose the sentence that correctly describes the situations that they talked about.

1. (a) Peter didn't hear the announcement because he wasn't at the meeting.
   (b) He heard the announcement because he was at the meeting.
2. (a) The meeting wasn't important.
   (b) The meeting was important.
3. (a) Peter thinks Denise did good work.
   (b) He thinks she was careless.
4. (a) Peter finished the project in plenty of time.
   (b) He didn't finish it in plenty of time.
5. (a) Denise told Peter that she hadn't gone over the figures.
   (b) Denise didn't tell Peter that she hadn't gone over the figures.
6. (a) She didn't check the figures.
   (b) Maybe she checked the figures.
7. (a) There were many mistakes.
   (b) There weren't many mistakes.
8. (a) Denise said that she wanted to get Peter fired.
   (b) Denise said that she didn't want to get Peter fired.

ACTIVITY 8: WRITING

Write two to three paragraphs on the differences between what is expected of students in North America and students in another country with which you are familiar. Use your ideas from the Opening Task when they are appropriate.

SENSORY VERBS, CAUSATIVE VERBS, AND VERBS THAT TAKE SUBJUNCTIVE

UNIT GOALS:

- To correctly understand and use sentences with sensory verbs
- To correctly understand and use sentences with causative verbs
- To correctly understand and use sentences with verbs followed by subjunctive *that*-clauses

▶ **OPENING TASK**
Parenting Techniques

STEP 1 Think about the way your parents raised you. How did they reward your good behavior or punish your bad behavior? What kind of responsibilities did they give you? Complete the chart on the next page to identify some of the parenting techniques your parents used. Decide whether their techniques were effective, and whether you would use (or are using) them to raise your own children. Examples have been provided.

Parenting Techniques Your Parents Used	Effective? Yes/No	Would/Do You Use This Technique? Yes/No/Why
Discipline/Punishment 1. sent to my room	1. no	1. No. My children have toys in their rooms so it's not really an effective punishment.
2.	2.	2.
3.	3.	3.
Responsibilities 1. take care of younger sister	1. yes	1. Yes. It was good practice for being a parent myself.
2.	2.	2.
3.	3.	3.
Rewards/Motiviations 1. ice cream and candy	1. yes	1. No. I don't want to use food as a reward for good behavior.
2.	2.	2.
3.	3.	3.

STEP 2 Form a small group with three or four other students, and compare the information you have written in your charts. Based on your discussion, your group should make ten recommendations for parents.

Start five of them with **"Parents should . . ."**

Start five recommendations with **"Parents shouldn't . . ."**

STEP 3 Compare your group's recommendations to those of other groups. Compile a list of recommendations that the entire class agrees upon. Begin your recommendations with **"Good parenting requires that . . ."**

▶ **Overview**

The verbs that are dealt with in this unit are followed by simple verb forms or present participles that describe a second action.

TYPES OF VERBS	EXAMPLES
Sensory Verbs (*see, hear,* etc.)	**(a)** I **saw** the mother **spank** her child. **(b)** I **heard** the child **crying.**
Causative Verbs (*make, let,* etc.)	**(c)** My parents **made** me **go** to bed at 8:00 on school nights. **(d)** They **let** me **stay** up late on Fridays and Saturdays.
Subjunctive *That*-Clause Verbs (*demand, recommend,* etc.)	**(e)** Good parenting **demands that** parents **be** consistent with discipline. **(f)** Educators **recommend that** a parent **try** to explain the reasons for punishment to children.

EXERCISE 1

Underline the simple verb form or participle that follows the highlighted verbs in the following passage. The first one has been done for you as an example.

Ideas about the best way to raise children differ a great deal from culture to culture. In some cultures, if a mother **hears** her baby <u>crying</u>, she will immediately go to pick it up and **try** to **get** it to stop. But in other cultures people **insist** that a mother ignore her child, because they feel that if you don't **let** a baby cry, it will become spoiled. In some cultures, any adult who **sees** a child misbehaving will **make** the child stop, but other cultures **prefer** that only the parent be allowed to discipline a child. In some cultures, people **have** slightly older children **help** take care of their younger brothers and sisters, but in other cultures people rarely **let** children be responsible for their brothers and sisters unless they are at least twelve or thirteen years old.

In the United States, most parents prefer to **get** a child to behave by persuasion rather than force. You rarely **see** parents spank their children in public, and schools don't usually **let** teachers use physical punishment as discipline. Parents who are **seen** hitting their children may even be reported to the police. American child-care experts **recommend** that children be given responsibility from a relatively early age. As a result, many parents **let** their small children make their own decisions about what kind of clothes they want to wear, or what they want to eat. They prefer to **get** children to obey instead of **making** them obey.

► Sensory Verbs

EXAMPLES	EXPLANATIONS
(a) Mary **heard** us laughing. **(b)** I **saw** the dog jump into the water.	Sensory verbs use either a **present participle (verb + _ING_)** or the **simple form** of a verb to express the second action. Depending on which is chosen, the meaning differs.
(c) Bob heard the thieves **breaking** into the house, so he called the police. **(d)** I saw Mary **leaving** school, **so I ran to catch her.** **(e)** We saw the fireworks **going off** on New Year's Eve. **(f)** The police watched the demonstrators **overturning trucks** and **setting them** on fire.	Use a Present Participle to describe actions that are: in progress (c) unfinished (d) repeated (e & f)
(g) Bob saw the thieves **load** the TV into the car and **drive** away. **(h)** I saw Mary **leave** school, so **I'm sure she's not coming to the teachers' meeting.** **(i)** We saw the fireworks **go off** at midnight. **(j)** The police watched the demonstrators **overturn a truck** and set **it** on fire.	Use the simple form of a verb to describe actions that are completed (g & h) or happen just once (i & j)
(m) I saw the bicycle **lying** by the side of the road. **(n)** **NOT:** I saw the bicycle **lie** by the side of the road.	Use present participles with verbs of position (_lie, stand, sit_, etc.), if the thing that performs the second action cannot move by itself.
(o) We **caught** the thief **taking** money out of the cash register. **(p)** **NOT:** We caught the thief **take** money out of the cash register. **(q)** We **found** the security guard **sleeping** at his desk. **(r)** **NOT:** We found the security guard **sleep** at his desk.	Use present participles with verbs of interception (_find, catch, discover_, etc.), where the second action is interrupted or not completed.

EXERCISE 2

Answer these questions by using sensory verbs with a second action.

▶ **EXAMPLE:** What can you see at a disco?

You can see people dancing.

1. What can you hear at a concert?
2. What can you see at a skating rink?
3. What can you smell at a bakery?
4. What can you hear at the beach?
5. What can you see at a shopping mall?
6. What can you hear at a playground?
7. What can you hear in an English class?
8. What can you see at a gym?

EXERCISE 3

Restate the lettered sentences in these paragraphs as sensory verbs followed by a participle or simple form of a verb.

▶ **EXAMPLE:** Here is what Tom saw: (a) Three boys were swimming in the river. (b) They were splashing and playing. (c) One of them shouted that it was time to go. (d) They picked up their towels and left.

(a) *Tom saw three boys swimming in the river.* (b) *He watched them splashing and playing.* (c) *He heard one of them shout that it was time to go.* (d) *He watched them pick up their towels and leave.*

1. Here is what Doris observed: (a) A man came into the bank. (b) He got in line. When he reached the teller's window, he handed her a piece of paper and a brown paper bag. (c) The teller was putting money in the bag, when a loud alarm began to ring. (d) Guards rushed in, but the man had escaped through the side entrance.

2. When Mrs. McMartin looked out the window, this is what she saw: (a) There were a few children playing on the swings. (b) Others were climbing on the monkey-bars. (c) One little boy was running very fast around and around the playground. (d) Suddenly he fell down. (e) He screamed in pain. (f) All the other children looked around to see where the noise was coming from. (g) One child ran toward Mrs. McMartin's office.

3. Here is what I saw, heard, and felt during the hurricane. (a) The wind grew louder. (b) The windows and doors shook. (c) The trees swayed in the garden outside. I thought the house was moving. (d) A tree crashed against the house. (e) There was a sound of breaking glass upstairs. I went upstairs. (f) Rain was pouring through the broken window. (g) A strong wind blew into the room. (h) The wind howled louder and louder.

EXERCISE 4

Decide on which form of the verb to use, based on the context. In some sentences both forms may be correct.

▶ **EXAMPLE:** I saw smoke (come/(coming)) from the storeroom, so I called the fire department.

1. I hear the phone (ring/ringing), but I'm not going to answer it.
2. Brian heard the phone (ring/ringing), but by the time he reached it, the person at the other end had hung up.
3. The principal watched the students (take/taking) the test, so she was sure there had been no cheating.
4. Matt felt himself (get/getting) angry as he and Jeff argued about who should do the dishes.
5. On my way to the store I saw Morris (ride/riding) his new bike.
6. As Mary listened to the radio (play/playing) her favorite song, she began to cry and hurried out of the room.
7. I heard the workers (leave/leaving) earlier today. I'm sure they haven't returned yet.
8. We could all smell something (burn/burning). Apparently somebody had tossed a lighted cigarette into the waste paper basket.
9. As the hurricane grew stronger, they heard many branches of the big oak tree (snap/snapping) and (fall/falling) to the ground.
10. John was relieved when he saw his lost wallet (sit/sitting) next to his checkbook on the shelf.
11. Deborah heard Evan (cry/crying), so she went in to see what was wrong.
12. When we arrived we found the dog (wait/waiting) at the door for us.

FORM MEANING

Causative Verbs

Many causative verbs are followed by infinitives. But a few common causative verbs (*make, let, have, help*) are followed by the simple form of the verb. Causative verbs show how much force or persuasion is necessary to cause a person to perform an action.

CAUSATIVE VERB + INFINITIVE	CAUSATIVE VERB + SIMPLE FORM OF THE VERB
(a) Parents should **force** naughty children **to stand** in the corner.	**(b)** Parents should **make** naughty children **stand** in the corner.
(c) Parents should **get** their children **to read** instead of watching TV.	*no synonym for this form*
(d) Parents should **employ or hire** a doctor **to examine** their children at least once a year.	**(e)** Parents should **have** the doctor **examine** their children at least once a year.
(f) Good parents should **allow** their children **to play** outside on sunny days.	**(g)** Good parents **let** their children **play** outside on sunny days.
(h) Good parents **help** their children **to learn** good manners.	**(i)** Good parents **help** their children **learn** good manners. (*help* can occur with either form)

EXERCISE 5

Underline the causative verbs and circle the infinitive or base form of the verb that follows.

(1) Kilroy hated his life in the army from the very first day. (2) When he arrived at Fort Dix for basic training, a drill instructor had him join all the other new recruits on the parade ground. (3) The officers made them stand in the hot sun for several hours, while clerks filled out forms. (4) They wouldn't allow the new recruits to joke, or talk to each other, or even to move their

heads. (5) Then they had Army barbers cut their hair so short that Kilroy felt like he was bald. (6) An officer ordered Kilroy to report to a long building called Barracks B, along with about twenty other men. (7) The sergeant at Barracks B had each man choose a bed. (8) He let them put their personal possessions in lockers next to each bed. (9) Kilroy helped the man in the next bunk make his bed, and that man helped Kilroy to do the same thing. (10) The sergeant then required the recruits to sweep the floors and clean the bathrooms. (11) Kilroy had wanted to join the army to learn how to be a soldier, but now he was beginning to worry that the army would only teach him how to be a janitor.

EXERCISE 6

Decide whether you think the policies suggested below are good ideas or not. Make statements with *should* or *shouldn't*. Then give a reason with *because*.

▶ **EXAMPLE:** *Parents should let their kids play actively every day, because vigorous physical exercise is important for growing bodies.*

causer	caustive verb	doer of action	action
EXAMPLE: *parents*	*let*	*kids*	*play actively*
1. parents	make	children	go to bed at 6:00
2. teachers	help	students	learn things by themselves
3. police	allow	people	break laws
4. people	have	a dentist	examine their teeth regularly
5. dog owners	let	pets	run around freely
6. a government	require	all citizens	take drug tests
7. a good manager	allow	employees	do whatever they like
8. a good manager	motivate	employees	do their best

EXERCISE 7

Match the verbs listed in Group A with the verbs in Group B which have the same or similar meaning.

Group A		Group B		
let	get	convince	assist	employ
help	make	hire	encourage	force
have		require	permit	allow

EXERCISE 8

What should a teacher do in order to help students learn to speak English?

Make sentences stating your opinion, using the causative verbs in Focus 3. Be careful to use the right form (infinitive or base form of the verb).

▶ **EXAMPLES:** Teachers should have students do homework every night.

Teachers should help students guess the meaning of unfamiliar vocabulary.

EXERCISE 9

Use this chart to make sentences about what governments should expect citizens to do and what citizens should expect governments to do. Choose three actions from each category and make sentences that express your real opinion. Write two sentences that express your opinion: one with a causative verb followed by a simple verb and one with a verb + infinitive.

▶ **EXAMPLE:** **causer:** government **doer:** citizens **action:** vote in regular elections

Governments should let their citizens vote in regular elections.

Governments should allow their citizens to vote in regular elections.

causer	doer	action
government	citizens	pay taxes read any books and magazines they wish be of service to the nation meet national goals defend the country
citizens	government	be responsive to their wishes work without corruption establish national goals maintain law and order provide for basic defense

Passive Causative Verbs

The causative verbs *make* and *help* can be made passive, especially when the causer or agent of the action is obvious or not stated, or is a law or an institution. When the verbs *make* and *help* are passive, they must be followed by an infinitive, not the base form of the verb.

PASSIVE CAUSATIVE VERBS	ACTIVE CAUSATIVE VERBS
(a) Children should **be made to brush** their teeth before bedtime.	**(b)** Parents should **make** their children **brush** their teeth before bedtime.
(c) Children should **be helped to learn** good table manners.	**(d)** Parents should **help** their children **learn** good table manners.

Other causative verbs (*get, have, let*) cannot appear as passive verbs in causative sentences. If the agent is unknown or unimportant, we must express the passive sentence with another causative verb + infinitive that has the same meaning.

(e) NOT: Children should **be gotten** to read.	**(f)** Children should **be inspired** to read not forced.
(g) NOT: Teachers should **be had** to teach.	**(h)** Teachers should **be employed** to teach, not baby-sit.
(i) NOT: Children shouldn't **be let** to stay up too late.	**(j)** Children shouldn't **be allowed** to stay up too late.

EXERCISE 10

Decide whether the causative verbs in these sentences can be made passive without omitting important information or being ungrammatical. If so, write the passive version of the sentence.

▶ **EXAMPLES:**   The law requires parents to send their children to school.

Parents are required to send their children to school.

The doctor got the patient to take the bitter tasting medicine.

No change possible

1. Tradition doesn't allow people to smoke in church.
2. Lack of time forced Kilroy to return to the barracks before the movie was over.
3. The law requires everyone who works to pay some income taxes.
4. People shouldn't let their dogs run free around the neighborhood.
5. We had the janitor clean up the mess.
6. When I was a child my mother didn't allow me to play in the street.

▶ Verbs of Urging Followed by Subjunctive *That* Clauses

EXAMPLES	EXPLANATION
(a) The doctor **suggested** that John **lose** fifteen pounds. **(b)** NOT: The doctor **suggested** that John **loses** fifteen pounds.	Certain verbs of urging (*advise, ask, demand, desire, insist, propose, recommend, request, require, suggest, urge*) are followed by a *that* clause. The verb of the *that* clause must appear in simple form.
(c) The children **demanded** that their father **give** them candy. **(d)** NOT: The children **demanded** that their father **gives** them candy.	

EXERCISE 11

Are these sentences correct or incorrect? For incorrect sentences, identify the mistake and fix it.

1. The students were got to do their homework.
2. The sergeant made the recruits to march for several hours.
3. A tailor was had to shorten my pants.
4. Parents shouldn't let their children watch too much television.
5. I had the waiter to bring the food to the table.
6. They encouraged all their children be independent.
7. We heard the protesters come closer and closer, so we left the area.
8. Companies should be required to provide their employees with health insurance.
9. The baby sitter made the children to fall asleep by singing quietly.
10. Kilroy had his hair to be cut.
11. The judge demanded that he was punished.
12. The army requires that every new soldier gets his hair cut very short.
13. My parents heard our coming in late from the party.

Use Your English

ACTIVITY 1: WRITING/SPEAKING

Seeing is the sense that we rely on most. But when we are deprived of sight, our other senses become sharper. Test your other senses through the following activity.

STEP 1 Go to a place you know well. It could be this classroom, or a favorite room in your house, or someplace outdoors. Close your eyes and keep them closed for three minutes. Listen for the sounds that you can hear, both inside and outside. Are there any smells that you notice? Are they pleasant or unpleasant? What can you feel? Is it hot, or cold? Make a list of things you have noticed about this place that you never noticed when your eyes were open. Try to think of at least three things for each of these categories:

I heard . . .   I smelled . . .   I felt . . .

STEP 2 Compare your list with several other people's lists. As a group, decide what other kinds of things escape your attention when you can rely on eyesight for information about the world around you. Present your ideas to the rest of the class.

ACTIVITY 2: SPEAKING/WRITING

In the previous activity you had an opportunity to experience the world as a blind person does. How are blind people able to move around independently? In what ways do they compensate for lack of sight? How do they get information about where they are and where they are going? Consider deaf people, who cannot hear. How are they able to communicate with each other and the rest of the world?

In a small group discuss ways that people with sensory handicaps can compensate for those handicaps. Use your experience in the previous activity, and any other experiences you have had with people who are blind or deaf. Present your ideas in a written or oral report.

ACTIVITY 3: SPEAKING/WRITING

There is a proverb in English that says. "You can catch more flies with honey than you can with vinegar." What do you think are the best ways to get someone to do something? Support your ideas by describing a situation when someone convinced you to do something you didn't want to do. How did that person convince you? Were you glad you did it or not?

Sensory Verbs, Causative Verbs, and Verbs that Take Subjunctive   **303**

ACTIVITY 4: LISTENING/WRITING

Here are some general statements about human nature.

- People are usually in too much of a hurry.
- Children are spontaneous.
- Teenagers like to spend time together in groups.
- Older people are usually slower than younger people.

Do you think such generalizations are true or not? Test the validity of such generalizations by doing the following:

STEP 1   Choose a generalization that you want to test. It could be one of the statements listed above, or some other generalization. You may want to test a generalization that involves cultural differences, such as *North Americans are very outgoing* or *Asians are studious.*

STEP 2   Go to a place where you can watch lots of people. A shopping mall, a cafeteria, a busy corner—these are all good places. Watch how people behave. Look for examples of behavior that reflect the generalization you are testing. Find as many examples as you can that either support or contradict the generalization, and write a paragraph describing what you have observed. Here's an example:

> They say that most people are friendly, and I have found that this seems to be true. At the mall yesterday I saw many people smiling at each other, I saw two people meet by chance. They must have been old friends because I saw them hug each other. I heard many people laughing and joking. I heard many of the salespeople say "Have a nice day" to customers. I saw one family arguing with one another, but strangers tended to be polite.

ACTIVITY 5: SPEAKING

What routine jobs do you hate? Pretend that you don't have to worry about money. What things would you have other people do for you?

STEP 1   Decide on five to ten personal tasks that you would have someone else do, if money were no problem. (For example: *If money were no problem, I would have somebody else do my homework.*)

STEP 2   Compare your list to those of other students in class. Based on your discussion, decide what the three most unpopular tasks are that people have to do.

ACTIVITY 6: SPEAKING

If you were the leader of the country, what things would you change?

- What laws would you establish for people to follow?
- What would you require people to do?
- What privileges would you allow people?
- What things would you not allow them to do?
- How would you get people to support you?

Think of at least three answers to each of these questions. Then tell the class why they should let you be their leader. Take a vote to see who is the most convincing candidate.

ACTIVITY 7: LISTENING/ SPEAKING/WRITING

In the radio, TV, and movie business they use the term "sound effects" to refer to the noises that are added to make the program or movie seem more real.

STEP 1 You will hear some common sound effects that are used in radio and TV broadcasts or movies. After you hear each sound, write a description of what you heard. Here's an example.

▶ **EXAMPLE:** I heard a dog barking.

STEP 2 Once you have identified all the sounds, compare you descriptions to those of another student to make sure you both interpreted the sound effects in the same way. Together, use your descriptions to write the story that the sounds tell you.

ACTIVITY 8: LISTENING

Listen to this conversation between Matt and his doctor, and answer the following questions. You may need to listen to the conversation more than once. The first question has been answered for you as an example.

1. What does Dr. Wong recommend that Matt do?

She recommends that _____ he change his eating habits.

2. How does she suggest that Matt do this?

She suggests that _____

3. What is the problem Matt has with following her advice?

His roommate Jeff, _____

4. How does Jeff insist that food be cooked?

He insists that _____

5. What does Dr. Wong urge that Matt demand?

She urges that _____

6. What other solution does Dr. Wong suggest?

She suggests that _____

ARTICLES IN DISCOURSE

UNIT GOALS:

- To correctly distinguish generic and particular statements
- To correctly understand and distinguish specific and nonspecific reference in particular statements
- To use correct articles with specific, non-specific and unique nouns

▶ OPENING TASK

Proverbs

Common American Proverbs

A *dog is man's best friend.*

Time is money.

A *fool and his money are soon parted.*

Experience is the best teacher.

An idle mind is the devil's playground.

Absence makes the heart grow fonder.

The leopard cannot change its spots.

Actions speak louder than words.

Beauty is only skin-deep.

Every cloud has a silver lining.

Time heals all wounds.

Money is the root of all evil.

You are known by the company you keep.

STEP 1 Proverbs are well-known sayings that express general truths. On the previous page are some common American proverbs. Choose one that you agree with, and think of an example from your own life (or the life of someone that you know) that proves the truth of that proverb.

STEP 2 Write a paragraph about that example. Show why the proverb is true from your own experience. The first proverb has been done for you as an example.

A DOG IS MAN'S BEST FRIEND.

I once had a dog named Poppy. She was a very faithful friend. Every afternoon when I came home, the dog would greet me with kisses and a wagging tail. I liked the wagging tail, but I didn't enjoy the kisses very much. Even so, she was always glad to see me, and I was happy to see her, too. There was a time in my life when I was feeling very lonely. I didn't think I had any friends. Every day I came home to an empty house with an empty heart. But Poppy was always at the door waiting for me. She seemed to know whenever I was sad or lonely, and at those times she would be extra friendly. One time she even gave me a "gift": an old bone. Somehow she knew that I was especially sad. She must have thought the bone would cheer me up. Those bad times passed eventually, but they would have been a lot more difficult without my faithful companion, Poppy. She proved to me that a dog really is a wonderful friend.

▶ **O**verview of Determiners

Most noun phrases in English require a determiner.

EXAMPLES	EXPLANATIONS
	Determiners can be:
(a) We need **this** pen. **That** pen is out of ink.	• **Demonstratives** (see Unit 20 for more information)
(b) **Peter's** information surprised us more than **his** appearance.	• **Possessives** (see Unit 21 for more information)
(c) Denise has **few** friends. She doesn't make **much** effort	• **Quantifiers** (see Unit 22 for more information)
(d) Denise has **a** new position. She has **some** work to do. She feels **the** work is quite important.	• **Articles** (see Focus 2 for more information)
(e) NOT: Here is **a this** pen. **(f)** NOT: **That my** pen is green.	There is only one determiner of these types in each noun phrase.

The form of most determiners depends on whether the noun is count or noncount, singular or plural.

EXAMPLES	EXPLANATIONS
one bottle/two bottles one dollar/two dollars one man/two men one chair/two chairs	Count nouns can be counted and must indicate singular or plural.
water (one liter of water/two liters . . .) money (one dollar/a hundred yen . . .) furniture (two pieces of furniture)	Noncount nouns cannot be counted without using words that tell a unit or amount. They usually have no plural form.

Many nouns can have both a count and a noncount meaning.

NONCOUNT MEANING	COUNT MEANING
(g) There is **much beauty** in nature.	(h) There were **many beauties** at the beach.
(i) They grow **coffee** and **tea** in Sumatra.	(j) We ordered **two coffees** and **a tea** in addition to dessert.

EXERCISE 1

Underline and identify the determiners in the sample paragraph of the Opening Task. Are they demonstratives, possessives, quantifiers, or articles? Are the nouns count or noncount, singular or plural?

▶ **Overview of Articles**

There are two kinds of articles: definite and indefinite.

Definite Articles

EXAMPLES	EXPLANATIONS
the pencil/**the** pencils **the** rice **the** information	There is only one form for definite articles: *the*. *The* can be used with any kind of noun: count, singular and plural, and non-count.

Indefinite Articles

EXAMPLES	EXPLANATIONS
a book **a** shiny apple **a** church **a** university **a** hotel	*a/an*: Used with singular count nouns. *A* precedes nouns (or their modifiers) that begin with a consonant sound.
an apple **an** uncomfortable situation **an** honest man **an** easy lesson **an** hour	*An* precedes nouns (or their modifiers) that begin with a vowel sound.
(a) Please get me **some pencils.** **(b)** I've invited **some friends** for dinner. **(c)** I have **some ideas** about the party. **(d)** Would you like **some rice?** **(e)** **Some water** got on my notebook. **(f)** I'm looking for **some information.**	*some*: Used with plural count nouns and noncount nouns. *Some* indicates a nonspecific quantity or amount.
(g) Everyone needs **friends.** **(h)** **Teachers** want **students** to succeed. **(i)** **Ideas** can come from anywhere. **(j)** **Rice** is eaten all over Asia. **(k)** **Water** is necessary for life. **(l)** I'm looking for **information** about public transportation.	No article (ø): Used with plural count nouns and noncount nouns. Use ø to make generic statements (see Focus 3) and statements that do **not** refer to a quantity or amount. (See Focus 4 for other rules regarding *some* versus ø.)

NOTE: See Appendix 5 for a chart that reviews the process for deciding how to choose the correct article for most situations in English.

EXERCISE 2

Decide which articles (*a, an, the, some, ø*) can **NOT** be used with the following noun phrases.

1. pencils
2. water
3. apple
4. university professor
5. hourly employee

6. motherhood
7. bread
8. fast food
9. test

FOCUS **3**

Using Articles in Generic and Particular Statements

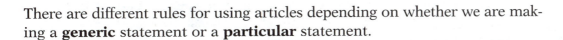

There are different rules for using articles depending on whether we are making a **generic** statement or a **particular** statement.

GENERIC STATEMENTS	PARTICULAR STATEMENTS
Generic statements describe concepts and ideas. They refer to general categories of things.	Particular statements describe real situations. They refer to individual members of a category.
(a) **Bicycles** are an excellent means of transportation. (a category)	**(b)** They went shopping for **bicycles** yesterday. (particular things they wanted to buy—they didn't buy all the bicycles in the world)
(c) **An angry customer** is a frightening sight. (a category of person)	**(d)** We saw **an angry customer** complaining about the high price of tickets. (a particular person—not all customers are angry)
(e) **The lion** is found throughout Africa. (a category of animal)	**(f)** I saw **the lion** at the circus. (a particular animal—not all lions are in the circus)

(g)	**Some people** never fall in love. (a category of people)	**(h)**	**Some people** are joining us for dinner. (particular people, not a class of people)
(i)	**Information** is increasingly communicated by electronic rather than printed media. (a category of things that are communicated electronically)	**(j)**	Please give me **some information** on medical treatments for heart disease. (particular written or spoken facts)

Both definite and indefinite articles can be used to express generic statements. The following examples are listed from most common to least common.

EXAMPLES	EXPLANATIONS
(k) **Lions** are mighty creatures. **(l)** **Rice** is eaten throughout Asia.	**ø with plural count or noncount nouns** is the most common way to make generic statements.
(m) **A** lion is a mighty creature.	**A**/*an* **with singular count nouns** is less common, but also acceptable.
(n) **The** lion is a mighty creature.	*The* **with singular count nouns** is also possible, but sounds very formal to most native speakers.

NOTE: Article usage in particular statements is explained in the rest of the focus boxes of this unit.

EXERCISE 3

Decide whether these sentences are generic statements (describing classes or categories) or particular statements (describing members of a category).

▶ **EXAMPLES:** **Computers** are cheaper now than they were ten years ago. *generic*

Computers for the new lab are being donated by a company in San Jose. *particular*

1. I wanted to buy **some mangoes** for the fruit salad, but they were too expensive!

2. **Mangoes** are a fruit found in most tropical places.

3. I saw **a doctor** about my cough.

4. **A doctor** is someone who has received training in medical science.

5. **Computers** have completely changed the way we live.

6. Don't go to that store for **computers.** They're cheaper at Radio Hut.

7. **Many people** don't like spicy food.

8. There weren't **many people** at Reiko's party.

9. If you really want to know how John is feeling, don't ask the **doctor,** ask the **nurses.** They will have better information.

10. There is a shortage of **nurses** in American hospitals today.

11. Many people in this country can't afford to go to **the doctor** when they are sick.

12. Raul is starting **a new company.**

13. **A company** needs to make sure that it is earning a profit.

EXERCISE 4

Write one generic statement and one particular statement for each of the cues listed here. The first one has been done for you as an example.

▶ **EXAMPLES:** **Generic:** Bicycles are a cheap and efficient means of transportation.

Particular: Both Billy and his sister got bicycles for Christmas.

1. bicycles
2. a new car
3. the English language
4. transportation
5. tea
6. salespeople
7. books
8. hard work
9. Chinese food
10. trouble

▶ **S**pecific Versus Nonspecific Nouns

In particular statements, article use is determined by whether a noun is specific or nonspecific.

SPECIFIC NOUNS	IMPLIED MEANING	EXPLANATION
(a) Please give me **the** red pen.	There is only one red pen.	Specific nouns require definite articles. Specific nouns refer to an identified object. **Both** the speaker and the listener know specifically which object is being talked about.
(b) Please pass **the** tea.	There is a teapot right here.	

NONSPECIFIC NOUNS	IMPLIED MEANING	EXPLANATION
(c) Please give me **a** red pen.	There are several red pens. Any red pen is O.K.	Nonspecific nouns require indefinite articles. A noun is nonspecific when **either** the speaker or the listener or both do **not** know specifically which object is being referred to.
(d) Let's go to **a** restaurant and have **some** tea.	We don't know which restaurant it will be, or what kind of tea we will have.	

EXAMPLES	IMPLIED MEANING	EXPLANATIONS
(e) I bought **a new car.**	You haven't seen it yet.	Use indefinite articles (*an/an, ø, some*) when: • the speaker has a specific mental image of the noun, but the listener doesn't.
(f) I had **some cookies** with lunch today.	I know which cookies I had, but you don't.	
(g) There are **students** in my class who always do their homework.	I know which ones they are, but you don't.	

(h) I hear you bought **a new car.** What kind is it?	You know, but I don't.	Use indefinite articles (*an/an*, *ø, some*) when: • the speaker doesn't have a specific mental image or idea, but the listener does.
(i) You said you were holding **some mail** that came for me.	You know what kind and how much mail there is, but I don't.	
(j) Mary tells you **secrets** that she never tells me.	You know which secrets, but I don't.	
(k) I hope you have **a wonderful time** on your vacation.	We don't know what events will make it a wonderful vacation.	• neither the speaker nor the listener has a specific mental image.
(l) Let's get **some spaghetti** when we go out tonight.	We don't know what kind of or how much spaghetti we're going to get.	
(m) We're supposed to bring **dessert** to the picnic	We haven't been told a specific kind of dessert to bring.	

EXERCISE 5

Decide whether the nouns in the sentences below are specific or nonspecific. Is the noun phrase identified for the speaker, the listener, or both? Write the number of the sentence on the appropriate line below. The first two have been done for you.

Listener and speaker know which one: _____

Listener knows which one, but speaker doesn't: _____

Speaker knows which one, but listener doesn't: ___#2_____

Neither listener nor speaker know which one: ____#1_____

1. Do you want to go to **a movie** tonight?

2. The Jordans just bought **a beautiful new house.** You really ought to see it. I'm sure you'll think it's wonderful.

3. I want you to meet **a friend** of mine. You both have the same interests.

4. Did you have fun at **the party?**

5. Let's have **some friends** over for dinner on Saturday.

6. I heard Ali has **a new girlfriend.** What's she like?

EXERCISE 6

Choose the correct implied meaning for each of these sentences. (*I* refers to the speaker. *You* refers to the listener.)

1. The student from Japan is here to see you.
   (a) There are several students from Japan who had appointments.
   (b) There is only one student from Japan who had an appointment.

2. Let's go to a restaurant.
   (a) We've already decided which restaurant to go to.
   (b) Let's choose a restaurant.

3. Some friends are coming to dinner.
   (a) You know who's coming to dinner.
   (b) You don't know who's coming to dinner.

4. Let's invite the neighbors to dinner.
   (a) You know which neighbors will be invited to dinner.
   (b) You don't know which neighbors will be invited to dinner.

5. You should see a doctor about that cough.
   (a) I am thinking about a specific doctor.
   (b) Any doctor should be able to help you.

EXERCISE 7

Add the appropriate article (*a/an, the, some,* or *ø*) in the blanks. There may be more than one correct answer.

1. I didn't bring _____ roses that you asked for. I completely forgot them.

2. Sally wanted to buy _____ new dress, so she's gone out to find one.

3. _____ teacher was here to see you. I think it was your English teacher.

4. Did you give _____ musicians a nice tip? They certainly played beautiful music for your party.

5. Would you like _____ cold iced tea?

6. How did you enjoy _____ Chinese food last night?

7. I have _____ problems that I don't want to talk about.

8. John sent Mary _____ card for her birthday, but she says she never received it.

9. (a) _____ bank where Dora works was robbed by
   (b) _____ masked man with (c) _____ gun.
   By the time (d) _____ police officer arrived, it was too late. (e) _____ robber had disappeared.

FOCUS **5**

▶ **Using Articles in Discourse**

A noun is usually used with an indefinite article the first time it is mentioned because it is nonspecific: It is the first time the listener has encountered it. In later sentences the same noun is used with a definite article because it has become specific; both the speaker and the listener now know exactly which noun is being talked about.

EXAMPLES	EXPLANATIONS
(a) There once was **a** little old man who lived in **a** house by **a** river. **The** shack was rather dirty, and so was **the** man. **(b)** I once had **a** big black dog and **a** little white dog. **The** black dog kept itself very clean, but **the** white dog loved to roll in mud.	A noun is usually used with an indefinite article the first time it is mentioned because it is nonspecific: it is the first time the listener has encountered it. In later sentences the same noun is used with a definite article because it has become specific; both the speaker and the listener now know exactly which noun is being talked about
(c) I had **a dog** named Poppy. Every afternoon when I came home **the dog** would greet me with **kisses** and **a wagging tail.** I liked **the wagging tail,** but I didn't enjoy **the kisses** very much.	A noun becomes specific • **by direct reference.** (The noun is repeated.)
(d) If you have **a dog** as **a pet,** you can always look forward to going home because of **the kisses** and **the wagging tail** that are there to greet you when you arrive. **(e)** I read **an interesting book. The author** suggested that all life came from visitors from another planet. **The first chapter** tells stories of visitors from outer space that are found in many different cultures.	• **by indirect reference.** (The noun itself is not repeated, but the reference is still clear from the context.)

EXERCISE 8

Write articles (*a/an, ø, some, the*) in the spaces. More than one answer may be correct.

1. I have (a) _____ foolish friend who is really careless with (b) _____ money. He has (c) _____ good-paying job, but he doesn't even have (d) _____ bank account. He says he doesn't need one because he spends his salary right away. He gets (e) _____ paycheck once (f) _____ week. (g) _____ money is always gone before (h) _____ week is over. I can't tell you what he spends it on. And you know what? Neither can he!

2. I saw (a) _____ interesting play last night. (b) _____ actors were excellent, and (c) _____ set was beautiful. However, (d) _____ play itself was unfortunately not very well written.

3. Would you like (a) _____ cake? (b) _____ frosting is (c) _____ special recipe from (d) _____ friend of my mother's. I made (e) _____ cake and (f) _____ frosting myself.

4. Little Billy doesn't like (a) _____ school. He says (b) _____ teachers are boring. He doesn't like doing (c) _____ homework. He much prefers to watch (d) _____ cartoons on TV. As (e) _____ result, his teachers aren't very happy with (f) _____ way he performs in class. If he doesn't take (g) _____ responsibility for doing (h) _____ assignments, he may have to repeat (i) _____ same grade next year.

▶ **Repeating the Indefinite Article**

USE

There are certain situations in which the usual rule of replacing an indefinite article with a definite article after the first time it is mentioned is not followed.

EXAMPLES		EXPLANATIONS
(a) There once was **a** little old man who lived in **a** house by *a river.* **The** house was rather dirty, and so was **the** man. Although *there was a river* right next to **the** house, **the** old man had to walk quite far to get clean drinking water.		• sentences with *there is/there are.*
(b) I once had **a** dog. Her name was Poppy. She was **a** good dog.	**Implied Meaning:** She was a member of the category "good dogs."	• sentences that identify someone or something as a member of a category.
(c) You know John. He's **a** teacher.	He's a member of the category "teachers."	
(d) John is **a** teacher. John and Fred are teachers. **(e)** NOT: John and Fred are **some** teachers. **(f)** Paris is **a** city. Paris, Rome, and Munich are cities. **(g)** NOT: Paris, Rome, and Munich are **some** cities.		Do not use *some* for plural nouns that identify things as part of a group.

EXERCISE 9

Add the correct article to the blank spaces in these sentences.

I once had (1) _____ experience that proved to me that
(2) _____ idle mind is (3) _____ devil's
playground. Miss Kersell was my eighth grade science and math teacher.
She was (4) _____ very strict teacher, and wouldn't allow any
misbehaving in class. To my friend Billy this presented (5) _____
irresistible challenge. He found math and science very easy, so he was

frequently bored in class. As (6) _____ result, he would try to play (7) _____ tricks on her without getting caught. It was (8) _____ challenge that he could never resist, especially when he didn't have anything else to do. One day we were taking (9) _____ arithmetic quiz. It was (10) _____ easy quiz, but I have never been good at arithmetic, so it was taking me (11) _____ long time. But Billy had finished (12) _____ quiz in just (13) _____ few minutes. I heard (14) _____ strange noise coming from the back of the room. It was (15) _____ noise like no other I had ever heard. Someone in (16) _____ front of the class began to giggle. Then there were (17) _____ giggles in the back. Soon there was (18) _____ laughter everywhere. Miss Kersell was furious and looked everywhere to find out where (19) _____ noise was coming from. Billy had found (20) _____ way to make (21) _____ strange noise by rubbing his foot against (22) _____ leg of his chair.

FOCUS **7**

▶ **Unique Nouns**

There are certain nouns that are specific for both the speaker and the listener the first time they are mentioned. These are called unique nouns.

EXAMPLES		EXPLANATIONS
(a) I hear someone knocking at **the** door.		Unique nouns are used with definite articles. We do not need to "introduce" them in a specific context.
(b) **The** sun is too hot. Let's sit in **the** shade.		
Unique Nouns **(c)** We were all having dinner. We were sitting around **the table,** and I asked my brother to pass **the butter.**	**Implied Meaning** There was only one table and one dish of butter.	A noun can be unique: • because of a particular situation or setting.
(d) "How did you do on **the exam** yesterday?" "Terrible! **The questions** were really difficult!"	The speakers both know which test is being discussed.	
(e) I hope you remembered to ask **the neighbors** to pick up **the mail** while we're on vacation.	We've previously decided which neighbors we will ask to pick up the mail.	
(f) **The sky** is so beautiful tonight. **The moon** is bright.		• because it is a universal reference (there is only one)
(g) **The street that John lives on** is lined with trees.		• if it is immediately identified by a relative clause or prepositional phrase
(h) First we went to a hotel where **the man at the desk** told us we had no reservations.		
(i) **The book the teacher told us about** is available at **the bookstore across the street.**		

Articles in Discourse **321**

EXERCISE 10

Why do you think the highlighted nouns in the following sentences are unique? Decide whether they have been specified:

(a) by being mentioned previously by direct or indirect reference (identify the reference)

(b) by a specific context/situation (identify the context or situation)

(c) by a universal context or situation

(d) by being immediately identified by a relative clause or prepositional phrase (identify the modifier)

1. An idle mind is **the devil's** playground.
2. I saw a great movie last night. **The camera work** was fantastic.
3. **The newspaper** said it was going to rain tonight.
4. **The tallest mountain** in **the world** is on **the border** between Nepal and China.
5. **The place** we went last year is great for a vacation.
6. Let's go to **the club** for dinner tonight.
7. **The teacher** said we have to finish **the assignment** before Friday.
8. **The town** that I grew up in was quite small.
9. **The noise** Billy made was like no other noise I had ever heard before.
10. What did **the doctor** say about **the medicine** you've been taking?

EXERCISE 11

Write the appropriate article (*a, an, the,* or *ø*) in the blanks. There may be more than one correct choice.

Peter Principle believes that every cloud has (1) _____ silver lining. He is (2) _____ very optimistic person. He thinks that (3) _____ problem is really (4) _____ opportunity in disguise. As (5) _____ result, he is always happy and reasonably content with (6) _____ things that (7) _____ life has given him. (8) _____ people like being around him, because he's (9) _____ cheerful, positive person.

Denise Driven is just (10) _____ opposite. She always looks on (11) _____ dark side of (12) _____ things. If she encounters (13) _____ problem, she sometimes blames it on

(14) _____ fact that she is (15) _____ woman in
(16) _____ man's world. She believes that (17) _____
world isn't (18) _____ fair place, and she in particular has always
had (19) _____ bad luck. Although she's not (20) _____
optimistic person, she doesn't spend much time feeling sorry for herself.
She rarely has time to listen to anyone's troubles or tell you about
(21) _____ troubles she is facing. But whenever
(22) _____ friend does something nice for her, she always
suspects that the person actually has (23) _____ hidden motive.
She believes that every silver lining has (24) _____ cloud.

EXERCISE 12
Write the appropriate article in the blanks. There may be more than one correct
choice.

The tall person in this picture is one of (1) _____
most beautiful people I know: (2) _____
woman by (3) _____ name of Big Sue.
She proves (4) _____ truth of
(5) _____ saying "Beauty is only skin
deep." Perhaps people who don't know her well would
say that she is not (6) _____
beautiful person. I guess that compared to (7) _____
movie star or (8) _____ fashion model
she isn't that attractive. But anyone who knows her
well thinks that she has (9) _____ beautiful and courageous spirit.
Her beauty is in her personality. She has (10) _____ deep,
booming laugh that makes other people laugh with her. She's not self-conscious
about her size. She makes (11) _____ jokes about it. She
was (12) _____ person who invented (13) _____
name "Big Sue." She says there are plenty of Sues in (14) _____
world, but only one Big Sue. If she gains (15) _____ few pounds
she doesn't worry. She just says "There's more of me to love." She is
(16) _____ incredible dancer, and moves around (17) _____
dance floor with (18) _____ grace and style. She is

(19) _____ wonderful comedian. She can tell (20) _____ stories in (21) _____ way that has (22) _____ people falling down with laughter. She has (23) _____ friends all over (24) _____ world. She has turned down (25) _____ dozens of proposals for marriage. People can't help falling in love with her, once they get to know her well. But she's not in (26) _____ hurry to find (27) _____ husband. She says "I'll wait till I'm old and skinny. Right now I'm having too much fun."

EXERCISE 13

Write the appropriate article in the blanks. There may be more than one correct choice.

When I first went to (1) _____ university I learned the truth of the proverb "Absence makes (2) _____ heart grow fonder." It was (3) _____ first time I had lived away from home. I was surprised to discover how homesick I got, even after just (4) _____ few days. When I lived with my family, my brother and I used to fight about everything. He wanted to watch one TV program and I wanted to watch another. We fought about whose turn it was to do certain chores like feeding (5) _____ dog, sweeping (6) _____ garage, cutting (7) _____ grass, and taking out (8) _____ garbage. We argued about whose turn it was to use (9) _____ car on Saturday night. (I was allowed to use it one week, and then he was allowed to use it on (10) _____ other.)

But when I moved away, I realized that there were (11) _____ lot of things about my brother that I missed. I began to forget about all (12) _____ tricks he used to play on me. I started to remember only (13) _____ happy times we had spent together. By (14) _____ time (15) _____ year ended and I went back to spend (16) _____ summer at home, I was really anxious to see him again.

Use Your English

ACTIVITY 1: SPEAKING

Every country has different proverbs. In America we say "Don't bite off more than you can chew," to remind people not to be too ambitious or try to do too many things at once. In Afghanistan the same idea is expressed by this proverb: "You can't hold two watermelons in one hand."

STEP 1 Work with a partner from a different cultural background, and come up with three pairs of proverbs. Each pair should express the same idea in two different ways.

STEP 2 Share each message and its two different proverbs with the rest of the class.

ACTIVITY 2: SPEAKING/WRITING

Describe an object that you found once, and what you did with it. Compare your story with the stories of other people in the class. Can you create a proverb that talks about finding objects, and what should be done with them? (For example, "Find a penny, pick it up, all day long you'll have good luck.")

ACTIVITY 3: SPEAKING

A time capsule is a metal or concrete box (usually about one cubic meter) that is sometimes built into the floor or walls of a building. The designers of the time capsule fill it with objects that they think are important, or interesting, or characteristic of the time when the building was built.

STEP 1 Imagine that you are organizing a time capsule to be placed in a sky-scraper being built today. The building is expected to remain stand-ing for several hundred years. What objects would you place in the time capsule, and why would you choose those particular objects?

STEP 2 Work with several other people and decide on the contents of a time capsule that will not be opened for at least 500 years. Present your list of items and your reasons for choosing them to the rest of the class.

ACTIVITY 4: WRITING

Write a short paragraph about a discovery or invention that has changed the course of history.

ACTIVITY 5: WRITING

What are three things that everybody needs? Write a short composition describing your three choices and why you think everyone should have them. Start your essay with: *"There are three things everyone needs: . . ."*

ACTIVITY 6: SPEAKING

Here are four pictures. What story do you think they tell? Tell your story to a partner or write it down for your teacher to correct

ACTIVITY 7: LISTENING

Listen to the following short conversations and then choose the statement from the pairs listed below that can be correctly implied from the conversation.

Conversation #1

_____ There is one ACME sales representative.

_____ There are several ACME sales representatives.

_____ There is one vice president.

_____ There are several vice presidents.

Conversation #2

_____ There is only one snack bar in the building.

_____ There are several snack bars in the building.

_____ John has already decided what he is going to eat.

_____ John hasn't decided what he is going to eat yet.

_____ Mary already knows what snack John will bring her.

_____ Mary doesn't know what John will bring her from the snack bar.

Conversation #3

_____ This is the first time Bob and Betty have discussed the idea of having a party.

_____ They've discussed the party before.

_____ They have already decided who they are going to invite.

_____ They haven't decided who they are going to invite.

_____ They have already decided which restaurant to go to.

_____ They haven't decided which restaurant to go to.

UNIT 20

DEMONSTRATIVES IN DISCOURSE

UNIT GOALS:

- To correctly understand and use determiners and demonstrative pronouns
- To correctly understand and communicate differences in reference by using determiners
- To correctly understand and communicate differences in focus and emphasis by using determiners

▶ OPENING TASK

This, That, or It?

Read the following dialogue and look at how the words *it, this,* and *that* are used. What is being referred to each time one of these forms is used? Can you substitute other forms? Does this change the meaning? What can you say about when to use *it* instead of *that*?

Denise Driven: Mr. Green has informed me that you're not going to be here this afternoon. **That's** outrageous, Peter! What about the Davis contract? **It's** due first thing Monday morning.

Peter Principle: Well, my son's in a play at school. **It's** his first big role. He's one of the Three Wise Men.

Denise Driven: He certainly didn't learn **that** role from his father! Is some stupid school play more important than your job?

Peter Principle: You'd better believe **it!** Besides, I spoke with Mr. Green. I told him **it** would get done sooner or later.

Denise Driven: If he believes **that,** he'll believe anything. **That's** what makes me so annoyed, Peter. **This** isn't the first time you've left work early. You're always asking for permission to take time off, and I get left having to do all the work. I'm getting real tired of **it,** Peter. **It's** all I can do to keep this office running professionally!

Peter Principle: I'm sure Mr. Green would be happy to give you time off, too. Just ask for **it,** Denise. **That's** all you have to do.

Denise Driven: That's not the point. **It's** true that most of us would probably rather be playing instead of working. But some of us have a sense of responsibility and a respect for hard work.

Peter Principle: That's true. My responsibility is to my son, and I respect the hard work he's put into learning his lines. **It's** not easy when you're only six years old.

Denise Driven: Don't give me **that** nonsense, Peter. I don't much fancy **it.**

Peter Principle: That's your trouble, Denise. You need a little nonsense in your life.

Denise Driven: My personal life is none of your business!

Peter Principle: Denise Driven has a personal life? Fancy **that!**

Denise Driven: That's it! I'm leaving. I'm making a formal complaint about **this** with Mr. Green.

Peter Principle: Well, **that's that,** then, isn't **it?** I guess there's nothing I can do to calm you down. I may as well leave a little early for the play. **It's** important to get there early if you want to get a good seat.

STEP 2 Discuss your ideas with a partner. Together decide on two things you have noticed about how *this, that,* and *it* are used in English and report them to the rest of the class.

▶ **O**verview of **Demonstratives**

Demonstratives can be used as determiners or as pronouns.

EXAMPLES	EXPLANATIONS
(a) Does **this** pencil belong to you?	Demonstrative determiner
(b) Yes, **that** is mine.	Demonstrative pronoun

The form of the demonstrative depends on whether the thing being referred to is singular or plural, and near or far.

	NEAR	FAR
singular	**(c)** You should read **this book.** **(e)** **This** is delicious.	**(d)** Does **that pencil** belong to you? **(f)** Is **that** yours?
plural	**(g)** **These problems** aren't so serious. **(i)** If you like peaches, try **these.**	**(h)** **Those people** live down the street from my parents. **(j)** **Those** are the cutest puppies I have ever seen!

EXAMPLES	EXPLANATIONS
(k) Please sit in **this** chair **(by me.).** **(l)** **That** chair **(over there)** is broken.	Near and far distinctions can be determined by: • physical distance.
(m) I've been to two parties in the last week, but **this** one (today) is much more enjoyable than **that** party Denise had (a few days ago) at the club.	• time distance.
(n) What are we going to do about **this** budget deficit? **(o)** I don't know. **That's** for you to worry about, not me!	• whether the speaker feels involved with the situation or distanced from it

EXAMPLE	EXPLANATION
(p) There once was **a** wicked king who live in **a** castle. Every day **this king** would go to **a** secret room. **This** room was where he liked to count this money.	Use demonstratives with nouns that have been specified by being mentioned previously (see Unit 19 for more information).

A demonstrative is not usually repeated to refer to the same item. A personal pronoun (*he, it*, etc.) or a definite article (*the*) is used instead.

(q)	Have you tried **these** pears? **They** are quite delicious.	**(r)**	NOT: Have you tried **these** pears? **These** are quite delicious.
(s)	**This** is the problem Denise was talking about. **It** will continue to get worse if we don't find a solution.	**(t)**	NOT: **This** is the problem Denise was talking about. **This** will continue to get worse if we don't find a solution.
(u)	I bought **that** pen and notebook at a drug store. **The** pen was a little expensive, but **the** notebook was cheap.	**(v)**	NOT: I bought **that** pen and notebook at the drugstore. **That** pen was a little expensive, but **that** notebook was cheap.

EXERCISE 1
Add appropriate demonstratives (*this, those*, etc.), personal pronouns (*he, it*, etc.), or articles (*a/an, the*) in the blanks. More than one answer may be possible. The first one has been done for you as an example.

1. When Denise came to Mr. Green with her complaints about Peter, he realized that they had talked about (a) __these/those__ issues before. He told her there was no point in discussing (b)__them__ any further.

2. I got these new skirts and blouses on sale. I'd like you to take a look at (a) _____. Which of (b) _____ dresses do you like better, (c) _____ red one or (d) _____ green one? What about (e) _____ blouses? Which do you prefer? (f) _____ one or (g) _____ one?

3. I got a new bike for my birthday. (a) _____ was a gift from my parents. I'm glad they got (b) _____ bike instead of another kind. (c) _____ will be much more practical.

4. The essay that John wrote didn't receive a passing grade.

(a)_____ didn't contain any of the guidelines Dr. Montaigne had explained when she had first assigned

(b) _____ essay. (c) _____ guidelines were not simple, but (d)_____ had to be followed in order to get a passing grade on (e) _____ essay.

(f) _____ grade made John rather upset, but Dr. Montaigne had made (g) _____ guidelines quite clear.

5. Where did you get (a) _____ ring? (b) _____ is really beautiful. (c) _____ looks like

(d) _____ came from Mexico. Is (e) _____ silver?

FOCUS 2

Demonstratives for Reference

EXAMPLES	EXPLANATIONS
(a) Everyone started laughing. **This** made John very angry (b) I knew it was going to rain! **That's** why I didn't want to come to this picnic in the first place.	There are two kinds of demonstrative reference: • **backward-pointing reference:** where demonstratives refer to information that has been previously mentioned
(c) **This** is why I can't come to your party: I don't have the time, I don't have the clothes, and I have no way to get there. (d) I like **these** kinds of Asian food: Chinese, Japanese, Indian, and Thai.	• **forward-pointing reference:** where demonstratives refer to information that is about to be introduced.

Using a particular demonstrative form depends on whether it refers forward or backward in the text.

EXAMPLES	EXPLANATIONS
(e) **This** is why I wasn't at your party: I had a terrible case of the flu.	*This/these* can be used to point both forward or backward.
(f) I had a terrible case of the flu. **This** is why I wasn't at your party.	
(g) I had a terrible case of the flu. **That** is why I wasn't at your party.	*That/those* are usually only used for backward pointing reference (except with modifiers that follow a noun—see Focus 4).
(h) Paris is a beautiful city. **That** is why everyone wants to go there.	

EXERCISE 2

What do the demonstratives refer to in these sentences? Circle the demonstratives in these passages, and draw an arrow to what each one refers to. Is it an example of forward-pointing or backward-pointing reference? The first passage has been done for you as an example.

1. Most people find it difficult to sleep during the day and work at night. This is why people who work "swing shift" (as that work schedule is called) are usually paid a higher wage than those who those work during the day.

2. We hold these truths to be self-evident, that all men are created equal, and have a right to life, liberty, and the pursuit of happiness.

3. Let me make this perfectly clear: No new taxes!

4. Frank said that he wanted to leave New York because he was tired of big city life. But I don't think that was the real reason for his move to California. The real reason was that his wife wanted to live in a place with warmer winters. At least, this is what Stuart told me.

5. These soldiers must report to Barracks B: Private Rebecca Adams, Private Mary Collins, and Corporal Marsha Powell. These soldiers have been assigned to patrol duty: Sergeant Kitty Westmoreland and Corporal Mary MacArthur. Those are your orders, soldiers.

6. The causes of the American Civil War were not very different from those of other wars that have taken place between different regions of any country. This is one of the things that can be learned by studying history.

7. The chemical composition of baking soda is similar to that of any compound containing sodium. This is what allows baking soda to enter into a chemical reaction with any compound containing acid, such as those found in vinegar or even orange juice.

8. Management techniques of many American companies now tend to resemble those used in Japan much more than they did a few years ago. This is due to the success those techniques have had in raising worker productivity.

▶ *This/That* Versus *It*

EXAMPLES	EXPLANATIONS
"Did you hear the news? Scott is in jail?" **(a)** "I knew **it**! That boy was always a trouble-maker!" (*Implied Meaning:* I'm not surprised!) **(b)** "I knew **that**. His mother told me last week." (*Implied Meaning:* I'd already heard that news.)	Both demonstrative pronouns **(this/that)** and personal pronouns **(it)** refer back to ideas or items in previous sentences, but there is often a difference in emphasis or implied meaning.
They say that Mary is getting married to Paul. **(c)** Has John heard about **this**? (*Implied Meaning:* Has this important information been told to John?)	Using *this/that* emphasizes that the idea being referred to is the most important information in the new sentence.
They say that Mary is getting married to Paul. **(d)** I don't *believe* **it**! (*Implied Meaning*: That's unbelievable!)	Using *it* indicates that some other part of the sentence (the subject or verb) is the most important information. We do not generally use pronouns to talk about significant new information.

In some cases we **must** use *that* instead of *it*.

(e) Don't leave your keys in the car. Someone might steal **it**. **(f)** Don't worry. I'm smarter than **that**. **(g)** **(NOT)** I'm smarter than **it**.	This is especially true in cases where *it* could refer to a physical object (*the car* or *the dog*) rather than the general idea or situation.
(h) Aunt Martha is planning to bring her dog when she visits us. **(i)** I was afraid of **that**! No wonder she was asking if we had cats. **(j)** **(NOT)** I was afraid of **it**!	

EXERCISE 3

Decide which form, demonstrative pronoun (this/that) or personal pronoun (it), to put in the blanks. In most sentences, both forms are possible, but native speakers would tend to choose one form instead of the other to indicate a particular emphasis. Compare your choices with those of other students and your teacher.

1. Someone took your wallet? I was afraid _____ would happen!

2. I'm glad Sunyoon hasn't had her baby yet. She was afraid _____ would happen while her husband was out of town.

3. I'm sorry you had to spend such a beautiful, sunny day in the library. _____ isn't really fair, is it?

4. I assume you have all heard the news about Ali. _____ is why I have asked you here to this meeting.

5. I love the wonderful California climate. _____ is why I moved here.

6. Did you say George's son is involved in another financial scandal? Are you completely sure of _____?

7. I just know Mary's dating someone else. I'm sure of _____!

8. If you don't take advantage of this great opportunity, I know you'll regret _____ in the future.

9. Don't worry about making such a mess. _____ really doesn't matter.

10. Don't worry about making such a mess. _____ is why I put newspapers over everything.

11. A: You said "seventeen." Don't you mean "seventy"?
    B: Oh yes, _____'s what I meant.

12. Don't complain to me. _____ is why we have a complaint department.

▶ *That/Those* with
Forward-Pointing Reference

EXAMPLES	EXPLANATIONS
(a) **Those who cannot learn from history** will repeat the mistakes made in the past. **(b)** I'm not very fond of dogs, but **those that are well behaved** are O.K. **(c)** The boss only gives raises to **those he really likes.** (**whom** has been omitted) **(d)** This script is really confusing I can't tell the difference between **that which is supposed to be spoken** and **that which is supposed to be sung.**	*That* and *those* can be used for forward pointing reference only when they occur with: • relative clauses.
(e) Compare your paragraph to **that of another student** in the class. **(f)** This problem will have to be decided by **those in charge.**	• prepositional phrases

EXERCISE 4

Identify the demonstratives that are followed by modifying clauses or phrases in these passages. Not all sentences contain these structures.

1. There is an old proverb that says fate helps those that help themselves.

2. Please put those in the refrigerator.

3. My brother is very fussy about eating certain vegetables. He won't touch these, but those he likes won't stay on his plate for very long.

4. Those in the stock brokerage business think that this is a bad time to invest.

5. One must learn to distinguish between that which is necessary and that which is only desirable.

6. Those who can't tell the difference between the colors teal and aquamarine shouldn't become interior decorators.

7. That is not my responsibility. You'll have to speak to those in charge of that part of the operation.

8. I read about that in the newspapers.

FOCUS **5**

► **Special Uses of Demonstratives**

Using *This/These* with Nonspecific Nouns

EXAMPLES	EXPLANATIONS
(a) I'm walking down the street and I see **this** man on the corner. He's talking with **these** two other guys.	In very informal speech or written narratives we can use *this* and *these* in place of indefinite determiners to introduce nouns for the first time.

Using *That* to Refer to Humans

EXAMPLES	EXPLANATIONS
(b) **That** man over there is married to **that** woman in the red dress.	**That** is not usually used to refer to humans, except when the speaker is pointing to the person.
(c) Were you talking to **that** boy again? I told you not to speak to him!	When it is used in other kinds of reference, it usually indicates the speaker is annoyed, or is insulting the person being referred to.

EXERCISE 5

Make this paragraph more informal by replacing the underlined articles with demonstratives. Decide which demonstratives are appropriate for the blanks.

I went to (1) <u>a</u> party where I met (2) <u>some</u> rather strange people. They had all read (3) <u>an</u> article in the newspaper about (4) <u>a</u> new invention that was supposed to help people lose weight. Mary, the hostess, was the strangest of all. She went around the room, asking all the guests to put on (5) <u>some </u>very dark glasses. Apparently (6) _____ is supposed to help people eat less. Now I ask you: Why does a person go to all the trouble of giving (7) <u>a</u> party if she doesn't want her guests to eat? (8) _____ 's Mary for you! She'll believe anything she reads in the paper.

Use Your English

ACTIVITY 1: SPEAKING/WRITING

Here is a puzzle. Can you punctuate this so that it makes sense?

that that is is that that is not is not isn't that it it is

There are four sentences in the correct answer. The solution is on page A-12.

ACTIVITY 2: WRITING/SPEAKING

STEP 1 Write a dialogue like the one in the Opening Task on page 329. Work with a partner. First, decide what the argument will be about. Then write your dialogue. Try to use some of the phrases that Peter and Denise used.

STEP 2 Perform your dialogue for the rest of the class.

ACTIVITY 3: LISTENING

Listen to an argument on a television comedy or drama. Write down the examples you hear using *that* or *it*. Why do you think the speakers used a particular form?

ACTIVITY 4: WRITING/SPEAKING

Compare two products from different countries or people from two different settings. For example: How does the coffee of Guatemala differ from that of Sumatra? How do students in high school differ from those in college? Present your comparison in either written or spoken form.

ACTIVITY 5: SPEAKING

Tell a story in informal spoken English. Use the present time frame and demonstratives (*this* and *these*) instead of indefinite articles. See Exercise 5 for an example to get you started.

ACTIVITY 6: LISTENING

STEP 1 Denise and Peter are arguing again. Listen to their conversation and write answers to the questions below. You may need to listen to the conversation more than once. Use *it* or *that* in your answers. The first question has been answered for you as an example.

1. When did Denise finish the Davis contract?
   She finished it late last night.

2. What did Denise think of Peter's offer to help?

3. When did Denise write her official complaint to Mr. Green?

4. How does Denise react when Peter offers to show her pictures of his son's play?

5. What does Denise threaten to do with the computer terminal if Peter doesn't stop telling her to be less serious about work?

6. Why does Peter decide to leave the office to take his children to the beach?

7. What effect does Denise think that firing Peter would have on the office?

STEP 2 When you have finished, compare your answers to those of another student in the class.

POSSESSIVES

UNIT GOALS:

- To correctly identify and use possessive forms (possessive determiners, possessive pronouns, possessive phrases and possessive nouns)
- To know when to use possessive nouns and when to use possessive phrases
- To correctly understand the various meanings of possessives

▶ **O PENING TASK**
What's Wrong with this Picture?

How observant are you? There are at least ten strange things about the picture on the next page. For example, the legs of the table seem to be a person's legs. Find as many other strange things as you can and write descriptions of them on the next page.

Strange Things

1. _____
2. _____
3. _____
4. _____
5. _____
6. _____
7. _____
8. _____
9. _____
10. _____
11. _____
12. _____

▶ Possessive Forms

EXAMPLES	EXPLANATIONS
(a) Peter, John, and I left **our** shoes on the porch.	There are four kinds of possessive forms: **Possessive determiners:** (*my, your, his, her, its, our, their*) Possessive determiners precede the noun.
(b) Mine were covered with mud.	**Possessive pronouns:** (*mine, yours, his, hers, its, ours, theirs*) Possessive pronouns can take the place of a noun phrase.
(c) The steps **of the porch** looked like a meeting place for old, dirty shoes.	**Possessive phrases:** (*the leg **of the chair,** the end **of the story,*** etc.) Possessive phrases are formed by adding the preposition *of* to the noun phrase. Possessive phrases follow the noun.
(d) John's shoes were wet, and **Peter's** were dirty.	**Possessive nouns:** (*the **student's** answers, the **children's** laughter, those **babies'** cries, **Phyllis'** cousin,* etc.) Possessive nouns are formed by adding *'s* (pronounced **apostrophe-s**) to a noun, or simply adding an apostrophe to nouns ending in *-s*.

EXERCISE 1

Underline and identify all the possessive structures in the following passage. Are they: (a) possessive determiners, (b) possessive pronouns, (c) possessive phrases, or (d) possessive nouns? The first paragraph has been done for you as an example. Do all the structures you identified describe possessive relationships?

(1) Have you ever tested (a) your memory? (2) There have been many studies of (d) people's ability to remember things. (3) These studies have found that there are two types (c) of memory: short-term memory and long-term memory.

(4) Short-term memory depends on the "length" or number of items that someone needs to remember. (5) A person's ability to remember a series of numbers for more than a minute is limited to about twelve or fourteen digits. (6) An individual's ability to remember strings of unconnected words seems to average about eight items. (7) Most people's performance on such memory tests will drop quickly if they are tested again, even after only a few hours' time.

(8) Long-term memory seems to be determined by the item's usefulness to the person being tested. (9) For example, people do a better job of remembering one of Shakespeare's sonnets if they can apply the "message" of the poem to some part of their own lives. (10) The more important a piece of information is to a person's life, the longer and more accurately it can be retained.

▶ Possessive Nouns Versus Possessive Phrases

EXAMPLES	EXPLANATIONS
(a) **The tall man's** face appeared in the window. **(b)** The face **of the tall man** appeared in the window.	Possessive noun (-'s) mean the same thing as nouns with a possessive prepositional phrase (*of . . .*), but one form is usually preferred over the other in specific situations.
(c) the **boy's** cap NOT: the cap **of the boy** **(d)** the **horse's** mouth NOT: the mouth **of the horse**	Use possessive nouns (with *-'s*) for: • most animate (living) nouns
(e) the **razor's** edge **(f)** the **train's** arrival	• objects that perform an action
(g) the **moon's** orbit **(h)** the **river's** mouth **(i)** the **earth's** atmosphere	• natural phenomena
(j) the back **of the chair** NOT: the **chair's** back **(k)** the roof **of the house** NOT: the **house's** roof **(l)** the cause **of the problem** NOT: the **problem's** cause	Use possessive phrases (with *of* + noun phrase): • for most inanimate (nonliving) nouns
(m) the daughter **of a well-known local politician** NOT: **a well-known local politician's daughter**	• when the possessive noun phrase is very long
(n) the that **of Mary's tall old-fashioned mother** NOT: **Mary's tall old-fashioned mother's** hat	• when a multiple possessive is long

EXERCISE 2

For each noun + possessive, write the best possessive form in the blank in the sentence. Add articles where necessary.

▶ **EXAMPLES:** hat/boy: _The boy's hat_____ blew into the sea.

cover/*Time* magazine: Being on _the cover of Time magazine_____ made Elvis Presley even more famous.

1. results/investigation: _____ were reported in the newspaper.

2. restaurant/Alice's mother: We had dinner at _____.

3. ability/individual: _____ to remember something depends on how important the information is.

4. rights/women: Suffragettes were early activists in the battle for

   _____.

5. opening/novel: _____ begins with the famous words, "Call me Ishmael."

6. take-off/rocket: _____ was quite an amazing spectacle.

7. music/Elvis Presley: _____ has been heard all over the world.

8. discovery/penicillin: Sir Alexander Fleming was responsible for

   _____.

9. children/a very famous American movie star: I went to school with

   _____.

10. rotation/earth: _____ is what causes night and day.

EXERCISE 3

Change the cues in parentheses to the correct possessive constructions. Add articles where necessary.

Last week Matt went shopping. It was (1) _____ (his roommate Jeff/birthday), and he wanted to buy a really "unusual" gift. He drove (2) _____ (Jeff/car) downtown. When he got there he realized that the (3) _____ (shopping district/center) was already quite crowded, and most (4) _____ (stores/the parking lots) were already full. He was in a hurry, so he decided to park in front of a hotel. He thought the (5) _____ (hotel/doorman) looked annoyed, but he wasn't really paying much attention. He visited several stores. In (6) _____ (one of the stores/window) he saw the perfect gift: a statue of a cowboy. In (7) _____ (cowboy/

hand) there was a container for toothpaste, toothbrush, and razor. He thought that the statue would look perfect in (8) _____ (their apartment/bathroom). He bought it and hurried back to where he had parked. The car was gone! At first Matt thought it had been stolen, but then he realized that it had probably been towed away. He called the police, and they verified that the car was at the station. When he got there, he found that (9) _____ (the car/front fender) had a dent, and there was a big scratch on (10) _____ (the car/side). Matt had to pay for the (11) _____ (repair/cost) and the towing charges. Jeff got a very expensive birthday present, and Matt got a long-overdue lesson about traffic laws and parking regulations.

FOCUS **3**

▶ Meanings of Possessive Forms

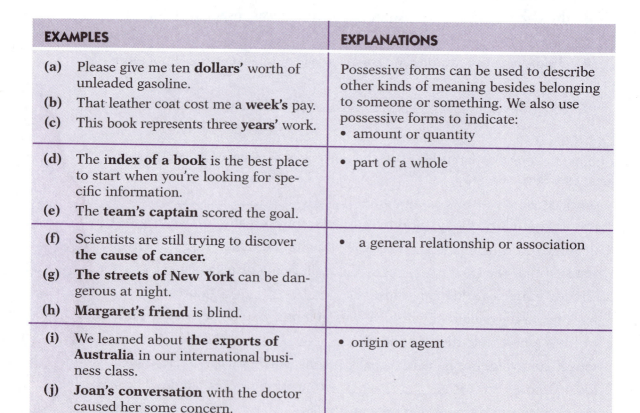

EXAMPLES	EXPLANATIONS
(a) Please give me ten **dollars'** worth of unleaded gasoline. **(b)** That leather coat cost me a **week's** pay. **(c)** This book represents three **years'** work.	Possessive forms can be used to describe other kinds of meaning besides belonging to someone or something. We also use possessive forms to indicate: • amount or quantity
(d) The **index of a book** is the best place to start when you're looking for specific information. **(e)** The **team's captain** scored the goal.	• part of a whole
(f) Scientists are still trying to discover **the cause of cancer.** **(g)** **The streets of New York** can be dangerous at night. **(h)** **Margaret's friend** is blind.	• a general relationship or association
(i) We learned about **the exports of Australia** in our international business class. **(j)** **Joan's conversation** with the doctor caused her some concern.	• origin or agent

EXERCISE 4

By yourself: Read the following article about Elvis Presley and underline all the possessives.

With a partner: Compare your answers. Find at least two examples of possessives that convey each of the following meanings, and write those examples in the space next to the meanings listed.

(a) quantity or amount _____

(b) part of a whole _____

(c) general relationship or association _____

(d) origin or agent _____

(e) actual possession _____

(f) phrases with *of* that should _____

     not be considered possessive

THE KING OF ROCK AND ROLL

(1) The most-visited residence in the United States is, <u>of course</u>, the White House, in Washington, D.C., the home <u>of the President of the United States</u>. (2) But the second most-visited residence may surprise you. (3) It is Graceland Mansion in Memphis, Tennessee, the home <u>of Elvis Presley</u>, the "King" <u>of Rock and Roll</u>. (4) Presley's influence on the popular music <u>of America</u> was profound. (5) He was one <u>of the first blues artists</u> to make rock and roll popular

with the middle class <u>of the United States</u>. (6) And <u>Elvis'</u> swinging hips and sexy voice made him the dream boyfriend <u>of an entire generation of teenage girls.</u>

(7) Presley's historic appearance on a 1958 broadcast of "The Ed Sullivan Show" caused an uproar. (8) His singing could not be heard because of the screams of his adoring fans. (9) And Presley's famous swinging hips were not seen at all, because of the objections of TV broadcasters, who felt his wild movements weren't suitable for family television. (10) Presley rapidly became America's most popular male singer of all time. (11) He made dozens of records and many films. (12) Everywhere he went crowds of screaming, adoring fans showered him with gifts, love, and devotion.

(13) But his personal life was marked by tragedy. (14) By the time he died in 1977, everyone had heard the rumors of his troubles with alcohol and drugs. (15) They had read about his failed marriage in the movie magazines. (16) His suspicions about his friends' loyalties and motivations had made a "living nightmare" of his life. (17) He died a prisoner of his own popularity.

(18) In spite of his death, Elvis is still called "The King of Rock and Roll." (19) Graceland Mansion is visited by hundreds of adoring fans every day. (20) His

records continue to be popular, and there are several radio stations that play nothing but Presley's music.

(21) Some people even believe that he is still alive and living in disguise. (22) There continue to be rumors that his mysterious death was just a trick to allow him to escape from the prison of his fame and his fans' adoration. (23) Many people still believe that he is living a quiet life with a new name and a thick beard to hide his famous face. (24) Today the Memphis post office still receives hundreds of letters addressed to Elvis at Graceland from fans who still await "The King's" return.

EXERCISE 5

Underline the possessive forms in the following sentences. There may be more than one possible interpretation. With a partner, discuss which of the following meanings the possessive forms indicate:

(a) an amount or quantity   (d) an origin or agent
(b) a part of a whole   (e) actual possession
(c) a general relationship/association

                           (b)   (c)

▶ **EXAMPLE:**   The <u>streets of San Francisco</u> are famous for <u>their</u> steep hills.

1. Scientists are studying the effects of alcohol on an individual's memory.

2. The wines of France are among the best in the world.

3. The teacher's assistant will hand back the homework.

4. That concept was introduced in the book's first chapter.

5. Chicago is four days' drive from Los Angeles.

6. An investigation of short-term memory has shown that items of personal importance are more easily remembered.

7. The steps of the porch looked like a meeting place of old, dirty shoes.

8. Matt's roommate likes ice cream.

9. Beethoven's symphonies still thrill listeners.

EXERCISE 6

Are these sentences correct or incorrect? If they are incorrect, identify the problem and correct it.

1. The fame of Elvis Presley spread across America.
2. The table's top was covered with newspapers.
3. The child of Bambang's classmate was sick with the flu.
4. Gladys' well-known next-door neighbor's dog's barking annoyed the entire neighborhood.
5. The scientists' studies' results indicate that memory is affected by such things as weather and time of day.
6. Memory's investigations have shown that the ability of people to remember things declines with age.
7. Rock and Roll's King died in 1977.
8. Elvis' death's circumstances are somewhat mysterious.

EXERCISE 7

Ask a classmate for his or her opinions on these topics, and the reasons for those opinions. Report your partner's answers to the rest of the class.

▶ **EXAMPLE:** best place to sit in a classroom

You: Where's the best place to sit in a classroom?

Your partner: The front of the class is better if you're a good student, but the back of the class is better if you want to sleep.

1. most important part of the semester (beginning, end, or middle)
2. favorite object that belongs to someone else
3. most important period of history
4. favorite piece of music

Ask two additional questions of your own that use possessive forms.

Use Your English

ACTIVITY 1: SPEAKING

Work with a partner to fill in the missing parts of the diagrams. Student A, look at diagrams A and C below. Student B, look at Diagrams B and D on page A-12. Diagram A contains elements not contained in Diagram B. Help your partner complete Diagram B correctly. Your partner should help you complete Diagram C, which is incomplete. You should not look at Diagrams B and D. Your partner should not look at Diagrams A and C.

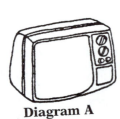

Diagram A

Diagram C

ACTIVITY 2: WRITING

Write a short description of a famous person. What are the things that made him or her famous? Here are some things you might mention in your description: his or her accomplishments, childhood, important experiences, influence on society.

ACTIVITY 3: SPEAKING

Check your short-term memory. Study the picture at the beginning of this chapter for thirty seconds. Then close your book and describe it to a partner. Your partner should look at the picture while you describe it and check your description for accuracy.

ACTIVITY 4: WRITING/SPEAKING

Oh no! There's been an automobile accident! Look at the picture and describe what has happened to the car and its passengers. After you have written your description, check the accuracy of your use of possessive forms.

ACTIVITY 5: LISTENING/SPEAKING

STEP 1 As you listen to the following talk, use the information to draw the diagram that is described by the speaker. Once you have finished, listen to the lecture again to check that you have completed your diagram correctly.

STEP 2 Compare your diagram with two or three others. As a group, decide on the correct answer to the two questions the speaker asks at the end of the lecture.

QUANTIFIERS, COLLECTIVE NOUNS, AND ADJECTIVES

UNIT GOALS:

- To correctly understand and use affirmative and negative quantifiers
- To correctly understand and use collective nouns
- To correctly understand and use collective adjectives

▶ OPENING TASK

Statistics About International Education

The Institute for International Education publishes statistical information about international educational exchange. Work with a partner. Examine these charts on the enrollment of international students in educational institutions in the United States. Using that information and your own knowledge, answer these three questions:

- What fields of study do international students pursue in the United States?
- How do they finance their education?
- Where do most students study?

A. Foreign Students by Field of Study, 1997/98

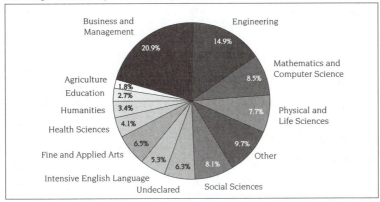

B. Primary Sources of Funding, 1997/98

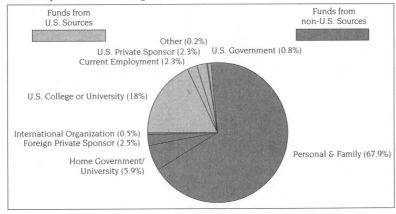

C. Host States for Foreign Scholars, 1997/98

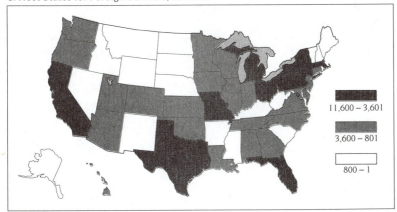

▶ **O**verview of Quantifiers in English

QUANTIFIERS Listed in Decreasing Order From All (100%) to None (0%)		PHRASES OF QUANTITY AND AMOUNT WITH SIMILAR MEANING
Affirmative Quantifiers		
Used with Count Nouns	**Used with Noncount Nouns**	
all/any *each/every*	*all/any*	the total number/amount
almost all	*almost all*	the vast majority
most	*most*	the majority
a great many *many* *lots of/a lot of* *plenty of*	*a great deal of* *much* *lots of/a lot of* *plenty of*	a large number/amount a substantial number/amount
a good number of	*a good deal of*	more than some
quite a few *quite a number of*	*quite a little* *quite a bit of*	more than a few/a little
some/any *a (certain/large/small) number of*	*some/any* *a (certain/large/small) number of*	an indeterminate number or amount
a few *several*	*a little*	a small number/amount

Negative Quantifiers		
Used with Count Nouns	**Used with Noncount Nouns**	
not all/every	*not all*	an unspecified number are not/do not
not many	*not much*	a small number/amount
few	*little*	an insufficient number/amount
hardly any *almost no/none*	*hardly any* *almost no/none*	the vast majority are not/do not
no/none/not any	*no/none/not any*	the total number/amount are not/do not

EXAMPLES	EXPLANATIONS
(a) **Most international students** study scientific or technical subjects.	You can use quantifiers: • as determiners with noun phrases
(b) **A few** study humanities or fine arts.	• in place of noun phrases to describe number or amount

EXERCISE 1

STEP 1 In the following passage, underline the quantifiers and circle the noun phrases they modify. The first sentence has been done for you as an example.

STEP 2 Are there quantifiers that do not appear with noun phrases? What sentences do they appear in, and what do they refer to?

▶ **EXAMPLE:** Clause 1 of the first sentence has a quantifier that does not appear with a noun phrase: **many.** It refers to **people** or **experts.**

Medical Education in the United States

(1) Even though American medical education is considered by <u>many</u> to be the best in the world, (2) there are relatively <u>few</u> (spaces) in American medical schools, and <u>a substantial number of</u> (Americans) are forced to go overseas to get their basic medical training. (3) As a result, not all the doctors practicing in the United States have received their training from American medical schools. (4) In fact, quite a few

---

have been educated in other countries. (5) However, all physicians must have clinical experience and pass qualifying examinations in order to receive a license to work in the United States.

(6) Most doctors currently working in the United States have completed their practical training in an American hospital or clinic. (7) Every hospital in this country accepts a few recently graduated medical students each year, (8) including graduates from many foreign medical schools. (9) While some popular hospitals receive a great many applications for each available space, (10) a number of hospitals in rural areas may receive only a few. (11) This period of practical training is called a "residency," and most last for two years. (12) A few are longer; some are shorter, depending on the specialization of the doctor.

(13) Many doctors study for an extra year before they begin their residency in order to become a specialist in a particular area of medicine. (14) No doctor is an expert in every area of medicine, but some doctors have more than one specialty. (15) Each area of medicine has its own period of residency and its own qualifying examinations.

EXERCISE 2

Based on the information you read in Exercise 1, write sentences that describe the training of medical doctors in the United States. Then write another set of sentences that describes medical training in another country that you are familiar with.

1. Most doctors . . .

2. Not all doctors . . .

3. All doctors . . .

4. A few doctors . . .

5. No doctors . . .

6. Many doctors . . .

EXERCISE 3

Use quantifiers to paraphrase the highlighted phrases of quantity or amount.

▶ **EXAMPLE:** **The vast majority of students** pass their qualifying examination on the first try.

Almost all students pass their qualifying examination on the first try.

1. **The vast majority of medical students** in the United States already have bachelor's degrees.

2. **An indeterminate number of students** have more than one major.

3. There are **a small number of scholarships** for international students.

4. It takes **a large amount of money** to fund a university education.

5. **A small number of students** apply to only one university for admission.

6. **An unspecified number of applicants** don't pass the qualifying exams such as TOEFL, GRE, or GMAT.

7. **The majority of international students** apply for admission to more than one university.

8. **A large number of students** study English before they begin their academic studies.

FOCUS **2**

Affirmative and Negative Quantifiers

	EXAMPLES	EXPLANATIONS
(a)	Do **all** foreign students have similar educational backgrounds?	Affirmative quantifiers can usually be used in both affirmative and negative statements and questions.
(b)	**Many** have different backgrounds, but **most** have graduated from high school, although **a few** haven't.	
(c)	NOT: **Few** doctors **don't** have medical degrees.	Negative quantifiers have a negative meaning, and usually do not occur in sentences with negative verbs.
(d)	BETTER: **Almost all** doctors **have** medical degrees.	

Negative quantifiers often imply that the amount or number is insufficient.

AFFIRMATIVE QUANTIFIERS (A SMALL AMOUNT)	NEGATIVE QUANTIFIERS (NOT ENOUGH)
(e) **A few** doctors have studied nonwestern medicine. (**Some** doctors have studied it.)	(f) **Few** doctors have studied nonwestern medicine. (**An insufficient number** have studied it.)
(g) There's **a little** money left after the bills are paid. (There is still **some** money for other things.)	(h) There's **little** money left after the bills are paid. (There is **not enough** money for other things.)

EXERCISE 4

Decide whether to use *few* or *a few, little* or *a little*. Compare your answers to those of a partner.

1. The students were discouraged because _____ people passed the examination.

2. Even very good students sometimes have _____ difficulty gaining admission to a good university.

3. I can loan you some money, but I've only got _____ dollars.

4. They were working in the laboratory for so long that now there's _____ time to get ready for the quiz.

5. There are _____ scholarships available for first-year medical students, so a medical education is expensive.

6. He put _____ effort into studying for examinations, and as a result, didn't pass on the first try.

7. The average medical student usually applies to at least _____ places for residency.

8. Bambang had _____ trouble finding a university. Several schools were willing to accept him.

EXERCISE 5

Using the following negative quantifiers, make true statements about the statistics on international education that you studied in the Opening Task.

1. few

2. not all

3. little

4. hardly any

5. no

▶ # Singular and Plural Quantifiers

EXAMPLES	EXPLANATIONS
(a) **All doctors know** basic first-aid techniques. **Most have** studied them in medical school. (b) **Every doctor knows** basic first-aid techniques. **Each has** studied them in medical school.	Most quantifiers are used with plural count nouns, but a few have a singular form.
(c) **Each student was** asked a question. (d) **Every student wants** to do **his or her** best in this class.	*Each* and *every* are only used with singular count nouns.
(e) **No student has** ever taken this test more than once. (f) **No doctors** in this country **are** allowed to practice without a license.	*No* can be used with both singular and plural nouns.
(g) When Bambang and Yanti took the TOEFL, **both students** passed on **their** first try. (h) **Both were** worried about doing poorly on the exam, but **neither has** to take it again. (i) They applied to the same two universities; **both universities have** acepted Yanti, and Bambang is willing to go to **either university** that **accepts** him.	*Both, either,* and *neither* are used in situations where there are only two nouns being described. *Both* is considered plural, but *either* and *neither* are considered to be singular.

EXERCISE 6

Change these statements with plural count nouns to statements with *any, each,* or *every.* Remember to make any other necessary changes to preserve the meaning of the original sentence. More than one answer may be correct.

▶ **EXAMPLE:**   All doctors know basic first aid.
    Every doctor knows basic first aid.
    Any doctor knows basic first aid.

1. All doctors must complete their residencies within two years.
2. All parents want their children to succeed in life.
3. Yanti spends all free weekends at the beach.
4. All the people who came to the examination brought calculators.
5. A wise student takes advantage of all opportunities to gain practical experience.

EXERCISE 7

Complete these sentences with true information.

1. Each student in this class . . .
2. Every teacher I have had . . .
3. Any English class . . .
4. No student . . .
5. No teachers . . .

EXERCISE 8

Use each of the following quantifiers—*both, either, neither*—to make true statements about similarities between each of the following categories.

1. two students in your class
2. two other people that you know
3. you and a good friend

FOCUS **4**

Using Quantifiers with *Of*

Quantifiers usually refer to nonspecific nouns (nouns that describe how many or how much, rather than identifying a specific item). But you can also use quantifiers with specific noun phrases, by adding *of* to the specific noun phrase. (See Unit 19 for more information and practice with specific and nonspecific reference.)

GENERIC/NONSPECIFIC REFERENCE	SPECIFIC REFERENCE
(a) **Any bus** will take you downtown.	(b) **Any of the buses** that stop here will take you downtown.
(c) **Most students** want to get good grades.	(d) **Most of the students** who Donna teaches have college degrees.
(e) **Several cars** have passed.	(f) **Several of the cars** at the police station had been stolen.

Note the exception for *all* and *no*.

(g) **All students** hate to take tests.	**(h)** **All the students** in this class hate tests.
	(i) **All of the students** in this class hate tests.
(j) **No buses** run after midnight.	**(k)** **None of the buses** that run after midnight stop here.

EXERCISE 9

Decide whether to use a *quantifier* or *quantifier + of* for these sentences.

1. (All) _____ laboratory equipment on this table should be sterilized before use.

2. (Almost all) _____ plants require sunlight to survive.

3. (Most) _____ coffee served in restaurants contains caffeine.

4. You won't need (much) _____ your warm clothing if you go to medical school in the Philippines.

5. (A great deal) _____ the population still believes in traditional medicine.

6. (Some) _____ the information in your report was incomplete.

7. I don't need (any) _____ your help.

8. Bob wasted (little) _____ the money he won on frivolous things.

9. (No/None) _____ students came to the party

▶ Quantifiers: Special Cases

EXAMPLES	EXPLANATIONS
(a) **Much of the financial support** for study in the United States comes from the students themselves. **(b)** How **much** money do you have? **(c)** **Not much.** We'd better stop at the bank and get a little. Are there any banks around here?	*Much* is **not** usually used in affirmative statements unless it is a specific reference (used with *of*). *Much* is used in questions and negative sentences.
(d) NOT: I'm having **much** trouble with finding a school. **(e)** I'm having **a lot of** trouble with finding a school.	*A lot (lots) of* is usually preferred in affirmative sentences.
(f) Is it true that **no students** failed the test? **(g)** That's correct. **None** did.	*No* cannot be used in place of a noun. *None* is used instead.
(h) Did **every** student pass the exam? **(i)** Yes, **every one** did. **(j)** NOT: Yes, **every** did.	*Every* cannot be used to replace a noun phrase without using *one*.

EXERCISE 10

Using the information in the article in Exercise 1, answer these questions with complete sentences, using quantifiers in place of noun phrases.

▶ **EXAMPLE:** Where are most doctors trained?

Most are trained here in America, but some study medicine overseas.

1. Do all doctors in the United States have to pass qualifying examinations?

2. How much money does it take to get a medical education in the United States?

3. How much competition is there for admission to American medical schools?

4. How many doctors have more than one specialty?

5. How many residency positions do most medical students apply for?

6. How many Americans study at medical schools overseas?

7. How many foreign students are enrolled in American medical schools?

8. How many doctors are experts in every area of medicine?

EXERCISE 11

Choose the correct form in these sentences.

1. I feel sorry for Albert. He's so shy and he has (few/a few/quite a few) friends he can talk to if he has problems.

2. Hardly any people (came/didn't come) to the meeting.

3. Ivan went to (quite a bit of/a bit of/only a bit of) trouble to get those tickets, so you must remember to thank him.

4. (Not every/Not all/None of) people like to go dancing on Saturday nights.

5. Do you have (many/much/every) time to help me?

6. Sure I do. I've got (a lot/lots of).

7. Why are Albert and Britta so sad? (Both/Neither/None) passed the chemistry exam.

8. Learning English takes (several/a certain amount of/any) practice.

FOCUS **6**

▶ # Collective Nouns

One category of collective nouns refers to groups of people or animals.

EXAMPLES		EXPLANATION
a **troupe** of dancers two **teams** of ball players several **committees** of experts a **delegation** of officials	a **flock** of birds that **herd** of goats **packs** of dogs a **swarm** of insects a **school** of fish	These collective nouns function like other count nouns. You can use them alone or with *of* + *a noun phrase*. They can have both singular or plural forms.

A second kind of collective nouns refers to social or political categories.

EXAMPLES		EXPLANATION
the government the middle class the media the opposition the arts community	the administration the aristocracy the public the establishment	They always occur with *the*. Their grammatical form is singular: **NOT**: **a** public, **a** media. **NOT**: the **publics** of the United States

Although the form of this kind of collective noun is singular, it can be used with either singular or plural verbs and pronouns.

SINGULAR	PLURAL
Using singular verbs and pronouns usually implies that the group operates as a whole. American English tends to use singular forms with singular collective nouns.	Using plural verbs and pronouns focuses on the individual behavior of the members of the group. British English tends to use plural forms with singular collective nouns.
(a) **The committee** of experts **has** decided to release **its** findings next week.	(b) **The committee** of experts **have** decided to release **their** findings next week.
(c) **The aristocracy has** opposed any challenge to **its** economic privileges.	(d) **The aristocracy have** opposed any challenge to **their** economic privileges.
(e) **The middle class** in America **has** begun to protest the accelerating decline in **its** standard of living.	(f) **The middle class** in America **have** begun to protest the accelerating decline in **their** standard of living.

EXAMPLES	EXPLANATION
(g) The beginning class **likes its** teachers to give **it** lots of homework. (h) The beginning class **like their** teachers to give **them** lots of homework. (i) NOT: The beginning class **likes their** teachers to give **them** lots of homework.	Although either singular or plural can be used, it is bad style to change from singular to plural within a single sentence or single reference.

EXERCISE 12

In the following sentences, underline each collective noun and any pronouns and verbs which refer to it. Decide why the author chose to consider the collective noun singular or plural.

▶ **EXAMPLE:**   The French Revolution was caused in part by the refusal of <u>the aristocracy</u> to give up <u>its</u> social privileges.
   Reason: Reference to a single social class—not a collection of individuals.

1. The victorious team all waved to their supporters while the crowd roared its approval.

2. The media is aware of the important role it plays in American presidential elections.

3. The herd of sheep bleated nervously to its shepherd as a pack of wolves made their way through the forest.

4. The military continues to fight further reductions in its funding.

5. The middle class is facing a greater tax burden than it has ever faced before.

6. A rash of new developments have made a great change in the government's priorities, and it is just beginning to respond to them.

EXERCISE 13

Decide whether the collective nouns in these sentences should be used with singular or plural verbs and pronouns, and choose the correct form. Although both choices may be grammatically correct, there may be a clear preference for one form instead of the other, so be prepared to explain why you have chosen the forms you did.

1. The staff took a vote about what kind of holiday party (it/they) (want/wants). (It/They) decided to rent a hall and hire a band.

2. The college administration (want/wants) a basketball team that (is/are) able to win enough games to place (itself/themselves) in the final play-offs.

3. The rowing team raised (its/their) oars as (its/their) boat crossed the finish line.

4. The advanced grammar class never like to turn in (its/their) homework right after a long vacation. (It/They) prefer(s) to finish all assignments before (it/they) leave(s) for vacation.

5. The crowd showed (its/their) approval by letting out a deafening roar.

6. The opposition voiced (its/their) disapproval of the policies the government had released in (its/their) latest report, by making more than three dozen speeches in Parliament.

▶ **C**ollective Adjectives

EXAMPLES	EXPLANATION
(a) **The rich** get richer and **the poor** get poorer. (b) These laws are designed to protect **the young** and **the helpless** from exploitation. (c) **The elderly are** making **their** opinions a growing force in American politics.	***The* + adjective** can be used to refer to a group that is defined by a particular characteristic. These structures are plural, and the verbs and pronouns reflect this.

EXERCISE 14

Rewrite each *the* + adjective construction below as a noun + relative clause.

▶ **EXAMPLE:** The French aristocracy didn't care about the poor.
   The poor = people who were poor.

1. Elvis Presley was very popular with the young.

2. Dear Abby writes an advice column in the newspaper for the lonely and the confused.

3. Nelson Mandela is an important hero for the oppressed.

4. Albert and Florence became doctors so they could help the sick.

5. The government should establish more comprehensive programs to help the underprivileged.

EXERCISE 15

Circle the correct form of the underlined phrases below.

The Problem of Homelessness in America

(1) The homeless are/is an increasing problem in most American cities. (2) The homeless consist/consists of several different categories of people. (3) The first category consist/consists of the mentally disabled. (4) In the early 1980s the Reagan administration ended most of its/their funding for treatment programs for the mentally ill. (5) As a result, quite a few mental hospitals were closed, and many of the mentally ill was/were released, and left to make its/their own way. (6) A substantial number have/has been unable to establish normal lives, and, as a result, it/they has/have ended up living on the streets.

(7) A second category of the homeless is/are the unemployed. (8) Typically, the unemployed is/are part of the homeless for a relatively short period of time—usually less than a year. (9) Some of it/them have/has lost its/their jobs; or the factories where it/they worked were closed without warning. (10) As a result, it/they didn't have enough money to pay rent. (11) Many of the unemployed has/have also ended up living on the streets or sleeping in its/their automobiles. (12) But the majority of the people in this category of the homeless is/are able to find housing again, once they have found other jobs.

(13) A third category of the homeless is/are the people who is/are addicted to drugs or alcohol. (14) Like the mentally ill, this category of homelessness represent/represents a persistent social problem. (15) The unemployed can hope for better times, and is/are usually able to escape from poverty and life on the streets, but the government has/have been very slow in giving its/their support to programs that help the mentally disabled or the addicted work on its/their recovery.

EXERCISE 16

Are these sentences correct or incorrect? If they are incorrect, identify the problem and correct it.

1. None of doctors are allowed to practice without a license.
2. I watched the flock of birds as it landed in the field across the road.
3. Few students never pass their qualifying exams.
4. The rich is always trying to avoid giving its money to pay taxes.
5. Quite a bit of time that doctors spend in their residencies is clinical training.
6. Students usually apply to several of universities for admission.
7. The herd of sheep was frightened by a pack of wolves, and it bleated nervously in their pen.
8. We had much trouble with the examination this morning.
9. A great many of traditional medicines are still used in rural areas.
10. No unlicensed physicians are allowed to practice in the United States.
11. Foreign students need lots of opportunities to get used to American educational techniques.
12. A few doctors don't stay up-to-date, but a lot of do.
13. Few students don't take their studies seriously.

Use Your English

A C T I V I T Y 1 : S P E A K I N G

English used to have many different collective nouns to refer to specific animals. These nouns usually indicated a quality or characteristic that these animals had.

- a pride of lions (because lions are proud)
- a parliament of owls (because owls are wise)
- a leap of leopards (because leopards leap)

Such collective words are rarely used in modern English. But sometimes for humorous reasons, people will invent collective words to apply to a particular group of people. Here are some examples:

- a sweep of cleaning ladies
- a hustle of salesmen
- a splash of swimmers

Working with a partner, decide on some humorous collective terms for some of these categories of people:

flight attendants	English teachers	puppies
lawyers	magicians	computer programmers
accountants	kittens	real estate agents

A C T I V I T Y 2 : W R I T I N G

Write a brief paragraph on one of these topics:

(a) Compare two athletic teams that play a sport you are familiar with. Why do you think one team is better than the other?

(b) Discuss one or more famous performing troupes (opera, drama, circus, dance, orchestra). Why are they famous, and do you feel that reputation is justified?

(c) What lessons can the old teach the young?

ACTIVITY 3: SPEAKING/WRITING

There is a joke that says, "A camel is a horse that was designed by a committee." Some management experts think that committees result in a product that is better than one made by a single individual. Others feel that committees tend to be inefficient and badly organized.

Based on your experience, identify the strengths and weaknesses of working in a committee. What are the advantages of having a group work together on a single task?

What are the disadvantages? Present your ideas to the rest of the class as a list of pros and cons.

▶ **EXAMPLE: Pro:** *A committee is able to assign tasks to each member, so the work can be divided.*

Con: *A committee doesn't reach decisions quickly, because each member has to agree about the issue before they can take action.*

How are you going to do this activity? By yourself or in a group?

ACTIVITY 4: SPEAKING

Should the rich pay more taxes or higher penalties (for traffic tickets, etc.) than the poor? Why do you think so? Discuss your ideas in a small group, and present a report on your group's opinion to the rest of the class. Your report should use phrases like "Our group feels that . . ."

ACTIVITY 5: WRITING/SPEAKING

Have you ever seen a political demonstration? Where and when did it occur? What was the demonstration about? What did the crowd do? What did the police do? Write a description of what happened.

ACTIVITY 6: SPEAKING

What is a good way to organize a complicated group project? Business managers have found that certain organizational techniques can make any group or committee run more smoothly and efficiently. Bad organization can result in a few people doing all the work, duplication of effort, or wasted time and energy. Here's an opportunity for you to explore techniques for streamlining group processes and decision-making.

STEP 1 Suppose the class has decided to all take a weekend trip together. In a small group, decide on the best way to organize such a complex project to make sure that work is done efficiently and everyone is involved in the process.

- Decide on the **tasks** that need to be done in order to organize and carry out such a trip.
- Establish a list of **committees** to accomplish these tasks, and specify the duties and members of each committee. Make sure that the work is evenly distributed, and that no single committee has too much to do.

STEP 2 When you have decided on your organizational plan, make a report to the rest of the class. Describe your plan. Tell what committees you have established, what responsibilities each committee has, and who each committee has as members.

STEP 3 Report on the decision-making process of your group. Identify any problems you had working as a committee. Present any techniques you used that helped you work together more efficiently.

STEP 4 The class should decide who has the best-organized plan for the trip.

ACTIVITY 7: SPEAKING

STEP 1 Conduct a poll of your classmates to find out about their educational backgrounds.

- How many years of school do they have?
- What subjects have they studied?
- Did most of them enjoy school?
- Decide on two more questions to ask them.

STEP 2 Present your information by constructing charts similar to the ones in the Opening Task of this unit.

ACTIVITY 8: SPEAKING

Conduct a public opinion poll on some aspect of current events.

STEP 1 In a group, choose some topic of current interest from the news, and develop a list of five to eight questions to determine how people feel about this issue.

STEP 2 Poll your classmates, and also interview ten to fifteen people outside of class.

STEP 3 Devise a graphic representation of your results similar to the charts in the Opening Task of this unit.

STEP 4 Using your charts, make a presentation of your findings to the rest of the class. Report any interesting differences between the opinions of your classmates and the people you interviewed outside of class.

ACTIVITY 9: LISTENING

STEP 1 Listen to the following brief news reports and answer the following questions. You may need to listen to each report more than once.

Report 1

1. What happens every year on March 19th?
   _____

2. Who provides publicity about this event?
   _____

3. Who else arrives on March 19th besides the swallows?
   _____

Report 2

1. What did the Canadian government ask the committee to do?
   _____

2. What is being anxiously awaited by the press and the public?
   _____

Report 3

1. What is different about the theater company described in this report?
   _____

2. When was it founded?
   _____

3. What effect has the company had?
   _____

STEP 2 Compare your answers with a classmate's.

PAST TIME FRAME

Using Adverbs and Aspect to Indicate Time Relationships

UNIT GOALS:

- To use correct sequence of tenses in past time to indicate time relationships
- To correctly understand and use clauses with *when* and *while* in past time
- To correctly understand and use progressive and perfect aspect in past time

▶ **OPENING TASK**

I'll Never Forget . . .

Write a paragraph or tell a partner about an experience that you will never forget. You can tell about a time when you heard about an important world event (for example, *"I will never forget the moment I heard that Yitzak Rabin had been assassinated,"* or *"I will never forget the moment I heard that the Berlin Wall was being torn down."*), or it could be something more personal (*"I will never forget the day my mother told me that I was going to have a new baby brother or sister."*). Your description should include what you were doing at the time, what you had been doing, and how you reacted. See the example on the next page.

Anyone living in San Francisco on October 17, 1989, can tell you exactly what he or she was doing when the earthquake occurred at 5:08 P.M. Here is Jeff's story about his experience in that earthquake.

(1) I will never forget the moment the earthquake struck San Francisco. (2) I was still in my office. (3) I had been trying to finish a project before I left for the day. (4) Suddenly, the building began to sway. (5) Books fell off their shelves. (6) People were screaming. (7) It seemed like things were moving for several minutes, but I guess the actual time was pretty short. (8) As soon as the building had stopped moving, I tried to get out as quickly as possible. (9) This wasn't easy, because I work on the seventeenth floor, and of course the electricity went out the moment the earthquake struck, so no elevators were working. (10) I ran down the emergency stairs in darkness and got out to the street. (11) Hundreds of people were just standing around, wondering what to do. (12) Pretty soon someone appeared who had a radio, so we all gathered around and heard about what had happened and what was happening. (13) After about twenty minutes, I realized that, of course, all public transportation had stopped, and if I wanted to get home, I'd have to walk, so I did. (14) When I finally got home, there was no electricity, but the apartment was O.K., and my roommate Matt and the dog were both sitting outside talking to the neighbors, watching the news broadcasts on a portable battery-operated TV. (15) We all sat around and told each other about our experiences.

Overview of Time Relationships in Past Time Frame

EXAMPLES	EXPLANATIONS
(a) He **walked** up the stairs. He **turned** the knob, and **opened** the door.	Time relationships in past time can be indicated by: • sequence Things happened in the order they are mentioned.
(b) **As he entered the room,** he realized something was different. **Before he had a chance to turn around,** he knew something was missing. **In a moment,** he realized what it was.	• adverbial information Adverbial clauses and phrases describe the order in which things happened.
(c) The television **had disappeared.** The antenna wires **were hanging** from the wall. He **had been watching** TV a few hours ago, but now there **was** nothing there.	• perfect and progressive aspect Choice of a particular verb tense and aspect describes the order in which things happened.

EXERCISE 1

Work with a partner to examine how time relationships are indicated in these passages. Passage 1 has been done for you as an example.

STEP 1 Place the highlighted verbs on a timeline in the order that they occurred.

STEP 2 Tell how you think that the order was indicated (by sequence, adverbials, or using perfect or progressive verb tenses). Sometimes there is more than one indication.

Passage 1

As he **entered** the room, he realized something was different. Before he **had** a chance to turn around, he **knew** something was missing. In a moment, he **realized** what it was. The television **had disappeared.** The antenna wires **were hanging** from the wall. He **had been watching** TV a few hours ago, but now there **was** nothing there.

STEP 1 Timeline

1. he **had been watching** TV	2. the TV **had disappeared**	3. the wires **were hanging** from the wall	4. there **was** nothing there	5. he **entered** the room	6. he **knew** something was missing	7. he **had** a chance to turn around	8. he **realized** what it was

STEP 2 How is the order of events indicated? (Example from #1)

1. perfect progressive; adverbial (a few hours ago) aspect
2. perfect aspect
3. progressive aspect
4. adverbial (now)
5. adverbial (as) aspect
6. sequence aspect
7. adverbial (before) aspect
8. sequence, adverbial (in a moment) aspect

Passage 2

Police **reported** yesterday that they **had uncovered** a large amount of stolen property from a warehouse in the southern part of the city. The warehouse **had been** under surveillance for some time. A suspiciously large number of people **had been seen** going in and out of the building. Once the police **had obtained** a search warrant, they **entered** the warehouse in the middle of the night and **discovered** large amounts of electronic equipment and other supplies. Police **announced** that this discovery **may lead** to the solution of a number of robberies.

Passage 3

1.	2.	3.	4.	5.	6.	7.	8.	9.

At the time of the earthquake Jeff **was** still in his office. He **had been trying** to finish a project before he left for the day. Suddenly, the building **began** to move. Books **fell** off their shelves. People **were screaming.** Although it seemed as if things were moving for several minutes, the actual time was just fifteen seconds. Even before the building **stopped** moving, people were trying to get out as quickly as possible. This wasn't easy for people who **had been working** on the higher floors of the building. The electricity **had gone off** the moment the earthquake struck, so no elevators **were working.** Most people **ran** down emergency strains in darkness and **got** out to the street.

1.	2.	3.	4.	5.	6.	7.	8.	9.	10.	11.

When, While, and Progressive Aspect in Past Time

Using *When*

EXAMPLES	TIME SEQUENCE	EXPLANATIONS
(a) When the books **fell** off the shelf, Jeff **hid** under his desk.	First the books fell off the shelf; then Jeff hid under his desk.	If you use *when* to connect two clauses with simple past tense verbs, the action described in the *when*-clause happened before the action in the main clause.
(b) When the books **fell** off the shelf, Jeff **was hiding** under his desk.	First Jeff hid under his desk; then the books fell off the shelf.	Use past progressive with the main clause to describe situations where the action described in the main clause happened before the action described by the *when*-clause.

Using *While*

EXAMPLES	EXPLANATIONS
(c) While the books **fell** off the shelf, Jeff **hid** under his desk.	*While* indicates that the action was **in progress at the same time** as the action described by the verb in the main clause.
(d) While the books **were falling** off the shelf, Jeff **was hiding** under his desk.	We can use either past progressive or simple past, since *while* makes the meaning clear.

EXERCISE 2

Answer these questions about the example passage in the Opening Task on page 373.

1. What was Jeff doing when the building started to sway?
2. What did he do when the building stopped swaying?
3. What happened to the elevators when the earthquake struck?
4. What was happening when Jeff reached the street?
5. What happened when Jeff reached the street?
6. What was happening when Jeff finally got home?
7. What happened when Jeff finally got home?

FOCUS **3**

USE

Other Uses of Progressive Aspect

EXAMPLES	EXPLANATIONS
(a) In 1997, while I **was researching** the economic consequences of the American Civil War, I found a fascinating piece of information.	Use progressive aspect to express: • actions that were in progress or uncompleted
(b) During the last few years of his life, Mozart **was constantly trying** to borrow money from anyone who would loan it to him.	• actions that were repeated or continous
(c) Before John found an apartment in Paris, he **was staying for a short while** at the house of a shopkeeper and his family.	• temporary situations

EXERCISE 3

Identify all the past progressive verb forms in the example passage of the Opening Task and tell why you think the author chose to use past progressive.

Circle the appropriate form of the verbs in parentheses. There may be more than one correct choice. The first sentence has been done for you as an example.

The Search for the Northwest Passage

(1) The St. Lawrence Seaway, the waterway that (links/is linking) the Great Lakes of North America with the Atlantic Ocean, was discovered by explorers who (looked/were looking) for the Northwest Passage. (2) Geographers at that time (believed/were believing) that there was a water course that (connected/was connecting) the Atlantic and Pacific oceans. (3) Throughout the sixteenth and early seventeenth centuries, both England and France constantly (sent/were sending) one expedition after another to attempt to find the passage. (4) Early explorers (investigated/were investigating) every large inlet and river along the entire eastern coast of North America.

(5) Even though they never (found/were finding) the Northwest Passage, these early explorers (made/were making) a valuable contribution to the knowledge of North American geography. (6) While they (explored/were exploring) the coast they (made/were making) many other very useful discoveries. (7) Not only the St. Lawrence Seaway, but also Hudson Bay, Chesapeake Bay, the Hudson River, and the Delaware River all (were discovered/were being discovered) by explorers who actually (looked/were looking) for something else.

FOCUS **4**

Using Perfect Aspect in Past Time Frame

You can use both adverbials and perfect aspect to indicate that a particular action happened before others.

ADVERBIALS	PERFECT ASPECT
(a) **Before** we left on the trip, we checked the car thoroughly. (b) **After** we checked the oil, we made sure the tires had enough air.	(c) But we **hadn't gotten** more than a few miles when we realized that we **had forgotten** something: We **had left** our suitcases on the front porch. We **had been worrying** so much about the mechanical condition of the car that we left without thinking about its contents.

We don't usually use both adverbials and perfect aspect in the same sentence, and tend to avoid the past perfect tense if the time sequence is clear from other information.

EXAMPLES	EXPLANATIONS
	In general, we indicate time relationships with perfect aspect only when it is necessary:
(d) He **had seen** the movie, and **therefore** didn't want to go with us.	• to communicate a logical connection between the two events
(e) They only **started** the project when I **arrived,** but they **had finished** it when I **left.**	• to clarify a time relationship
(f) I **had finished** all my homework before I went to Jane's party.	• to describe an action that was fully completed
(g) They **told** me that the doctor **had just left.**	• to change the time frame in reported speech.

EXERCISE 5

With a partner, examine how adverbials and aspect are used to indicate time relationships in these passages.

- For each sentence, identify the verb phrases that happened **before** the verb phrases listed in the first column of the chart, and write them in the "Time Before" column.
- Then decide whether each time relationship is indicated by adverbials, by aspect or by both. Record that information in the "How Indicated" column.
- Compare your answers with another pair of students.

The first two sentences in each passage have been done for you as examples.

1. (1) Before we left on the trip, we checked the car thoroughly. (2) After we checked the oil, we made sure the tires had enough air. (3) But we hadn't gotten more than a few miles when we realized that we had forgotten something: We had left our suitcases on the front porch. (4) We had been worrying so much about the mechanical condition of the car that we left without thinking about its contents.

	TIME BEFORE	HOW INDICATED
1. we left on the trip	we checked the car	adverb (before)
2. we made sure the tires had enough air	we checked the oil	adverb (after)
3. we realized that . . .		
4. we left without thinking about its contents		

2. In the fifteenth century, a new social and economic order was born in Europe. (1) By the end of the fourteenth century, the population of Europe was about a third smaller than it had been at the beginning of the century. (2) It was one of the few times in history when the population had actually decreased. (3) This smaller population was caused by repeated outbreaks of bubonic plague which had swept through the continent several times during the century, (4) and by the time the century had ended, this disease had caused some fundamental changes in society. (5) So many people had died that the traditional feudal landlords were forced to intermarry with wealthy merchant families, instead of the aristocracy. (6) People who had previously only had the opportunity to make a living as farmers or serfs were able to become craftsmen and artisans. (7) The plague had killed so many people that the traditional social boundaries were wiped out, and this created a period of great social mobility and economic change.

	TIME BEFORE	HOW INDICATED
1. the population was one third smaller	than it had been at the beginning of the century	adverbial (By the end of the fourteenth century) aspect
2. it was one of the few times in history	the population had actually decreased	aspect
3. the smaller population was caused by repeated outbreaks of plague		
4. the disease had caused some fundamental changes in society		
5. landlords were forced to intermarry with wealthy merchants		
6. people were able to become crafsmen and artisans		
7. this created a period of great social mobility and economic change		

EXERCISE 6

Use past perfect in these sentences only if it is necessary to the meaning of the sentence. Otherwise use simple past or past progressive.

1. Peter (a) _____ (went) to talk with Mr. Green about the fight he (b) _____ (have) with Denise earlier in the day.

2. As soon as the building (a) _____ (stop moving), Jeff
   (b) _____ (try) to call Matt, but the telephones
   (c) _____ (stop working).

3. It was too late to put out the fire because it _____
   (grow) too big for anything to control.

4. I (a) _____ (look) everywhere for my wallet, but I
   (b) _____ (not find) it anywhere. It (c) _____
   (disappeared).

5. Denise (a) _____ (go) to Peter's office to complain about
   his attitude, but he (b) _____ (leave) early to take his
   children to the circus.

6. Mary (a) _____ (be) extremely worried about John
   since she (b) _____ (not receive) any letters from him
   in over a month.

Perfect Progressive Aspect in Past Time Frame

USE

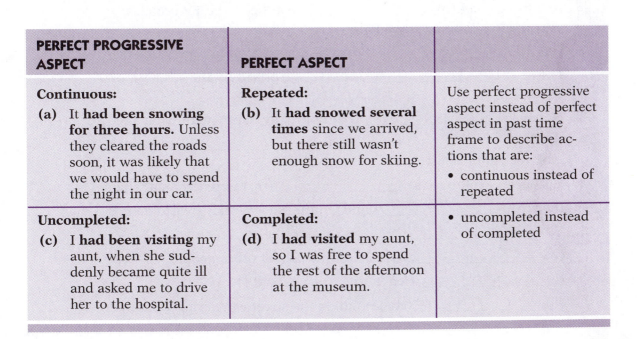

PERFECT PROGRESSIVE ASPECT	PERFECT ASPECT	
Continuous: (a) It **had been snowing for three hours.** Unless they cleared the roads soon, it was likely that we would have to spend the night in our car.	**Repeated:** (b) It **had snowed several times** since we arrived, but there still wasn't enough snow for skiing.	Use perfect progressive aspect instead of perfect aspect in past time frame to describe actions that are: • continuous instead of repeated
Uncompleted: (c) I **had been visiting** my aunt, when she suddenly became quite ill and asked me to drive her to the hospital.	**Completed:** (d) I **had visited** my aunt, so I was free to spend the rest of the afternoon at the museum.	• uncompleted instead of completed

EXERCISE 7

Fill in the blanks with the appropriate form of the verbs in parentheses (past perfect or past perfect progressive).

1. When the earthquake struck, Jeff was still in the office because he
   _____ (try) to finish a project before he left for the day.

2. Denise _____ (look) for a reason to complain about Peter
   even before he took time off from work to see his son's school play.

3. By the beginning of the fifteenth century, the bubonic plague
   _____ (cause) some fundamental social and political
   changes.

4. The police _____ (keep) the warehouse under surveillance
   for some time when they finally obtained a search warrant and inves-
   tigated.

5. They first became suspicious because so many people
   _____ (go) in and out of the warehouse at strange hours
   of the day and night.

EXERCISE 8

Fill in the blanks with the appropriate form of the verbs in parentheses (simple past, past perfect, or past perfect progressive). More than one answer
may be correct.

1. I (a) _____ (work) on my homework for about twenty
   minutes when I (b) _____ (overhear) the TV broadcast
   announcing Rabin's assassination.

2. Jeff (a) _____ (experience) several minor earthquakes,
   but he (b) _____ (be) still surprised by the strength of
   this one.

3. Nancy (a) _____ (be) not really happy with what she
   (b) _____ (do) so she (c) _____ (decide) to
   look for another job.

4. European explorers (a) _____ (try) to reach Asia, when
   they (b) _____ (land) in the New World "by accident."

5. When Jeff (a) _____ (get) to the street, he
   (b) _____ (see) that hundreds of other people
   (c) _____ (leave) their offices and
   (d) _____ (stand) out on the street wondering what to do.

EXERCISE 9

Fill in the blanks with the correct forms of the verbs in parentheses (present, present perfect, simple past, past perfect, past progressive, or past perfect progressive). There may be more than one correct answer.

George Washington (1) _____was_____ (be) the first President of the United States, and (2) _____served_____ (serve) as the leader of American troops during the War of Independence. According to a famous story, when George (3) _____was_____ (be) a young boy, and (4) _____learned_____ (learn) how to use farming tools, his father (5) _____gave_____ (give) him a hatchet for his birthday. George (6) _____was_____ (be) anxious to use the hatchet, so he (7) _____ran_____ (run) out of the house and (8) _____chopped_____ (chop) down a cherry tree in his father's garden. When his father (9) _____discovered_____ (discover) that someone (10) _____chopped_____ (chop) down the tree, he (11) _____was_____ (be) very angry. He (12) _____demanded_____ (demand) to know who (13) _____chopped_____ (chop) down his cherry tree. When little George (14) _____heard_____ (hear) his father's angry shouting, he (15) _____went_____ (go) to his father and (16) _____told_____ (tell) him that he (17) _____did_____ (do) it with his new hatchet. He said, "I (18) _____am_____ (be) sorry you (19) _____are angry_____ (be) angry, and I (20) _____know_____ (know) you will punish me, but I must admit my crime, because I cannot tell a lie." George's father (21) _____was_____ (be) so impressed with his honesty, that he (22) _____decided_____ (decide) not to punish the boy after all, and, in fact, (23) _____rewarded_____ (reward) him, by giving him a silver dollar.

This incident actually never (24) _____ (happen), but millions of American children (25) _____ (read) this story in school. Parents and teachers (26) _____ (think) that it is a good way to teach children to always tell the truth.

Use Your English

ACTIVITY 1: WRITING

Write a paragraph about an experience that happened to you or to someone you know that supports the truth of one of the following proverbs.

- An idle mind is the devil's playground.
- Too many cooks spoil the broth.
- Two heads are better than one.
- If at first you don't succeed, try, try again.
- Never count your chickens before they have hatched.

ACTIVITY 2: WRITING

Form groups of three to five people. You are going to write a group story.

STEP 1 Each person should take a piece of paper and start a story with this sentence: "It was a dark and stormy night. Suddenly, (your teacher's name) heard a terrible scream."

Then each person in the group should write for three minutes. When the three minutes is up, fold the paper so that only the last sentence or two can be read.

STEP 2 Pass your story to the person on your right, and take the paper of the person on your left. Then each person should write for three minutes to continue that person's story. Repeat the process until the papers have gone completely around the group.

STEP 3 Unfold the papers and read the resulting stories to each other. Which story is the funniest? Which story is the clearest? Choose the story you like best to read aloud to the rest of the class.

ACTIVITY 3: SPEAKING/WRITING

Every country has famous stories in its history that all children learn about when they are growing up. In the United States, for example, all school children have heard the story of George Washington and the cherry tree (Exercise 9).

Do you know any similar kinds of famous stories about real people that you were told as a child? Write down the story or tell it to a partner or the rest of the class.

ACTIVITY 4: SPEAKING

Listen to other people tell their stories of their unforgettable experience from the Opening Task. Compare your account to other people's stories. In a group decide an answer to this question:

- Are there any common feelings or reactions that all or most people share in situations when they hear about or experience some very important or surprising event?

Present your list of shared reactions to the rest of the class.

ACTIVITY 5: LISTENING

Listen to this story of one person's unforgettable experience and answer the questions below.

1. What was the speaker doing when she heard the news about John F. Kennedy (JFK)?

   _____

2. What did the speaker do when she heard the news about JFK?

   _____

3. What were her classmates doing when they heard the news about JFK?

   _____

4. What did they do when they heard the news about JFK?

   _____

UNIT 24

MODALS IN PAST TIME

UNIT GOALS:

- To correctly use *could* versus *was able to* to describe abilities in past time
- To correctly use *would* versus *use to* to describe habitual actions in past time
- To correctly use *would* versus was *going to* to describe future events in past time

▶ OPENING TASK
Identifying the Benefits of Growing Older

386

STEP 1 Think about these questions:

- In what ways are you different than you were in the past?
- What are some things that you used to do but don't do anymore?
- What are some things that you do now, but you couldn't or wouldn't do five or ten years ago?
- How do people change as they grow older?

STEP 2 Discuss your ideas with two or three other students in the class. Your group should decide on two general ways that people's lives change for the better as they grow older, and present those ideas to the rest of the class. You can read the paragraph below as an example of the kind of changes you may want to consider.

GROWING OLDER

Growing older makes people less worried about what other people think. In high school I used to be really shy. I would avoid talking to people, and I couldn't express my ideas in class without feeling very uncomfortable. I guess I was afraid that people were going to laugh at me, or that they would think I was strange. In high school people were supposed to "fit in." They weren't allowed to be different. So I used to wear the same kind of clothes and try to behave the same way as everybody else. I felt I had to be "one of the crowd." Now that I am older, I can stand up in front of other people and tell them what I think. I certainly couldn't do that in high school. I wear clothes because I like them, not because other people like them. I think I'm much more independent and self-confident than I used to be in high school.

▶ **O**verview of Modals in Past Time Frame

MEANING/ USE	ONE-WORD MODALS	EXAMPLES	PHRASAL MODALS	EXAMPLES
necessity	*(No one-word modals for these uses.)*		*had to*	**(a)** I **had to** do my homework before we went to the movies.
permission			*was allowed to*	**(b)** John **was allowed to** bring a guest.
advice/ obligation			*was supposed to*	**(c)** You **were supposed to** be at the doctor's office at 2:00.
ability	*could* *couldn't*	**(d)** John **could** speak French when he was younger.	*was able to*	**(e)** I **was able to** get tickets to the concert.
habitual actions	*would* *wouldn't*	**(f)** When he lived in France he **would** always have his meals at a bistro.	*used to*	**(g)** He **used to** play tennis, but he doesn't anymore.
future events in past time	*would* *wouldn't* *might* *might not*	**(h)** Naomi hoped that she **would** have the kind of vacation where she **might** meet someone and fall in love.	*was going to* *was about to* *was to*	**(i)** Nora **was about to** leave for the airport She **was going to** spend a couple of months in Japan.

EXERCISE 1

Decide whether the modals in these sentences are requests in present time or questions about past habits and abilities.

1. Could you tell me how to get to Carnegie Hall?
2. Would you cry when your mother punished you?
3. Could you ride a bicycle when you were five?
4. Would you mind putting out that cigar?
5. Do you think you could tell that joke without laughing?
6. When you were little, would you always do everything your parents wanted?

FOCUS **2**

Expressing Necessity, Permission, and Advisability in the Past Time

EXAMPLES	EXPLANATION
	Use phrasal modals in the past time frame to describe:
(a) When I was a child my brothers and sisters and I **had to** do a number of chores.	• necessity
(b) If we didn't, we **weren't allowed to** watch TV.	• permission
(c) I **was supposed to** wash the dishes on Mondays.	• advisability

EXERCISE 2

Make five statements about things you **were allowed to do** when you were a child. Make five statements about things you **weren't allowed to do.**

EXERCISE 3

Work with a partner, and ask if he or she was allowed to do the things you talked about in Exercise 2.

▶ **EXAMPLE:** When you were a child, were you allowed to stay out after dark?

Identify one privilege that was the same for both of you, and report it to the rest of the class.

EXERCISE 4

Make five statements about things that you **had to do** when you were a child. Make five statements about things that you **were supposed to do** when you were a child but didn't always do.

EXERCISE 5

Work with a partner, and ask if he or she had to do the things you talked about in Exercise 4.

▶ **EXAMPLE:**   When you were a child, did you have to come home before dark?

When you were a child, were you supposed to do your homework before you could watch TV?

Identify one responsibility that was the same for both of you, and report it to the rest of the class.

FOCUS **3**

MEANING

▶ **Ability in Past Time:**
Could Versus *Was Able To*

EXAMPLES	EXPLANATIONS
(a) John **could speak** French. **(b)** John **was able to speak** French.	In statements of general ability (skills that exist over time), there is no difference in meaning or use between *could* and *was able to*.
(c) I **was able to** get two tickets to the concert. **(d)** NOT: I **could** get two tickets to the concert.	In statements of specific ability (specific events or actions), use *was able to*.
(e) I stood in line for over an hour, but **I couldn't** get tickets. **(f)** I stood in line for over an hour, but **I wasn't able to** get tickets.	In negative statements of specific ability both *couldn't* and *wasn't able to* can be used.

EXERCISE 6

Fill in the blanks with *could* or *be able to*.

▶ **EXAMPLE:** <u>Were you able to</u> go to Joan's party?

No, I <u>couldn't/wasn't able to.</u> But I <u>was able to</u> send her a birth-day card.

1. George (a) _____ get tickets to the play. However, he (b) _____ (not) find them when it was time to go to the theater.

2. Peter (a) _____ convince his boss to let him do anything he wanted. As a result, he (b) _____ stay home from work last week.

3. Professor Katz (a) _____ speak Russian. Because of this, she (b) _____ translate the ambassador's speech to the United Nations.

4. Bambang (a) _____ (not) pass the TOEFL, so he enrolled in an English course. He still (b) _____ (not) pass the TOEFL last semester, but he succeeded this semester.

EXERCISE 7

1. Which of the following activities were you able to do ten years ago? Use complete sentences to identify things that you could do ten years ago and things that you couldn't do.

2. Describe two other things not listed below that you could do ten years ago and two other things that you couldn't do.

ride a bike	run a mile in eight minutes
speak fluent English	drive a truck
understand American films	support my family
play a musical instrument	shop for food in a foreign country
read and write English	swim
speak a second language	play soccer
drive a car	translate things into English

EXERCISE 8

Underline the structures that describe past abilities in these short passages. Why do you think the author decided to use the form he did?

1. (a) Matt stood in line for four hours, but he wasn't able to get tickets for the concert. (b) When he got home, Jeff could tell that he was frustrated and a little angry. (c) He wanted to cheer Matt up, but he couldn't do much to improve Matt's mood.

2. (a) Nigel was a genius. (b) He was able to do many things that other children his age couldn't do. (c) He could solve complicated mathematical equations. (d) He could write poetry and quote Shakespeare. (e) He was even able to get into college when he was only fourteen years old. (f) But he couldn't make friends with other children his own age.

FOCUS **4**

▶ # Habitual Actions in Past Time: *Would* Versus *Used To*

EXAMPLES	EXPLANATIONS
(a) I **used to** live in Washington, D.C. (b) Every day I **would** go jogging past all the famous monuments. (c) No matter how hot or cold it was, I **would** run around the Tidal Basin and along the Mall.	Habits and regular activities in the past are described by using *used to* and *would*. *Used to* is often used in the first sentence to establish the topic. *Would* is used in other sentences to supply the details.
(d) When I was a child I **would wait** at the bus stop for my father to come home. (e) When I was a child I **used to wait** at the bus stop.	Habitual **activities** can be expressed by both *would* and *used to*.
(f) When I was a child I **used to have** lots of toys. (g) When I was a child I **had** lots of toys. (h) NOT: When I was a child I **would have** lots of toys.	Habitual **states** must be expressed by *used to* or simple past tense. We do not use *would*.

EXERCISE 9

Below is a list of things many children do.

1. From this list choose five things that you used to do when you were a child.

2. Choose five things that you didn't use to do.

3. Think of three additional examples for each category.

4. Describe these activities in complete sentences. Be sure to use the correct form for verbs that describe habitual states rather than activities. You should have eight sentences describing things you used to do as a child and eight sentences about things you didn't used to do.

believe in ghosts	have a secret hiding place
be afraid of the dark	play with dolls
eat vegetables	like going to the doctor
play "cops and robbers"	enjoy going to school
pretend to be able to fly	obey older brother or sisters
ride a bicycle	cry when hurt
spend the night at a friend's house	

EXERCISE 10

Work with a partner, and ask questions about the things you described in Exercise 9.

▶ **EXAMPLE:** When you were a child, did you ever pretend that you could fly?

Report some of your partner's answers to the rest of the class.

▶ Future in Past Time Frame

EXAMPLES	EXPLANATIONS
(a) My parents got married almost fifty years ago. In 1937 my father first met the woman that he **would marry** a few years later. From that very first day my father knew that he **was** eventually **going to marry** her.	The past time-frame often includes references to future events. The actual time of these events may be in the past (in relation to **now**), but it is in the future in relation to our moment of focus. The moment of focus in Passage (a) is "that very first day" in 1937.
(b) Although Lincoln **wasn't to become** president until 1860, he started running for political offices quite early in his career. At that time he had no idea that he **was going to have** three unsuccessful attempts before he **would** finally **win** his first election.	In passage (b) the moment of focus is when Lincoln "started running for political offices." We use the one-word and phrasal modals for future activity in their past tense forms (*would, was/were going to*, and *was/were to*). See Unit 15 for more practice with these modals in the present and future time frames.
(c) Naomi hoped that she **would** have a vacation where she **might** meet someone and fall in love. Perhaps it **could** even become a more permanent romance.	"Past tense" one-word modals (*might, would, could*) of future activity can be used to talk about future events in the past time frame.

EXAMPLES	EXPLANATIONS
(d) Elizabeth didn't have much time to get ready for the dance She **was going to** do all her errands in a single afternoon. First she **would** pick up her dress. Then she **would** get her hair done. That **would** leave her the rest of the afternoon to get ready.	*Was going to* is preferred over *would*: • to introduce a topic
(e) Yuri didn't want to leave the house It **was going to** rain any minute.	• to indicate immediate future
(f) At first my parents **weren't going to** let me stay up late but I convinced them to let me do it. **(g)** Oh, here you are! I **was going to** call you. But now I don't have to. **(h)** We **were going to** go skiing tomorrow, but there's no snow, so we'll just stay home instead.	• to describe unfulfilled intentions—intended actions that did not actually take place

EXERCISE 11

Underline all the modal structures that refer to future events or intentions in these paragraphs. The first sentence of each passage has been done for you as examples.

1. (a) When I was a child I used to dream that I <u>would have</u> a bright future. (b) I thought I was going to be a doctor or a movie star. (c) I would have a university medical degree. (d) I would have a job where I could do what I wanted, and wouldn't have to go to an office every day. (e) I was going to be famous, and I was definitely going to have lots of money. (f) I would have a big house in Hollywood and ten children.

2. (a) Nora <u>was going to spend</u> a month in Japan before she started her new job, which <u>was to begin</u> in six weeks. (b) She was going to fly to Japan last Monday, but a strange thing happened as she was about to leave for the airport. (c) Suddenly she had a strong sensation that she shouldn't get on the plane. (d) She had a strange feeling that there might be an accident or that there would be some other problem. (e) She knew that she could take a flight later in the week, so that's what she decided to do.

EXERCISE 12

Do these sentences describe unfulfilled intentions or future activities in the past time frame? In sentences that describe future activities, substitute *would* for *was/were going to*.

▶ **EXAMPLE:** Nora and Jim aren't here right now. They said they **were going to** be studying at the library.

If describes future activity. They said they would be studying at the library.

1. I **wasn't going to** mention the money you owe me. But since you brought it up, I guess we should talk about it.

2. My teacher **wasn't going to** postpone the test, so we studied for the entire weekend.

3. The committee organized the refreshments for the party. Mary **was going to** bring cookies. John **was going to** take care of beverages.

4. I'm not finished painting the house. Jim **was going to help,** but I guess he had something else to do.

5. **Were you going to** send me a check? I haven't received it yet.

6. I never thought this party **was going to** be so much fun.

7. We **weren't going to** extend our vacation, but the weather was so nice that we decided to stay for a few more days.

EXERCISE 13

Decide which form, *would* or *was/were going to*, should be used in the following sentences. In some cases both answers may be correct.

1. As soon as Charlie heard about Maria's party he decided that he
   (a) _____ (not go). Sofia (b) _____ (be)
   there, and she and Charlie didn't get along. He was afraid that she
   (c) _____ (probably) to tell everyone about how they
   used to be engaged to be married.

2. Last week Jeff stood in line for five hours to get a ticket to the
   opera, but he knew it was worth the long wait. It (a) _____
   (be) a great performance. Pavarotti (b) _____ (sing) the
   part of Falstaff. Jeff had heard him before so he was sure it
   (c) _____ (be) wonderful.

3. Naomi didn't know what to do for her vacation. Perhaps she
   (a) _____ (go) to Mexico. The plane ticket
   (b) _____ (be) expensive, but she didn't want to travel
   by herself on the bus.

4. When I talked to Lin last Sunday night she wasn't planning on getting
   much sleep. Her project was already a week late, and she couldn't ask
   the professor for another extension. She (a) _____
   (finish) her assignment, even if she had to stay up until dawn. It
   (b) _____ (not be) easy. She had to finish reading *War and
   Peace* and then write a ten-page paper. She (c) _____
   (probably be) up all night.

5. We performed a very difficult experiment in our chemistry class the
   other day. I was very nervous because we had to put just the right
   amount of chemicals into a solution in order for the reaction to
   occur. Too much phosphorous (a) _____ (cause) the
   wrong reaction. If there was too little, nothing (b) _____
   (happen) at all. If I (c) _____ (do) the experiment
   correctly, it (d) _____ (be) necessary to measure very,
   very carefully.

Use Your English

ACTIVITY 1: WRITING/SPEAKING

In the Opening Task on page 387 you read about ways in which people change for the better as they grow older. Now think about ways that people change for the worse.

STEP 1 Make a list of things that you can no longer do that you used to be able to do. These may be activities or privileges. If you wish, compare your list to those of other students in the class.

STEP 2 Write a paragraph or give a short speech to the rest of the class describing one general way that people's lives change for the worse as they grow older. Be sure to provide examples to support your ideas.

ACTIVITY 2: SPEAKING

In 1989 political changes in Eastern Europe resulted in important changes in worldwide economics, politics, and military alliances. In 1991 the outbreak of war in the Middle East caused similar unexpected changes in world affairs.

STEP 1 What predictions did people make about world events before these changes occurred? What things are happening now that seemed impossible a few years ago? With other students develop two lists:

- Things people thought were going to happen that no longer seem likely to happen.
- Things that are happening now that people never thought would happen.

STEP 2 Make a presentation to the class about other great surprises in history.

ACTIVITY 3: WRITING

Write a short paragraph about one or more of these topics:
- bad habits that you used to have, but don't have anymore.
- things you would do as a child when you were unhappy.
- a time when you were going to do something but weren't allowed or weren't able to do so.
- how your life has turned out differently from your expectations (things you thought were going to happen that didn't, and vice versa).

ACTIVITY 4: LISTENING

Listen to the following short lecture on science fiction and match the predictions listed below to the authors who imagined them, by writing the initials of the author (JV—Jules Verne; HGW—H.G. Wells; GO—George Orwell; or AH—Aldous Huxley) next to the prediction Then put a check by those predictions which have actually come true, and compare your answers with a partner's.

_____ The government will control all aspects of people's lives.

_____ Anyone who tries to disagree with the government will be put in prison.

_____ Many people will own airplanes.

_____ There will be exploration of the moon.

_____ People will be able to travel through time.

_____ Children will be raised in state-run nurseries, instead of in individual families.

_____ There will be a single world language.

_____ People will use solar power to get energy.

_____ Aliens from Mars will invade and conquer the Earth but will eventually die from common bacterial infections.

_____ Scientists will discover a way to make people invisible.

_____ People will be watched by police, by hidden cameras and microphones.

_____ Children will be born through artificial means.

_____ There will be movies that are so realistic that people will think they are actually happening.

_____ There will only be three or four huge governments, and they will constantly be at war with each other.

_____ The use of mind-altering drugs will be widespread, and encouraged by the government.

ACTIVITY 5: SPEAKING

Based on the information you learned from the lecture in Activity 4, discuss the following question in a small group and present your opinion and your reasons to the rest of the class.

- Which writer did the most accurate job of predicting the future?

ACTIVITY 6: WRITING/SPEAKING

Think about these questions:

- How has the social role of women changed?
- What things were your grandmothers not allowed to do, simply because they were women?
- What things wouldn't women consider doing fifty years ago that are commonplace today?

Write a paragraph or make a presentation to the rest of the class discussing the five biggest differences between women's lives fifty years ago and today.

U N I T   25

R E P O R T E D   S P E E C H

UNIT GOALS:

- To restate direct quotations and indirect thought by using reported speech
- To know when to make necessary changes in verb tenses and reference forms
- To correctly report questions and commands when using reported speech

▶ ## O P E N I N G   T A S K
What Are They Saying?

Look at this series of pictures. It is the photographic record of a conversation between Jack and Jean.

STEP 1 What do you think these people are talking about? Write down the exact conversation that you think occurred between them.

Photo 1:

Jack: _____

Jean: _____

Jack: _____

Jean: _____

Photo 2:

Jack: _____

Jean: _____

Jack: _____

Photo 3:

Jean: _____

Jack: _____

Jean: _____

Photo 4:

Jack: _____

Jean: _____

Jack: _____

Jean: _____

STEP 2 Compare your conversation with that of another student. Discuss what you thought they were talking about in each picture and why you thought that. Your discussion might be something like this:

> **You:** In the first picture I thought that Jack was telling Jean that he had something important to tell her.

> **Your partner:** Oh really? I thought that he was trying to introduce himself for the first time. Why did you think he already knew her?

> **You:** Because they're sitting rather close together.

STEP 3 Report the three most interesting differences between your two conversations (and your reasons for thinking so) to the rest of the class.

► Reported Speech and Change of Time Frame

When we report information that was spoken, written, or thought in the past, we can use reported speech or direct quotation. **Direct quotation** is the actual words that were spoken in the conversation. **Reported speech** expresses the meaning of what was said. We use these same patterns to describe **indirect thoughts:** ideas that were thought but not actually spoken. Because we are describing something that has already occurred (the speaking or thinking), we need to change the time frame of the verb phrases of what we are reporting.

To refer to Present Time Frame:

DIRECT QUOTATION	REPORTED SPEECH
(a) Jack thought, "I**'m** really sick. I **am having** terrible headaches. I**'m going to try** to see my doctor this afternoon, if I **can get** someone to drive me to her office."	**(b)** Jack thought that he **was** really sick. He **was having** terrible headaches. He **was going to try** to see his doctor yesterday afternoon, if he **could get** someone to drive him to the doctor's office.

To refer to Past Time Frame:

DIRECT QUOTATION	REPORTED SPEECH
(c) Yesterday I spoke to Jack on the phone. Here is what he said: "My headache **was getting** worse all the time, so I **went** to the doctor yesterday. She **took** my temperature. She **prescribed** some pills. My condition **has improved**, but I still **haven't gone** back to work yet."	**(d)** Yesterday I spoke to Jack on the phone. He told me that his headache **had been getting** worse, so he **had gone** to the doctor the day before yesterday. She **had prescribed** some pills. Jack felt that his condition **had improved,** but when I spoke to him he still **hadn't gone** back to work.

EXERCISE 1

Denise Driven had a meeting with her boss, Mr. Green, to complain about Peter Principle's work in the office. Here are some of the complaints that Denise made about Peter. Change these direct quotations to reported speech, using the cue given.

▶ **EXAMPLE:** "I've been getting more and more annoyed by Peter's behavior."
Denise reported that . . .

> **Denise reported that she had been getting more and more annoyed by Peter's behavior.**

1. "Peter needs to be more serious about work."

   Denise felt that . . .

2. "Peter came to work fifteen minutes late for the second time in a month."

   Denise was angry that . . .

3. "Peter is going to leave the office early to see his child perform in a school play."

   She complained that . . .

4. "He is always whistling in the office."

   She didn't like the fact that . . .

5. "He has made rude comments about my personal life."

   She was upset that . . .

EXERCISE 2

Here are other complaints Denise had about Peter. How do you think she stated her complaints? Restate them as direct quotations, using "Denise said."

▶ **EXAMPLE:** She reported that she had been getting more and more annoyed by Peter's behavior.

> **Denise said, "I have been getting more and more annoyed by Peter's behavior."**

1. She was annoyed that he didn't always finish projects on time.

2. She was unhappy that he told so many jokes at staff meetings.

3. She didn't like the fact that he refused to come into the office on Saturdays.

4. She was upset that he was going to miss an important meeting because he had promised to take his children to the circus.

5. She was angry that he constantly allowed his personal life to interfere with his work obligations.

Modal Changes in Reported Speech

Change present modals to past modals in reported speech.

DIRECT QUOTATION	REPORTED SPEECH
(a) "I **will try** to see my doctor this afternoon, if I **can** get someone to drive me to her office."	**(b)** He said that he **would try** to see his doctor yesterday afternoon, if he **could** get someone to drive him to the doctor's office.

may
can   **changes to** ⟶   *might*
shall   *could*
will   *should*
                              would

EXERCISE 3

Here is the response Mr. Green made when he talked with Denise. Change his direct quotation to reported speech. Start your paragraph with *Mr. Green said that*. . . . Use *Mr. Green suggested that* . . . and *Mr. Green thought that*
. . . later in the paragraph.

Mr. Green said, "The personnel officer will be asked to speak to Peter. If Peter can't get to the office on time, he will just have to take an earlier bus. He may not be crazy about getting up at 5:30, but he will have to do it if he wants to keep his job. Personnel won't talk to Peter about the other problems he may be having, though. One of Peter's friends in the office can deal with him directly about his lack of responsibility. Peter probably won't change much, but he may be more willing to listen to the complaints if he can get the information from someone he likes and respects."

Changes in Pronouns and Possessive Determiners in Reported Speech

In reported speech we must change pronoun forms in order to keep the same meaning.

EXAMPLES	IMPLIED MEANING
(a) Jack said, "**I** am sick."	Jack is sick.
(b) Jack told me that **I** am sick.	I am sick—not Jack.
(c) Jack told me that **he** was sick.	Jack is sick.

Compare the pronouns in these two passages.

DIRECT QUOTATION	REPORTED SPEECH
(d) Jack said, "**You** will be happy to know that **my** condition has improved, but **I** still haven't gone back to **my** office yet."	**(e)** He said that **I** would be happy to know that **his** condition had improved, but **he** still hadn't gone back to **his** office yet.

If there is some confusion about what the pronoun or possessive determiner refers to, it may be necessary to substitute the actual noun.

DIRECT QUOTATION	REPORTED SPEECH
(f) Jack said, "I asked **my** brother Peter to bring **his** wife to the party."	**(g)** Jack asked **his** brother Peter to bring **his**—**Peter's**—wife to the party.

EXERCISE 4

Change these direct quotations into reported speech.

▶ **EXAMPLE:** Peter said, "My kids have an invitation for your kids."

Peter said that his kids had an invitation for my kids.

1. Peter said, "My kids are having a birthday party at my house on Saturday."

2. Peter told me, "My kids have invited your kids to come their party."

3. Peter said, "I've asked my friend to bring her three girls."

4. Peter said, "I've hired a clown to entertain all our kids."

5. Peter said, "While our kids are watching the clown, my wife and I can prepare the cake and ice cream for your kids."

6. Peter said, "I asked Denise's secretary to tell her about the party, because she wanted me to work all weekend."

7. Peter said, "My family is more important to me than Denise's project."

FOCUS **4**

▶ # Changes in Demonstratives and Adverbials in Reported Speech

You may also need to change demonstratives and adverbials to keep the same meaning.

DIRECT QUOTATION	REPORTED SPEECH
(a) On Saturday Maria said, "Please come **here** for lunch **this afternoon.**"	**(b)** On Saturday Maria asked me to go **there** for lunch **that afternoon.**
(c) Jack said, "I went to the doctor **yesterday.**"	**(d)** Jack told me that he had gone to the doctor **(on) the previous day.**

Here are some examples of common changes in reference that are required in reported speech:

this/these		that/those
here		there
today/tonight		(on) that day/that night
yesterday	**changes to**	(on) the day before/the previous day
tomorrow		the next day
two days from today		two days from then
two days ago		two days earlier

EXERCISE 5

Change these direct quotations into reported speech:

▶ **EXAMPLE:** Ali said, "I came here to get some groceries, but the store's closed until tomorrow."

Ali said that he had gone there to get some groceries, but the store was closed until the next day.

1. Yesterday morning Peter said, "I am coming to the meeting this afternoon."

2. When I saw Petra last week, she told me, "My father may be able to take this letter directly to the Immigration Office later today."

3. Last week my brother told me, "I have already completed all the assignments I have for my classes this week."

4. Two days ago I spoke to the doctor, and he said, "The results of your test will be here by tomorrow morning."

5. Yesterday my mother promised me, "Tomorrow when you come here, I'll give you some of my delicious fudge."

Statements in Reported Speech

In direct quotation, the same markers—quotation marks ("...")—are used for statements, questions, and imperatives.

EXAMPLES	EXPLANATIONS
(a) The doctor told me, "I'm afraid we'll have to do more tests."	Direct quotation of a statement
(b) "The doctor asked me, "Have you been having these headaches for a long time?"	Direct quotation of a question

In reported speech, different patterns are used for statements and questions. *That* is used for statements.

EXAMPLES	EXPLANATIONS
(c) The doctor told me **that** he was afraid we would have to do more tests.	*That* introduces reported statements.
(d) The doctor told me he was afraid we would have to do more tests.	*That* is often omitted in informal contexts and conversation.

EXERCISE 6

Underline the reported speech patterns in the following passage that tell what the narrator heard or thought. Restate each one as a direct quotation. The first paragraph has been done for you as an example.

▶ **EXAMPLES:** His parents told him, "We found you under a cabbage leaf."

He thought, "That probably isn't true."

He thought, "There are lots of new babies in my neighborhood and no cabbage plants at all."

    (1) When I was a child I had some very strange ideas about where babies come from. (2) My parents always told me <u>that they had found me under a cabbage leaf.</u> (3) I knew <u>that probably wasn't true,</u> since I realized

there were lots of new babies in my neighborhood and no cabbage plants at all.

(4) For several years I thought my parents had actually bought my younger sister at the hospital. (5) I figured hospitals were places that sold babies to any couple that wanted one. (6) This was because when my mother came back from the hospital after giving birth to my sister, I heard her remind my father that he had to be sure to pay the bill before that week was over. (7) I was a little jealous of my new sister, and I hoped that my father would forget to pay and that the hospital would decide to take her back and sell her to someone else. (8) It wasn't until several years later that I found out that babies were neither bought nor found.

FOCUS **6**

Questions in Reported Speech

Changes in Word Order: All reported speech occurs in statement word order, whether it is a statement or a question.

DIRECT QUOTATION	REPORTED SPEECH
(a) "Am I late?"	**(b)** Yuri asked **if he was late.**
(c) "Do you need money?"	**(d)** Paolo wanted to know **whether I needed money.**
(e) "How much do you need?"	**(f)** He asked **how much I needed.**

Adding Question Markers: We use different patterns depending on whether the question being asked is a *yes/no* question or *Wh*-question.

EXAMPLES	EXPLANATIONS
(g) He wanted to know **if** I could bring my notes to the meeting.	***Yes/no* Questions**
(h) He wanted to know **whether** I could bring my notes to the meeting.	We can use either *if* or *whether (or not)* to report *yes/no* questions. *If* is preferred for *yes/no* questions.
(i) He wanted to know **whether or not** I could bring my notes to the meeting.	

(j)	I applied for a job. They wanted to know **where I had worked, when I worked there, how many years of experience I had,** and **what kind of previous experience I had had** in sales.	**Wh-Questions** We use a *Wh*-question word to report *Wh*-questions.
(k)	Can you tell me **what your zip code is?**	**Embedded Questions** Direct *yes/no* and *Wh*-questions sound more polite if they are embedded in a conversational frame such as "Do you know . . . ," or "Can you tell me . . . ," or "I wonder . . . ." It is not necessary to change the tense of the questions from present to past.
(l)	Do you know **what time the store opens?**	
(m)	I wonder **if Dr. Tang is able to come to the phone.**	

EXERCISE 7

Here is a list of interview questions that were common in American businesses thirty or forty years ago. Some of them are no longer asked by employers these days. In some cases the law prohibits asking such questions.

Restate the questions as statements about old-fashioned hiring practices by adding such reporting phrases as "A number of years ago employers used to ask . . . ," "They wanted to know . . . ," "They often asked prospective employees to tell them . . . ," and other similar phrases you can think of.

Which questions do you think are still being used?

1. Are you married or single?
2. Does your wife work outside the home?
3. How many children do you have?
4. Are you a Communist?
5. Do you go to church?
6. How old are you?
7. Why do you want to work for this company?
8. Do you use drugs?
9. What is your racial background?
10. How much experience do you have?

EXERCISE 8

Change this report of a job interview into the list of questions that the interviewer actually asked.

▶ **EXAMPLE:** *Where did you graduate from high school?*

(1) Bob applied for a summer job as a computer programmer in a large company. (2) The head of the Personnel Office interviewed him. (3) <u>She wanted to know where he had graduated from high school</u>, and if he had ever studied in a college or university. (4) She wanted to know if he had ever been arrested, or whether he had ever needed to borrow money in order to pay off credit card purchases. (5) She wanted to know how fast he could type and what kind of experience he had had with computers, and whether he was more proficient in COBOL or BASIC. (6) She asked him what companies he had worked for in the past. (7) She wanted to know what his previous salary had been. (8) She wanted to know why he was no longer working at his previous job. (9) She asked him if he would voluntarily take a drug test. (10) He began to wonder if he really wanted to work for a company that wanted to know so much about his private life.

EXERCISE 9

Change these direct questions into more polite forms by making them embedded questions using phrases such as "Do you know," "Can you tell me," or "I wonder."

1. What time does the train leave?
2. Is the bookstore open yet?
3. Can Sunyoon come with us to the party?
4. How do I get to Carnegie Hall?
5. Where can I find a cheap apartment?

▶ **Commands and Requests in Reported Speech**

EXAMPLES	EXPLANATIONS
(a) Teacher to student: "Do the home-work." **(b)** The teacher **told me to do** the homework.	To report commands, use verbs like *tell* or *order* + infinitive.
(c) Roommate: "Can you help?" **(d)** My roommate **asked me to help** with the dishes.	To report requests or invitations, use verbs such as *ask* or *invite* + infinitive.
(e) The teacher told me **not to joke** with other students. **(f)** My roommate asked me **not to play** my stereo too loud.	Negative commands and requests are reported with *not* + infinitive.

EXERCISE 10

Rewrite these indirect commands and requests as direct quotations.

▶ **EXAMPLE:** On his first day in the army, Kilroy was told to report to the drill field by the master sergeant.

> **The master sergeant told Kilroy, "Report to the drill field."**

1. Another officer assigned him to clean the area for nearly an hour.
2. The officers ordered all the new recruits not to talk to each other.
3. They were told to stand at attention until their papers had been processed.
4. Kilroy asked to go to the bathroom, but this request was denied.
5. Finally the processing was over, and they were ordered to return to their barracks.
6. Several other recruits invited Kilroy to join them in a game of cards.
7. He told them he was too tired, and asked them not to be too noisy since he wanted to sleep.

When No Tense Changes Are Required in Reported Speech

In certain situations, English speakers do not always make the tense and modal changes we have practiced here. These situations occur when we are reporting:

CATEGORY	DIRECT QUOTATION	REPORTED SPEECH
• things that are always true	**(a)** My father always told me, "Time **is** money."	**(b)** My father always told me that time **is** money.
• things that are still true	**(c)** Jean told me, "Jack **is still living** with his parents after all these years."	**(d)** Jean told me (that) Jack **is still living** with his parents after all these years.
• hypothetical statements	**(e)** Peter said, "If I **had** the money, I **would make** a donation to the club, but I **am** a little short on cash this month."	**(f)** Peter said that if he **had** the money, he **would make** a donation to the club, but that he **is/was** a little short on cash this/last month.
• statements that were made only a very short time ago	**(g)** Bambang told me, "I **can't** understand a word you're saying"	**(h)** He **just** said that he **can't** understand a word **I'm** saying.
• future events that have not yet occurred	**(i)** Diane said, "I **am going** to Hawaii next month."	**(j)** Diane said that she **is going** to Hawaii next month.

EXERCISE 11

Decide whether tense changes are required in the following sentences when they are changed to reported speech. If a tense change is not required, state the reason.

▶ **EXAMPLE:** Shakespeare once observed, "Love is blind."

No change. Timeless truth—still true

Last week our teacher reminded us, "Do your homework before you come to class tomorrow."

Last week our teacher reminded us to do our homework before we came to class the next day.

1. A student in my geography class reported, "Not all the people who live in China speak Chinese as their first language."

2. My brother told me, "I wouldn't need to borrow money from you all the time if I had a better paying job."

3. It was only a minute ago that I asked, "Are you paying attention?"

4. Jae told me, "I couldn't get any tickets for the concert."

5. Yesterday Denise said, "If I were you, I would plan things a little more completely before you leave for vacation next week."

6. This morning Peter told me, "I'm still having problems with Denise, but I'm trying extra hard to get along with her."

7. Bob said, "We're all going to go skiing the second week in January."

Use Your English

ACTIVITY 1: SPEAKING/WRITING

Work with a different partner from the one with whom you worked on the Opening Task. Together, write a conversation that matches the photos in the Opening Task. Act out your conversation for the rest of the class. Other students should write a paraphrase of your conversation.

ACTIVITY 2: LISTENING/SPEAKING/WRITING

To *eavesdrop* means to secretly listen to someone else's conversation. Go to a public place, like a restaurant, a shopping mall, or a bus station, and eavesdrop on someone's conversation. It's important not to let people know what you're doing, so pretend to read a book, or study your English grammar, or read a magazine in another language (people might think that you don't understand English), or pretend to write a letter.

Report what the people were talking about, and tell or write two or three things that they said to each other. Did you learn anything interesting about their lives, or about English, as a result of this experience?

ACTIVITY 3: LISTENING/SPEAKING/WRITING

Listen to a news broadcast on television. Report one story that you heard on that broadcast to the rest of the class. Start with some sort of statement like this: *I heard on the news that. . .*, *It was announced that. . .*, etc.

ACTIVITY 4: LISTENING/SPEAKING

Play a game of "Telephone." Here's how to play:

Form two or more teams of ten people each. Student #1 should make a statement to Student #2 very quietly, so that only Student #2 can hear what was said. Student #2 then reports what was said to Student #3 using reported speech (*Student #1 told me that . . .*). Student #3 tells Student #4 and so forth. When the last student receives the report, he or she should announce the message to the rest of the class. Compare how close that message is with what was originally said by Student #1. The team that has the closest, most accurate report wins a point. Student #2 starts the next round.

ACTIVITY 5: WRITING

Write a paragraph discussing some of the misconceptions about life that you had when you were a child. Describe what you thought, and why you thought it. See Exercise 6 for an example.

ACTIVITY 6: WRITING

Tell about a time when you had an important conversation with someone. Perhaps you learned some important information about yourself or someone else. Perhaps you found out about a decision that had a big effect on your life in some way. Perhaps you got some valuable advice.

STEP 1   First, tell the **story** of the conversation. Write down who it was with, where, and when it took place. Then try to write the conversation word-for-word.

STEP 2   Next, write a paragraph telling what you learned from this conversation, and why it was important for you. You may want to begin your paragraph with *When I was . . . , I learned that . . . .*

ACTIVITY 7: LISTENING

STEP 1   Based on the short news broadcast you hear, complete the following sentences with the actual words that were probably used by the speaker.

1. The Police Department representative announced, " _____ ."

_____

2. He admitted, " _____ ."

_____

3. He predicted, " _____ ."

_____

STEP 2   Use the sentences you have written to perform the announcement.

Appendices

Appendix 1A

Present Time Frame: Use Present Time to talk about general relationships. Most scientific and technical writing is in Present Time. Anything that is related to the present moment is expressed by Present Time, so newspaper headlines, news stories, and spoken conversations, jokes, and informal narratives are often in Present Time.

Form	Meaning	Use	Example
SIMPLE PRESENT *I/you/we/they* + simple form of verb *he/she/it* + *-s* form of verb	true in the past, present and future	general relationships and timeless truths permanent states	**(a)** Time **changes** the way people live. **(b)** Bob **has** two brothers and one sister.
		habitual and recurring actions	**(c)** Bob **works** in the library every afternoon.
PRESENT PROGRESSIVE *am/is/are* + present participle (verb + *-ing*)	already in progress now or around this time	actions in progress	**(d)** Bob **is studying** for a midterm at this moment.
		repetition or duration	**(e)** Bob **is taking** a biology class this semester.
		temporary states and actions	**(f)** Bob's brother **is living** with his father for the summer.
		uncompleted actions	**(g)** **He is** still **looking** for a cheap apartment.

Form	Meaning	Use	Example
PRESENT PERFECT *have/has* + past participle (verb + *-ed* or past participle of irregular verbs)	began in the past but related in some way to the present	past events related to now by time past events related to now by logical relationship	**(h)** Bob **has visited** Canada twice, so he won't join the tour to Quebec. **(i)** Bob **has gotten** very good at the computer, so he doesn't need to take another class.
PRESENT PERFECT PROGRESSIVE *have/has* + *been* + present participle (verb + *-ing*)	in progress before and including the present	repeated and/or continuous actions	**(j)** Bob **has been spending** his weekends at home since he started living in the dorm. **(k)** Bob **has been singing** in a chorus ever since he was in high school.

Appendix 1B

Past Time Frame: Use Past Time to talk about things that are not directly connected to the present moment. Most fiction, historical accounts, and factual descriptions of past events are in Past Time.

Form	Meaning	Use	Example
SIMPLE PAST verb + *-ed* or irregular past form	at a certain time in the past	states or general relationships that were true in the past habitual or recurrent actions that took place in the past specific events that took place in the past	**(a)** Tuberculosis **was** a common cause of death 50 years ago. **(b)** Robert Lee **worked** 12 hours a day for low wages. **(c)** Robert Lee **went** to work in a factory at age 14.

Form	Meaning	Use	Example
PAST PROGRESSIVE *was/were* + present participle (verb + *-ing*)	in progress at a certain time in the past	interrupted actions	**(d)** Robert **was studying** in high school when his father died.
		repeated actions and actions over time	**(e)** Robert **was** always **trying** to get promotions at the factory.
PAST PERFECT *had* + past participle (verb + *-ed* or past participle of irregular verbs)	before a certain time in the past	actions or states that took place before other events in the past	**(f)** His father **had been** dead for several weeks when Robert quit school and started working to help his mother.
PAST PERFECT PROGRESSIVE *had been* + present participle (verb + *-ing*)	in progress until a certain time in the past	continuous versus repeated actions	**(g)** Robert **had been working** for 12 hours when the foreman told him to go home.
		uncompleted versus completed actions	**(h)** Robert **had been hoping** to complete school when he had to find a job to help his family.

Appendix 1C

Future Time Frame: Use Future Time for anything that is scheduled to happen or predicted to happen in the future. Notice that two tenses (simple present and present progressive) that are used in Present Time Frame can also be used to talk about future plans or scheduled events.

Form	Meaning	Use	Example
SIMPLE PRESENT	already scheduled or expected in the future	schedules	(a) The plane **leaves** at 6:30 tomorrow.
PRESENT PROGRESSIVE		definite future plans	(b) I **am spending** next summer in France.
SIMPLE FUTURE one-word (*will/might*/etc.) or phrasal modals (*be going to*) + simple verb	at a certain time in the future	predictions about future situations	(c) Roberta is **going to take** a vacation on the moon. (d) She **will** probably **get** there by space shuttle, and she **might stay** on an observation platform.
FUTURE PROGRESSIVE future modal + *be* + verb + *-ing*	in progress at a certain time in the future	future events in progress	(e) 100 years from now Roberta **will be living** on the moon.
FUTURE PERFECT modal + *have* + past participle (verb + *-ed* or past participle of irregular verbs)	before a certain time in the future	events happening before other future events	(f) Scientists **will have visited** the moon long **before** tourists **will be** able to.
FUTURE PERFECT PROGRESSIVE modal + *have* + *been* + verb + *-ing*	in progress until a certain time in the future	repeated and/or continuous actions	(g) When Roberta retires on Earth she will probably not be used to the earth's level of gravity because she **will have been living** on the moon for several years.

ASPECT:	Simple	Progressive	Perfect	Perfect Progressive*
TIME:	**TENSES:**			
Present	is/are studied	am/is/are being studied	has/have been studied	has/have been being studied
	is/are given	am/is/are being given	has/have been given	has/have been being given
Past	was/were studied	was/were being studied	had been studied	had been being studied
	was/were given	was/were being given	had been given	had been being given
Future	will be studied	will be being studied	will have been studied	will have been being studied
	will be given	will be being given	will have been given	will have been being given

*Although perfect progressive passive forms are theoretically possible in English, such forms are **very** rarely found in speech or writing.

Verb Patterns that Are Followed by Infinitives

(a) Norman **decided to specialize** in African stamps when a friend **offered to give** him some stamps from Ghana.	Pattern 1: verb + infinitive
(b) A friend **advised Norman to order** rare stamps from commercial companies, and **encouraged him to be** persistent.	Pattern 2: verb + noun phrase + infinitive
(c) Norman **likes to send** stamps to other people, and also **likes other people to send** stamps to him.	Pattern 3: verb (+ noun phrase) + infinitive

Verb Patterns that Are Followed by Gerunds

(a) Charlie **can't help falling** in love with a new woman every week. **(b)** The doctor told me that I've got to **quit smoking.**	Pattern 1: verb gerund
(c) Doctors **advise reducing** fats in one's diet. (It's good advice for everyone.) **(d)** The doctor **advised me to reduce** fats in my diet. (She gave this advice to me specifically.)	Pattern 2: verb { + gerund / + noun phrase / + infinitive
(e) I **don't mind sleeping** late when I get the chance, and **I don't mind other people doing** it either.	Pattern 3: verb (+ noun phrase) + gerund

Verbs that Are Followed by Infinitives			Verbs that Are Followed by Gerunds		
Pattern 1	**Pattern 2**	**Pattern 3**	**Pattern 1**	**Pattern 2**	**Pattern 3**
appear	advise	expect	can't help	advise	appreciate
refuse	remind	arrange	keep on	encourage	anticipate
seem	persuade	want	recommend	urge	dislike
agree	urge	intend	suggest	forbid	don't mind
claim	encourage	consent	deny	allow	enjoy
care	convince	ask	consider	permit	resent
deserve	force	need	admit	invite	consider
decide	forbid		give up	cause	delay
demand	command		avoid	teach	postpone
pretend	order		quit		excuse
hesitate	allow		practice		imagine
offer	permit		include		miss
tend	invite		resist		tolerate
learn	trust				understand
neglect	cause				
wait	tell				
	warn				
	teach				
	hire				

Meaning Categories	Beginning of the Clause	Middle of the Clause	End of the Clause
ADDITION	additionally also in addition	also in addition	also in addition too as well
EMPHASIS/ INTENSIFYING	actually as a matter of fact besides furthermore indeed in fact moreover	actually as a matter of fact furthermore indeed in fact moreover	as a matter of fact indeed in fact
CONTRAST	despite this however on the other hand	however on the other hand	despite this however on the other hand
CONCESSION	despite this even so in spite of the fact nonetheless	nonetheless	despite this even so in spite of the fact nonetheless regardless though
REASON	with this in mind for this reason therefore	therefore	therefore with this in mind for this reason
RESULT	accordingly as a result consequently thus	accordingly as a result consequently therefore thus	accordingly as a result consequently t
CONDITIONAL	providing if then under such circumstances		under such circumstances
SEQUENCE	next then first, second, etc.	and next then first, second, etc.	next first, second, etc.

1. What is the form of the noun? Noncount or count? Singular or plural?
2. Is the noun used to make a generic reference or particular reference? Does it describe a class of things or does it refer to a particular item?
3. If it refers to a particular thing, is the reference specific or nonspecific?

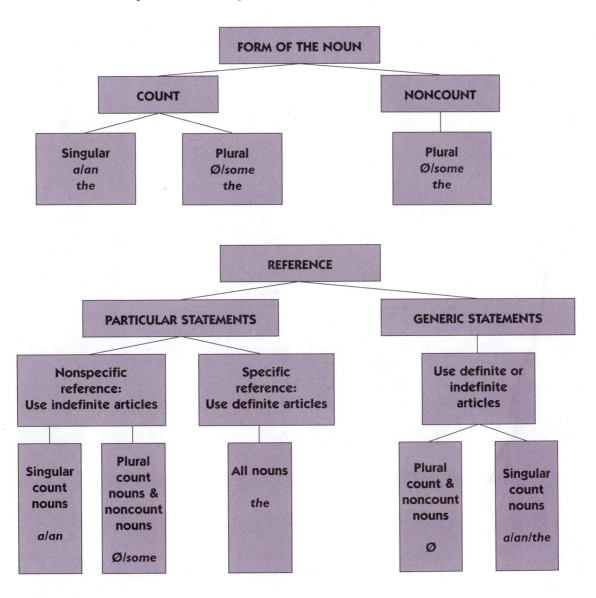

Simple Form	Past Tense Form	Past Participle	Simple Form	Past Tense Form	Past Participle
become	became	become	grow	grew	grown
begin	began	begun	hang	hung	hung
bend	bent	bent	have	had	had
bet	bet	bet	hear	heard	heard
bind	bound	bound	hide	hid	hidden
bite	bit	bit	hit	hit	hit
bleed	bled	bled	hold	held	held
blow	blew	blown	hurt	hurt	hurt
break	broke	broken	keep	kept	kept
bring	brought	brought	know	knew	known
build	built	built	lead	led	led
buy	bought	bought	leave	left	left
catch	caught	caught	lend	lent	lent
choose	chose	chosen	let	let	let
come	came	come	make	made	made
cost	cost	cost	mean	meant	meant
cut	cut	cut	meet	met	met
dig	dug	dug	put	put	put
do	did	done	quit	quit	quit
draw	drew	drawn	read	read	read
drink	drank	drunk	ride	rode	ridden
drive	drove	driven	ring	rang	rung
eat	ate	eaten	rise	rose	risen
fall	fell	fallen	run	ran	run
feed	fed	fed	say	said	said
feel	felt	felt	see	saw	seen
fight	fought	fought	seek	sought	sought
find	found	found	sell	sold	sold
fit	fit	fit	send	sent	sent
fly	flew	flown	set	set	set
forbid	forbade	forbidden	shake	shook	shaken
forget	forgot	forgotten	shine	shone	shone
forgive	forgave	forgiven	shoot	shot	shot
freeze	froze	frozen	shut	shut	shut
get	got	gotten	sing	sang	sung
give	gave	given	sink	sank	sunk
go	went	gone	sit	sat	sat
grind	ground	ground	sleep	slept	slept

Simple Form	Past Tense Form	Past Participle	Simple Form	Past Tense Form	Past Participle
slide	slid	slid	swing	swang	swung
speak	spoke	spoken	take	took	taken
speed	sped	sped	teach	taught	taught
spend	spent	spent	tear	tore	torn
split	split	split	tell	told	told
spread	spread	spread	think	thought	thought
spring	sprang	sprung	throw	threw	thrown
stand	stood	stood	understand	understood	understood
steal	stole	stolen	wake	woke	woken
stick	stuck	stuck	wear	wore	worn
sting	stung	stung	weave	wove	woven
strike	struck	stricken	weep	wept	wept
swear	swore	sworn	win	won	won
sweep	swept	swept	wind	wound	wound
swim	swam	swum	write	wrote	written

Answer Key (for puzzles and problems only)

UNIT 11

Answer to Activity 5 (page 201)

Secret: Silly Sally only likes things with double letters.

UNIT 16

Additional Clues for Opening Task (page 256)

Mystery 1	Mystery 2	Mystery 3
The man is very, very short.	There's a big puddle of water in the room, and the paper is a delivery bill from an ice company.	The police officer is a woman.

Answer to Activity 3 (page 268)

(A) Candle snuffer; **(B)** Hook to catch chickens; **(C)** Cherry pit remover; **(D)** Mechanical vegetable chopper; **(E)** Glove dryer/stretcher; **(F)** Ear protector for carriage horses

UNIT 20

Answer to Activity 1 (page 338)

That that is, is. That that is not, is not. Isn't that it? It is!

UNIT 21

Activity 1 (page 350)

Diagram B

Diagram D

Index

prediction
  in future time, 247
  modals describing, 73, 79, 256, 258–260
  perfect modals, 264–266
prepositional phrases, 30
  adjective, 30
  adverbial, 30
  coordinating conjunctions connecting parallel,
    190–191
  demonstratives and, 334
  following noun phrases, 160
  identifying unique noun, 321–324
  modifying phrases for noun phrases, 148
  possessive, 342, 344, 346
  relative clauses, 210
  that/those with forward-pointing reference,
    332–334
prepositions
  gerund as object of, 116
  gerunds and, 88
  infinitives and, 88
  object of, 205
present participle
  adverbs added to, 157
  agents modified by, 155
  meaning in, 155–156, 155
  modifiers in, modifying phrases for noun
    phrases, 153–154
  nouns added to, 157
  sensory verbs and, 293
present perfect progressive tense, 21
present perfect verbs, 230–243
  progressive tense, 239–240, 239
  relationship to the present and, 235–236, 235
  relationship to the present and, 236–237, 236
  still true vs. no longer true, 234
present perfect verbs, 230–243, 230
present progressive tense, 17
  future events and, 246
present tense, present time frame, 1, 2, 4, 5, 19, 48,
  218–229, 232–233
  future planned events and, 247
  present progressive, 220
  reported speech and, 402–403
  simple present, 220
pretty, 128
previous, 407
probability
  modals describing, 251–252, 258
  unlikely, 284
progress, present progressive tense in, 220
progressive aspect, 2, 4, 17–18, 48
  infinitives, 90
  past time frame and, 372, 374, 376–377
progressive tense, present perfect, 239–240
progressive verbs and relative clauses, 210
prohibition expressed using modals, 70
promises expressed using modals, 69
pronouns
  demonstratives as, 330
  gerund and, 111

infinitive and, 93, 97
personal, 331
possessive use of, 342
relative, 207–209, 210
reported speech and changes to, 405
providing, 186

quantifiers, 308, 352, 354–363
  affirmative, 357–358
  modifying phrases for noun phrases, 148
  negative, 357–358
  of used with, 360–361
  plural, 359
  singular, 359
  special cases for, 362–363
questions in reported speech, 409–411
quite/quite a few, 126, 128, 133, 168, 172, 176, 178,
  354
quotations, 400–416

rarely, 38
rather, 126, 128
really, 128, 133
reason, adverbial clauses of, 40
reasonably, 128
receiver of passive verbs, 51
  agent vs., 51
  past participle modifier of, 155
recurrent actions, simple verb tense to describe, 16
references
  backward-pointing, 332–334
  forward-pointing, 332–334
regardless of, 197
relationships
  adverbial phrases to describe, 38
  simple verb tense to describe, 16
relative clauses, 30, 202–217
  adjective phrase and, 210
  demonstratives and, 334
  indirect object of, 205
  modifying phrases for noun phrases and, 148
  nonrestrictive, 204
  object of, 205
  object of a preposition and, 205
  passive verbs and, 210
  prepositional phrases and, 210
  progressive verbs and, 210
  relative pronouns, 207–209
  relative pronouns, deletion of, 210
  restrictive, 204, 205
  subject of, 205
  whose, 213–214
relative pronouns, 207–209
  deletion of, 210
  direct object of, 210
  indirect object of, 210
  object of preposition and, 210
repetitive actions, past time frame and, 377, 381

Use the Entire Grammar Dimensions Series

Grammar Dimensions Book 1, Platinum Edition
High Beginning

Student Text:	0-8384-0260-7
Workbook:	0-8384-0266-6
Audiocassette:	0-8384-0261-5
Teacher's Edition:	0-8384-0267-4

Grammar Dimensions Book 2, Platinum Edition
Intermediate

Student Text:	0-8384-0268-2
Workbook:	0-8384-0274-7
Audiocassette:	0-8384-0269-0
Teacher's Edition:	0-8384-0275-5

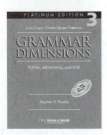

Grammar Dimensions Book 3, Platinum Edition
High Intermediate

Student Text:	0-8384-0277-1
Workbook:	0-8384-0284-4
Audiocassette:	0-8384-0278-X
Teacher's Edition:	0-8384-0285-2

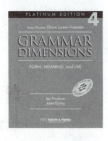

Grammar Dimensions Book 4, Platinum Edition
Advanced

Student Text:	0-8384-0286-0
Workbook:	0-8384-0291-7
Audiocassette:	0-8384-0287-9
Teacher's Edition:	0-8384-0292-5

Read the Definitive Source for Grammar Reference and Teaching Guidance
The Grammar Book: An ESL/EFL Teacher's Course, Second Edition
Marianne Celce-Murcia and Diane Larsen-Freeman ISBN:0-8384-4725-2

For more information about ***Grammar Dimensions, Platinum Edition*** and
The Grammar Book, please contact your Heinle & Heinle/Thomson Learning
representative or call (toll-free in the U.S.) 1-877-NEED-ESL

Heinle & Heinle
Thomson Learning™
20 Park Plaza
Boston, MA 02116